Enhancing Couples

About the Editors

Dr. Kurt Hahlweg is a professor of psychology at the University of Braunschweig, Germany. He is a clinical psychologist and has held research and teaching positions at the universites of Hamburg and Heidelberg, Queen's University Belfast, and UCLA. His research interests are in the fields of interpersonal factors in individual psychopathology, cognitive-behavioral couple therapy, the prevention of couple distress and childhood behavioral problems, and interactional diagnostics.

Dr. Mariann Grawe-Gerber is director of the Klaus Grawe Institute for Psychological Therapy in Zurich, Switzerland. She holds degrees in law from the University of Zurich and in social and clinical psychology from New York University. She is a licenced therapist who has worked in childhood and adolescent psychiatry in New York and has been active in the development of evidence-based interventions in Switzerland. Her research interests are in the areas of couple and family therapy and their empirical validation, resource activation in psychotherapy, and in the further development of therapy training that transcends individual schools of therapy.

Donald H. Baucom, PhD, is a professor of psychology at the University of North Carolina – Chapel Hill. He is a licenced clinical psychologist with extensive experience working with couples and an expert in the areas of relationship functioning and couples counseling. His research interests are in the field of intimate human relationships, particularly couple relationships, and their development throughout the lifespan. He is continuously active in the development of treatment interventions for couples experiencing relationship distress and currently involved in studies exploring the interactions of physical and mental health with relationship functioning.

Enhancing Couples

The Shape of Couple Therapy to Come

Kurt Hahlweg
Mariann Grawe-Gerber
Donald H. Baucom
(Editors)

HOGREFE

Library of Congress Cataloging in Publication

is available via the Library of Congress Marc Database under the
LC Control Number 2009927605

Library and Archives Canada Cataloguing in Publication

Enhancing couples: the shape of couple therapy to come / Kurt Hahlweg,
Mariann Grawe-Gerber, Donald H. Baucom, editors.

Includes bibliographical references and index.
ISBN 978-0-88937-373-0

1. Marital psychotherapy. I. Hahlweg, Kurt II. Grawe-Gerber, Mariann
III. Baucom, Donald H.

RC488.5.E65 2009 616.89'1562 C2009-904238-X

PUBLISHING OFFICES
USA: Hogrefe Publishing, 875 Massachusetts Avenue, 7th Floor, Cambridge, MA 02139
Phone (866) 823-4726, Fax (617) 354-6875; E-mail customerservice@hogrefe-publishing.com
EUROPE: Hogrefe Publishing, Rohnsweg 25, 37085 Göttingen, Germany
Phone +49 551 49609-0, Fax +49 551 49609-88, E-mail publishing@hogrefe.com

SALES & DISTRIBUTION
USA: Hogrefe Publishing, Customer Services Department,
30 Amberwood Parkway, Ashland, OH 44805
Phone (800) 228-3749, Fax (419) 281-6883, E-mail customerservice@hogrefe.com
EUROPE: Hogrefe Publishing, Rohnsweg 25, 37085 Göttingen, Germany
Phone +49 551 49609-0, Fax +49 551 49609-88, E-mail publishing@hogrefe.com

OTHER OFFICES
CANADA: Hogrefe Publishing, 660 Eglinton Ave. East, Suite 119-514, Toronto, Ontario M4G 2K2
SWITZERLAND: Hogrefe Publishing, Länggass-Strasse 76, CH-3000 Bern 9

Hogrefe Publishing
Incorporated and registered in the Commonwealth of Massachusetts, USA, and in Göttingen,
Lower Saxony, Germany

Printed and bound in the USA
ISBN 978-0-88937-373-0

Table of Contents

Preface

The Klaus-Grawe-Stiftung für Psychologische Therapy (Klaus Grawe Foundation for Psychological Therapy) in Zurich, Switzerland, decided to stimulate coordinated strategies in the field of clinical psychology and psychotherapy through the development of the Klaus Grawe Think Tank Meetings (KGTMs), which will bring together leading researchers, trainers, and clinicians in various fields of mental health. The goals of the KGTMs are to encourage cutting-edge, creative, daring ideas and research related to the prevention and treatment of psychological problems and disorders, as well as to disseminate empirically supported programs to the public through a variety of delivery systems for individuals, couples, families, businesses, and institutions.

Every two years a specific, socially relevant topic will be decided on. The five to seven best-known experts within the chosen topic area will be invited together with junior colleagues to discuss the latest findings in prevention of a psychological disorder and empirically based intervention procedures in order to bring them to the public and to develop an agenda for future research and dissemination into practice and into public awareness in general.

The participants at the meeting will emphasize new methodological approaches that are available to address complex issues relevant to the topic which might be of importance to the general public. They will also make efforts to integrate various specific findings into a comprehensive, cohesive organization to develop a set of actions that serve the public on various levels. This includes using new media to assist in disseminating findings as well as gathering data. Research findings will be put into an understandable and attractive language for the public and institutions. New means of reaching the population with a variety of delivery options will be developed. The invitation of junior researchers is a unique feature of these meetings and intends to support and encourage talented young researchers. The participants of the KGTMs will form an international network inspired by Klaus Grawe's research and his innovative, interdisciplinary way of thinking. Most important, these people will contribute in an important way to the dissemination of research results and their consequences for training and practice.

The first of these meetings was held in Zurich and Zuoz, Switzerland, in September 2007, focusing on couple therapy and prevention. As an outgrowth of that meeting, the current volume evolved. Investigators from several continents gathered to discuss the current status of the field and to make recommendations for the future.

The current volume includes two types of papers: (a) overviews of the field with recommendations for the future from more senior investigators and (b) representative research in these same areas from younger scholars who provide current relevant findings as well as glimpses of what is ahead in research for the future. These two types of papers are organized around several central themes in the couple area: models of intervention, models of prevention, new approaches to assessment, and transmitting programs to the consumer. It is our hope that the reader will find this volume to be informative regarding the current status of the field and join in our efforts to improve the quality of couple functioning in all its diverse forms, one of the richest and potentially most rewarding sets of relationships for adults across all cultures.

Zurich, Fall 2009
Kurt Hahlweg, Mariann Grawe-Gerber, and Donald H. Baucom

Acknowledgments

We give our sincerest thanks to Barbara, Franz, Lukas, and Thomas, who made the think tank meeting and this book possible.

Introduction

Strengthening Couples and Families

Dissemination of Interventions for the Treatment and Prevention of Couple Distress

Kurt Hahlweg,[1] Donald H. Baucom,[2] Mariann Grawe-Gerber,[3] and Douglas K. Snyder[4]

[1]Technical University Braunschweig, Germany
[2]University of North Carolina, Chapel Hill, NC, USA
[3]Klaus Grawe Institute for Psychological Therapy, Zurich, Switzerland
[4]Texas A&M University, College Station, TX, USA

Abstract

The quality of family life is fundamental to the well-being of the community. The stability of the family has a pervasive influence on the psychological, physical, social, economic, and cultural well-being of children and parents. Strengthening couple, parenting, and family skills has the potential to improve the quality of life and health status of children, our future generation. Over the past 30 years, approximately 100 clinical trials have demonstrated the efficacy and effectiveness of couple therapy and interventions to prevent relationship distress and divorce. However, the impact of these programs on a public health level is highly questionable. Few therapists and counselors actually use evidence-based interventions; likewise, few couples actually use counseling or treatment services whenever they experience a deteriorating relationship. Therefore, the most important question for the next 10 years is: Are we ready to disseminate our effective interventions to the public? This chapter describes the steps necessary to disseminate a public health model of couple therapy and prevention. For example, do we have sufficient knowledge of risk and protective factors? Are there "ready-to-use" resources (e.g., treatment manuals and psychoeducational materials)? Are there effective training and supervision programs available? Do strategies exist that help to build sustainability? And: Do we have continuous quality control measures to monitor the ongoing implementation of the interventions?
The field of couple therapy and prevention has made great strides over the past decades, and innovations continue to evolve as theoreticians, researchers, trainers, and clinicians employ recent findings to benefit couples and families. In order for the field to benefit maximally from these ongoing findings and recommendations, it is important that coordinated efforts be made, such as those in the recommendations discussed in this chapter.

Across all countries and cultures, most people are involved in intimate couple relationships at some point in their lives, whether it be marriage or cohabitation (Buss, 1995). Since 1970, marriage rates have been declining in most Western countries; the average age at marriage is increasing, and the rate of cohabitation is growing. Be that as it may, intimate couple relationships continue to be viewed as the best forum for meeting individual needs for affection, companionship, loyalty, and emotional and sexual intimacy, even among those individuals who have experienced prior relationships as unsatisfactory (Halford, Kelley, & Markman, 1997). Marriage remains the most popular means of expressing commitment in a couple's relationship. Based on data from the 1990s, within 5 years of cohabitation, between 50% and 66% of couples in most European countries (US: 82%) had married (with the exception of Sweden: 33%), while between 25% and 33% had dissolved their relationship (US: 47%; see Kiernan, 2004). At least until the 1990s, by the age of 50, approximately 90% of the population in Western countries had been married at least once (McDonald, 1995). In Germany, approximately 16 million married couples live in one household; of those 52% do not have children. In 2006, about 380,000 couples got married.

As common as intimate relationships and marriage are, in industrialized Western countries approximately 40% of marriages end in divorce. And in approximately 70% of the divorces, children are involved with negative consequences for their future well-being. In Germany alone, about 170,000 children were affected in 2004. Not only do children experience their parents' divorce, but they also witness or experience parental conflict and distress as well as the lack of a warm positive relationship with parents, insecure attachment, and harsh, inflexible, and inconsistent discipline tactics. These are risk factors for a range of poor child outcomes including depression, withdrawal, conduct disorder, poor social competence, health problems, and academic underachievement (Amato, 2001; Hetherington & Elmore, 2004; Zimet & Jacob, 2001). These negative effects impact upon children long term. Adult offspring of divorce have substantially higher rates of psychological disorders and an elevated risk to become divorced themselves when in their own marriage: For example, in Germany, boys have a fourfold increase in divorce compared to boys from a non-divorced family (girls: twofold increase). Therefore, divorce seems to be "socially inherited" (Diekmann & Engelhardt, 1995).

The quality of family life is fundamental to the well-being of the community. The stability of the family has a pervasive influence on the psychological, physical, social, economic, and cultural well-being of children and parents. Many significant health, social, and economic problems are linked to the breakdown of family relationships. Strengthening couples, parenting, and family skills has the potential to improve the quality of life and health status of children, our future generation.

Over the past 30 years, approximately 100 clinical trials have demonstrated the efficacy and effectiveness of couple therapy and interventions to prevent relationship distress and divorce (Hahlweg, 2004; Snyder, Castellani, & Whisman, 2006). The empirical evidence especially for programs with a cognitive-behavioral emphasis, is impressive. *However, the impact of these programs on a public health level is highly questionable.*

Few therapists and counselors actually use evidence-based interventions; likewise, few couples actually use counseling or treatment services whenever they experience a deteriorating relationship. Even when they ask for help, the data on the long-term outcome indicate that in many cases counseling is undertaken too late to repair the damage of years of destructive conflict.

Therefore, the most important questions for the next 10 years are: Are we ready to disseminate our effective interventions to the public? If the answer is yes, how do we organize the dissemination process and how will we motivate couples to use the services? This chapter describes the steps necessary to disseminate a public health model of couple therapy. Our ideas are heavily influenced by the successful implementation of the Triple P system, a parent-training model developed by Sanders and colleagues (1999). When treatments such as couple-based interventions are to be delivered on a broad, public health scale, several important questions must be addressed (Flay et al., 2005; Sanders, 2008):

(1) Is the base rate of relationship problems large enough to be of concern for society?
(2) Do we know enough about risk and protective factors, which are in principle modifiable?
(3) Do we have efficacious and effective interventions?
(4) Are the interventions culturally appropriate and available?
(5) Do we have "ready-to-use" resources (e.g., treatment manuals and psychoeducational materials) that can be made available to service providers?
(6) Is an effective training and supervision program available?
(7) Are the couple interventions widely available?
(8) Do strategies exist that help to built sustainability?
(9) Are continuous quality control measures to monitor the ongoing implementation of the interventions built into the system?

Is the Base Rate of Relationship Problems Large Enough to Be of Concern for Society?

Relationship Satisfaction

At the beginning of committed relationships, almost all couples report high levels of relationship satisfaction. There is some evidence that many of these couples are making unrealistically positive predictions about the stability of their own relationship. At the beginning of their partnership, most partners believe that there is a zero probability that they will ever divorce, despite the well-publicized evidence of how common divorce is (Fowers, Lyons, & Montel, 1996). The mean level of relationship satisfaction typically declines each year over at least 10 years (Glenn, 1998) and is particularly notable after the birth of the first child. For many couples, the erosion of satisfaction leads them to seek divorce. *This unrealistic expectation* (it will not happen with us) *seems to be a solid barrier for couples to participate in some form of relationship enhancement intervention.*

Divorce

About 55% of American, 40–45% of Australian, English, German, or Swiss first marriages end in divorce (Halford et al., 1997). About 50% of the divorces occur in the first seven years of the marriage. In 2006, 200,000 couples got divorced in Germany. Many other couples, about 10–25% (Gallup, 1990; Hahlweg, 2004; for Germany: 1.6–4 million), live in stable but unhappy relationships for various reasons: e.g., the financial implications of divorce, personal and cultural expectations about divorce, or because no alternative partner is available. As painful as the experience of divorce is for many people, about 75% of divorced men and 66% of divorced women remarry within 3 years. Unfortunately, the divorce rate in second marriages is even higher than in first marriages (Cherlin, 1992).

Often, the public and researchers have taken a pathogenic view of divorce and have focused on the stresses and adverse outcomes associated with marital breakup. However, it should also be recognized that divorce can offer an escape from an unhappy, abusive, conflictual, or demeaning marriage and an opportunity to build new, more harmonious, fulfilling relationships, and increase personal growth and individuation (Hetherington & Elmore, 2004).

Consequences of Relationship Dissatisfaction and Divorce

Marital distress and divorce are the most severe, commonly occurring stresses that adults experience. As highlighted in a NIMH report on prevention (Coie et al., 1993), marital distress and destructive marital conflict are major generic risk factors for many forms of dysfunction and psychopathology, and may have long-lasting consequences for the children.

Individual Psychopathology

Relationship distress is linked with the onset, course, and poorer response to the treatment of individual adult psychiatric disorders. Using data from over 2,500 married participants of the National Comorbidity Survey, Whisman (1999) reported that marital distress was correlated with the 12-month prevalence rate of 12 specific psychiatric disorders. In comparison to non-distressed individual patients, maritally distressed individuals are up to three times more likely to have a psychological disorder, including depression (particularly in women), alcohol abuse (particularly in men), and anxiety disorders. Children from high relationship conflict couples, divorced, and remarried families exhibit more problems in adjustment than do those in low conflict, non-divorced two parent families. These children are more likely to have academic problems, exhibit externalizing and internalizing disorders, be less socially responsible and competent, have lower self-esteem, and have more problems in their relationship with parents, siblings, and peers (Amato, 2001; Zimet & Jacob, 2001). Adolescents from divorced families are more likely to drop out of school, be unemployed, become sexually active at an earlier age, be involved in delinquent activities and substance abuse, and associate with antisocial peers (Hetherington & Elmore, 2004). In adulthood, the offspring of divorced and high conflict families are less satisfied with their lives, have lower socioeconomic status, have more problems with their intimate partners, and experience a higher rate of marital instability.

Physical Health

Relationship problems also are correlated with poorer physical health. Distressed individuals are more likely to have major somatic illness and recover more slowly when they become ill (Burman & Margolin, 1992; Kiecolt-Glaser & Newton, 2001). There are several mechanisms by which being distressed can have effects on health through health-related behaviors. For example, distressed partners smoke more tobacco, drink more alcohol, and exercise less than non-distressed partners. Moreover, distressed partners make less use of health promotion and early detection of disease services (Schmaling & Sher, 2000). Evidence for the influence of marital distress and divorce on longevity and death was reported in a study by Friedman et al. (1995). The authors followed up Terman's sample of 1,528 gifted children by collecting death certificates. Adult children of divorced parents faced a one third greater mortality rate than people whose parents remained married. Among men from divorced families, the mean age of death was 76 years; for men whose parents did not divorce the mean age was 80 years (for women: 82 and 86 years, respectively).

Family Violence

In the US, approximately 12.5% of men are physically aggressive (e.g., grab, push, and slap) toward their wives, and 1.5–2 million women are severely assaulted by their husbands per year (Holtzworth-Monroe, Smutzler, Bates, & Sandin, 1997). In Germany, the 1-year prevalence rate of physical aggression among partners between 20 and 45 years of age is about 8.5% (Wetzels, Greve, Mecklenburg, Bilsky, & Pfeiffer, 1995).

Bidirectionality of Effects

The cited consequences of relationship distress on adults are mainly based on correlational studies which do not imply causality. For example, the associations between marital distress and individual psychopathology or health may be explained bidirectionally: Marital problems may cause psychological disorder or the individual's psychological disorder may cause marital problems. With regard to health, marital distress may lead to drinking more alcohol or drinking may lead to marital distress. Thus, a simple unidirectional model of causality is inadequate: Marital distress and individual disorders likely reciprocally influence each other.

Do We Know Enough About Risk and Protective Factors Which are in Principle Modifiable?

An understanding of how relationships develop, succeed, and fail is best achieved with longitudinal data. Karney and Bradbury (1995) reviewed 115 longitudinal studies, representing over 45,000 couples, and evaluated how the quality and stability of relationships change over time. The weight of the evidence suggests that the quality of the relationship, whether warm and supportive or hostile and negative, relates to the risk for marital distress and instability. Good communication is strongly correlated with relationship satisfaction and stability, specifically the presence of self-disclosing communication, effective conflict management, partner mutual support, positive day-to-day interactions, satisfying sexuality, and shared positive activities. In contrast, negative reciprocity and destructive handling of relationship conflicts predict dissatisfaction and instability, while undermining love, sexual attraction, friendship, trust, and commitment. Consequently, these major dynamic factors (e.g., communication and conflict management) should be the key components of preventive and treatment programs.

Another implication of the longitudinal research on the determinants of marital satisfaction and stability is *when* the preventive intervention should be offered. Entry to a committed relationship or marriage is a good time because relationship roles, household routines, and means of conflict management and negotiation need to be developed using appropriate communication skills. In addition, other life events such as the transition to parenthood, major illness, and unemployment are associated with relationship deterioration. Interventions at that point in time may help the couple to sustain relationship satisfaction.

Do We Have Efficacious and Effective Interventions?

Empirically Supported Treatments for Couple Distress

Empirical findings from randomized clinical trials support the efficacy of six different couple-based treatments for couple distress. These approaches vary along a continuum anchored by traditional behavioral interventions emphasizing primarily behavior exchange and skill-building interventions at one end, to insight-oriented interventions emphasizing intrapersonal dynamics and enduring relationship patterns at the other end.

Traditional Behavioral Couple Therapy

By far, traditional behavioral couple therapy (TBCT) (Jacobson & Margolin, 1979) has been studied more extensively than any other single approach to couple therapy.

A meta-analysis of 30 randomized trials with distressed couples contrasting TBCT with a no-treatment control (Shadish & Baldwin, 2005) yielded a mean effect size of 0.59, indicating that the average individual receiving TBCT was better off at the end of treatment than 72% of individuals in the control condition. This composite effect size is smaller than previously reported effect sizes for TBCT, and likely results from inclusion of non-published dissertations with smaller sample sizes and small or negative effect sizes. Follow-up studies of TBCT indicate that approximately 30% of couples who had initially improved in response to therapy subsequently showed significant deterioration in the first two years after termination (Jacobson, Schmaling, & Holtzworth-Munroe, 1987).

Cognitive-Behavioral Couple Therapy

Cognitive-behavioral couple therapy (CBCT) builds upon TBCT by incorporating interventions targeting partners' relationship assumptions and standards, expectancies, and attributions that contribute to or maintain distorted emotions or maladaptive behaviors underlying couple distress. Initial studies of CBCT demonstrated pre- to post-treatment effect sizes averaging 0.72 and ranging from 0.54 to 0.78 across behavioral, cognitive, and affective criteria (Dunn & Schwebel, 1995). Various adaptations of CBCT have since been developed and shown to be efficacious for treating couple distress related to a variety of physical health and emotional/behavioral disorders (Baucom, Epstein, LaTaillade, & Kirby, 2008).

Integrative-Behavioral Couple Therapy

Integrative-behavioral couple therapy (IBCT) (Jacobson & Christensen, 1996) is a different variation of behavioral couple therapy that emphasizes interventions aimed at increasing acceptance, including promoting tolerance and encouraging partners to appreciate differences and to use these to enhance their marriage. In a large randomized clinical trial comparing IBCT with TBCT, Christensen and colleagues (2004) reported that both treatments produced similar levels of clinically significant improvement by the end of treatment; 71% of IBCT couples and 59% of TBCT couples were reliably improved or recovered, based on self-reports of overall relationship satisfaction. At 5-year follow-up, separation/divorce rates for couples in the two treatment conditions were virtually identical at slightly over 25% (Christensen, personal communication, July, 2007).

Emotionally Focused Couple Therapy and Integrated Systemic Couple Therapy

Emotionally focused couple therapy (EFCT) (Johnson, 2004) combines an experiential, intrapsychic focus on inner emotional experience with an emphasis on cyclical, self-reinforcing interactions. In four randomized trials, EFCT was superior to a wait-list control condition in reducing relationship distress, yielding recovery rates of 70–73%, and a weighted mean effect size of 1.31 (Johnson, 2002). Goldman and Greenberg (1992) compared integrated systemic couple therapy (ISCT) and EFCT with each other and a waiting-list control condition. ISCT sought to disrupt repetitive, self-perpetuating negative interactional cycles by changing the meaning attributed to these cycles. At the end of 10 one-hour weekly sessions, ISCT and EFCT were both found to be superior to the control condition and to be equally effective in alleviating marital distress; moreover, ISCT couples showed greater maintenance of gains at 4-month follow-up in marital satisfaction and goal attainment.

Insight-Oriented Therapy

Snyder and Wills (1989) compared insight-oriented marital therapy (IOMT) with traditional behavioral approaches to couple therapy in a controlled clinical trial involving 79 distressed couples. The insight-oriented condition emphasized the interpretation and resolution of conflictual emotional processes related to developmental issues, collusive interactions, and maladaptive relationship patterns. Couples in both treatment modalities showed statistically and clinically significant gains in relationship satisfaction compared to a waiting-list control group. Treatment effect sizes at termination for behavioral and insight-oriented conditions were 1.01 and 0.96, respectively; however, at 4-year follow-up, 38% of the behavioral couples had experienced divorce, in contrast to only 3% of couples in the insight-oriented condition (Snyder, Wills, & Grady-Fletcher, 1991).

When the above approaches to couple therapy are compared, meta-analyses of couple therapy affirm that various approaches to treating couple distress produce statistically and clinically significant improvement for a substantial proportion of couples, with the average couple receiving therapy being better off at termination than 80% of couples not receiving treatment (Shadish & Baldwin, 2003). However, tempering enthusiasm from this overall conclusion are additional findings that in only 50% of treated couples do both partners show significant improvement in relationship satisfaction, and that 30–60% of treated couples show significant deterioration at two years or longer after termination (Snyder et al., 2006). Meta-analyses provide little evidence of differential effectiveness across different theoretical orientations to couple therapy, particularly once other covariates (e.g., reactivity of measures) are controlled (Shadish & Baldwin, 2003).

Processes of Change

Although each of the empirically supported approaches to couple therapy posits specific processes or mechanisms of change, there has been little research explicitly indicating these proposed mechanisms as responsible for observed therapeutic effects (Snyder et al., 2006). For example, mediation regression analyses of data from TBCT clinical trials have failed to find an association between the magnitude of changes in communication behaviors and gains in relationship satisfaction. Similarly, although CBCT has been shown to produce positive change in targeted cognitions (e.g., expectancies and attributions), changes in these cognitions have not been linked to couples' gains in satisfaction following CBCT (see Whisman & Snyder, 1997, for a summary of relevant studies).

More encouraging results have been reported by Doss and colleagues (Doss, Thum, Sevier, Atkins, & Christensen, 2005) using hierarchical growth curve analysis to examine mechanisms of change in Christensen and colleagues' (2004) clinical trial comparing TBCT with IBCT. Both therapies were effective in increasing emotional acceptance and improving communication behaviors across the course of therapy; however, these changes differed by treatment modality in a manner consistent with their respective presumed change mechanisms. Specifically, acceptance increased significantly more for couples in IBCT than for couples in TBCT, whereas couples in TBCT showed larger initial gains in positive communication. Moreover, examination of change separately in the first and second halves of therapy indicated that change in targeted behaviors was a powerful mechanism of change early in therapy whereas, in the second half of therapy, emotional acceptance was more strongly related to changes in relationship satisfaction.

Several studies have examined change processes using task analysis to link proximal outcomes occurring within or between sessions to specific therapeutic events. In an initial pilot study comparing IBCT with TBCT, Cordova, Jacobson, and Christensen (1998) found that couples in IBCT showed relatively more constructive detachment over the course of therapy, and that these changes predicted couples' gains in relationship satisfaction. Three task-analytic studies of EFCT (Greenberg, Ford, Alden, & Johnson, 1993) showed that: (a) couples receiving EFCT demonstrated more shifts from hostility to affiliative behaviors than waiting-list couples; (b) best sessions as identified by couples were characterized by more depth of experiencing and affiliative and autonomous statements than were sessions identified as poor; and (c) intimate, emotionally laden self-disclosure by one partner was more likely to lead to affiliative statements by the other partner than were other randomly selected responses. A more recent task analysis of four EFCT sessions by Bradley and Furrow (2004) found that specific therapist interventions linked to "softening events" (reformulations of partners' hostile or critical comments as expressions of vulnerability) involved intensifying a couple's emotional experience and promoting intrapsychic awareness and interpersonal shifts in attachment-related interactions.

Predictors of Treatment Outcome

Research targeting predictors of couple therapy outcome has overwhelmingly emphasized prognostic rather than prescriptive indicators (Snyder et al., 2006). The former predict response to a particular treatment (or response across treatments, irrespective of specific approach), whereas the latter predict response to one versus another treatment. Although prescriptive indicators are essential to informed selection of specific interventions in tailoring treatment to partner or relationship attributes, empirical findings in this regard are virtually non-existent.

Studies examining demographic, individual, and relationship prognostic indicators of treatment outcome are more frequent, but their yield has been modest and mixed (see reviews by Snyder et al., 2006; Whisman, McKelvie, & Chatav, 2005). The most consistent finding (but of limited usefulness in selecting interventions) is that couples having the greatest difficulties in their relationship are less likely to benefit from treatment, with initial levels of relationship distress accounting for up to 46% of the variance in treatment outcome (Johnson, 2002). Lack of commitment and behavioral steps taken toward divorce have been associated with poor treatment outcome to BCT in two studies (Beach & Broderick, 1983; Hahlweg, Schindler, Revenstorf, & Brengelmann, 1984), but not in another (Jacobson, Follette, & Pagel, 1986). Snyder, Mangrum, and Wills (1993) found that poorer response to couple therapy was predicted by lower relationship quality, greater negative relationship affect and disengagement, and greater desired change in the relationship.

Effectiveness Investigations

The effectiveness of couple therapy in the field outside of research settings has not been researched sufficiently. In two uncontrolled prospective studies, Hahlweg and Klann (1998) and Klann (2002) investigated the effectiveness of marital counseling in Germany. In total, 139 counselors recruited 1,152 clients into the study. The interpretation of the results is difficult because the attrition rate was high: Only about 50% of the clients participated in the post-assessment six months later. Pre-post comparisons resulted in significant improvements in several scales. The effect size for the Global Dissatisfaction Scale (of the Marital Satisfaction Inventory, MSI; Snyder, 1981) was ES = 0.45, a medium effect size. About 26% reported happy relationships after couple counseling – considerably less than in the Christensen, Atkins, Yi, Baucom, and George (2006) study, which leaves room for improvement of everyday effectiveness.

Conclusions

To conclude, couple therapy has been investigated widely demonstrating strong effect sizes. Furthermore, it has been demonstrated that it is effective in changing risk factors: e.g., dysfunctional communication patterns. Research also demonstrates its effectiveness in treating generalized relationship distress as well as comorbid relationship problems and individual emotional and behavioral difficulties.

Couple Therapy and Child Functioning

As described, couple conflict, distress and the lack of a warm positive relationship with parents, insecure attachment as well as harsh, inflexible, and inconsistent discipline tactics are risk factors for a range of poor child outcomes. In the context of couple therapy and the prevention of couple distress, the relevance of these findings seems to be obvious: One of the major tasks in couple intervention is to lower the likelihood that children will experience the above-mentioned negative consequences. Between 66% (Christensen et al., 2004) and 78% (Hahlweg & Klann, 1998) of couples in marital therapy have at least one child, on average of 7 years old. Approximately 40% of treatment couples with children report that they frequently fight about child rearing. Couples with children are more distressed than childless couples at the beginning of therapy, and couples with children improve less in marital satisfaction than couples without children, immediately at post therapy and at the 2-year follow-up (Gattis & Christensen, 2004).

Couple therapy seems to have no effects or only small effects on child-related variables. At present, only two studies have investigated the effects of marital treatment on child-related problems. Christensen and colleagues (2004) compared two forms of behavioral couple therapy, and Hahlweg and Klann (1998) investigated the effectiveness of couple counseling in Germany. Both used the Dissatisfaction with Children (DSC) scale and the Conflict over Childrearing (CCR) scale from the Marital Satisfaction Inventory (MSI) by Snyder (1981). The pre-post effect sizes were somewhat similar and quite low – for DSC: 0.07 versus 0.09, and for CCR: 0.20 versus 0.08. BCT seems to be no more effective than eclectic marital counseling in changing parental attitudes and behavior toward children.

Conversely, parent training appears to have an impact on couple relationship satisfaction. Ireland, Sanders, and Markie-Dadds (2003) provided evidence that behavioral family intervention programs that primarily target the parent-child relationship can have pervasive effects on other aspects of the family system, including the marital relationship. The effects on the marital relationship were achieved without direct training in the specific marital communication skills hypothesized to comprise more supportive partner behavior. There is now considerable evidence to show that parenting interventions are often associated with decreased parental stress and depression, increased parenting efficacy, and improved marital functioning.

Despite the importance of child functioning in couples' relationships, most couple treatment manuals give only scant attention to child-related issues: e.g., Epstein and Baucom (2002), Jacobson and Christensen (1996), Halford (2001), and Schindler, Hahlweg, and Revenstorf (2006). In order to provide comprehensive interventions to families, it seems plausible and necessary to combine couple interventions with parenting skills training, with the goal of enhancing couple relationship functioning along with child well-being. In summary, couple therapists should recognize that to be of most assistance to couples, they can benefit from attending to parenting and child behavior problems. Such an emphasis would include:

(a) Routinely assessing the parenting skills (using, e.g., the Parenting Scale (Arnold, O'Leary, Wolff, & Acker, 1992)), conflicts over child rearing (MSI-R (Snyder, 1991)), and child behavior problems (child behavior checklist, CBCL (Achenbach & Resorla, 2000), or the Strength and Difficulties Questionnaire, SDQ (Goodman, Ford, Simmons, Gatward, & Meltzer, 2000)).
(b) Educating the couple about the deleterious effects that couple conflict can have on their child.
(c) Educating the couple how a temperamentally difficult child or a child with special needs (e.g., a mentally retarded or hyperactive child) can influence the couple's relationship.
(d) Teaching and actively training the couple in:
  1. Communication skills and problem-solving training with a focus on child-related problems;
  2. Dealing with stressors outside of the relationship (see Bodenmann, this volume);
  3. Parenting skills (e.g., using the Triple P system (Sanders, 1999)).

Prevention

A viable alternative to treating marital distress is to provide *preventive* interventions while the couple is still happy or at least in the early stages of distress. Based on a cognitive-behavioral approach, the working model of intervention assumes that the couple's communication difficulties, e.g., the inability to handle negative emotions and to solve conflicts, underlie the deterioration of a relationship. Consequently, the goal of preventive efforts is to decrease the frequency of negative and increase the frequency of positive exchanges during conflict discussions and to solve relationship issues more effectively.

Universal preventive interventions target an entire population, e.g., all couples planning marriage, rather than focusing on high-risk groups. There are a number of well-researched and effective preventive programs, including:

- Premarital Relationship Enhancement Program, PREP (Markman, Floyd, Stanley, & Stoorasli, 1988)
- Ehevorbereitung – Ein Partnerschaftliches Lernprogramm, EPL (Premarital Preparation – A Couples' Learning Program; Hahlweg, Markman, Thurmaier, Engl, & Eckert, 1998; Thurmaier, Engl, & Hahlweg, 1999)
- Freiburger Stress Präventions Programm, FSPP (Couples Coping Enhancement Training (CCET, see Bodenmann, this volume)
- Couple Commitment and Relationship Enhancement, Couple CARE (see Halford, this volume).

These programs can be delivered individually or in groups either in six weekly sessions of approximately 2.5-hour duration or at a weekend meeting (typically Friday evening to Sunday afternoon). Group sizes vary from three to five couples with two trainers for each group. The couples meet as a group for the lecture portions of the sessions but meet alone and work with a trainer for all other aspects of each session.

There is a general finding that most couples who complete pre-marriage education programs generally report high satisfaction with the programs. The Giblin, Sprenkle, and Sheehan (1985) meta-analysis of 85 relationship education and enhancement programs found an average effect size of 0.44 across all programs and relationship outcome measures, which corresponds to a moderate effect size. The Hahlweg and Markman (1988) meta-analysis included seven controlled studies, which all included relationship skills training. They found a large mean effect size of 0.79 for cognitive-behaviorally oriented education programs relative to controls. The most meaningful index of the efficacy of relationship education is its long-term effects. At the 3-year follow-up (Markman et al., 1988), PREP couples were more satisfied than control couples who showed the predictable declines that occur in most relationships over time. Furthermore, PREP couples were more satisfied with their sexuality, had lower levels of problem intensity, and reported significantly fewer instances of spousal physical violence than control couples. At the 4-year follow-up, there was a significantly lower dissolution rate among the PREP couples relative to controls (but no differences in divorce rate); and PREP couples showed more positive and less negative communication than control couples. The EPL was evaluated in a longitudinal prospective study (Hahlweg et al., 1998; Thurmaier et al., 1999). At the 5-year follow-up, the divorce rates differed significantly: 16% in the control versus 4% in the EPL group. EPL couples also demonstrated significantly greater use of positive verbal and non-verbal behavior than control couples. Control-group couples displayed significantly greater use of negative verbal behavior (e.g., criticism and disagreement) and non-verbal negative behavior than EPL spouses.

The results of these two prospective longitudinal studies demonstrate a significant impact of the universal interventions on couples' functioning over a 5-year period. The German findings replicate those of Markman, Renick, Floyd, Stanley, and Clements, (1993) cross-culturally and demonstrate the possibility of preventing relationship distress and dissolution through a short-term intervention focused on building skills in functional communication and conflict management for satisfied couples at the beginning of their relationship.

Selective preventive interventions target subgroups of the population who have elevated risk for developing a problem. One example is to provide premarital relationship enhancement programs only to those couples in which one or both partners come from a divorced family and are therefore at elevated risk for developing marital problems. Only PREP has been used as a selective preventive intervention. Van Widenfelt, Hosman, Schaap, and van der Staak (1996) and Halford, Sanders, and Behrens (2001) have explored the efficacy of PREP-based interventions for high-risk couples who came from divorced families and/or had experienced physical aggression in their families. Van Widenfelt et al. found essentially no treatment effects, but the findings are difficult to compare with other premarital interventions because their couples were significantly older than those in other studies, had been living together for a number of years prior to the intervention, and no observational measures were used.

Halford et al. (2001) conducted a randomized controlled trial of a skills-based relationship education program, with collection of relationship satisfaction and stability data at a 4-year follow-up. The relationship education program evaluated was Self-PREP, which is similar in content to PREP, but has a self-regulation component. A unique aspect of this study was that couples were stratified into high and low risk for relationship problems on the basis of negative family-of-origin experiences (parental divorce or inter-parental violence). Couples completing Self-PREP were found to have significantly higher relationship satisfaction at 4-year follow-up than couples in a control condition, but this effect was only evident for couples at high risk of relationship problems. The possibility that relationship education may have differential effects for low- and high-risk couples needs further exploration.

Indicated prevention involves selecting couples who self-identify with some symptoms of distressed relationships but who do not identify themselves as maritally distressed in need of therapy. This intervention format is similar to the many psycho-educational, enrichment programs offered to married couples by churches. In a study by Kaiser, Hahlweg, Fehm-Wolfsdorf, and Groth (1998) couples with a minimum partnership duration of 3 years were recruited. The EPL couples reported significantly fewer relationship problems after the intervention and also showed greater skill in positive verbal and non-verbal communication (namely self-disclosure, positive solution, and acceptance of partner) and fewer negative verbal communication behaviors (criticism and justification) than control couples. Recently, an 11-year follow-up interview study was conducted (Hahlweg & Richter, 2008). The response rate after 11 years was 93%. The divorce rate in those couples attending the EPL were 26%; in those who did not attend, it was 56%. For those couples still being together, the rate of happy relationships was 80%; thus, there is optimism for older couples who are willing to focus on improving their relationships.

Couples entering marriage and similar committed relationships are heterogeneous with respect to their relationship education needs, yet there has been little research on tailoring programs to the needs of couples. In the future, adaptations of existing universal, selective, or indicated prevention programs are needed to address issues specific to particular couples (see also Halford & Casey; Markman & Rhoades, this volume). For example, stepfamilies and couples in which a partner has a psychological disorder warrant special attention. Future research also should address the needs of couples at stages other than just the transition into the relationship. For example, couples making the transition to parenthood or facing health crises (see Baucom et al.; Halford & Casey; Heinrichs, this volume) may benefit from specialized relationship education.

Are the Interventions Culturally Appropriate and Available?

It is important to assess the cultural context within which relationship standards develop and may be reinforced (Epstein & Baucom, 2002; Halford, 1999). Partners who differ in their ethnic, racial, or cultural background often differ in their expectations and beliefs about relationships. This diversity in partner assumptions and beliefs can be a positive source for a relationship when the partners are able to draw on the wisdom and strength from different cultural traditions. At the same time, substantial differences in expectations can be a significant source of conflict between the partners, and marriages in which partners have very different cultural backgrounds tend to break down at somewhat higher rates than other marriages (Kurdek, 1993). At least for behavioral couple therapy, evidence exists that the interventions bring about change in couples from diverse cultures.

Do We Have "Ready-To-Use" Resources (e.g., Treatment Manuals and Psycho-Educational Materials) That Can Be Made Available to Service Providers?

Quality materials are needed that can be made readily available to service providers. Several resources, e.g., self-help books, videos, or DVDs, exist in different languages, published by the various developers of couple interventions, e.g., Baucom, Bodenmann, Christensen, Hahlweg, Halford, Schindler, Markman, or Snyder.

Is an Effective Training and Supervision Program Available?

To the degree possible, existing personnel should be employed to deliver the programs, persons such as those employed at marital counseling agencies, and church staff. Such persons know how their agencies operate and will require less effort to be accepted and assimilated into existing personnel than would occur with new staff hired to run new programs. These personnel will require standardized training programs to administer the skills-based programs. Any program must allow for a certain amount of individuality among presenters and trainers in the delivery of the program, but it is essential that the persons trained learn a standardized way to administer a given program. Understandably, many clinicians desire to be creative and put their own perspective on issues such as marriage. Lack of standardization runs the risk that the programs provided might differ widely from what we know to be effective. Similarly, there is a tendency for individuals to "drift" over time in the delivery of a standardized program; consequently, initial training in a standardized manner does not ensure that a program will continue to be offered in that fashion over time.

Therefore, continued periodic training of personnel and ongoing assessment of how a program is being delivered are important to maintain the integrity of the program. As a part of this process, the success of the training program itself should be evaluated. A model in this respect is the Triple P positive parenting program in which such standardized training programs and dissemination procedures have been developed (Sanders, 1999, 2008).

Professional change is more likely to occur when supervisors, managers, and professional colleagues support the adoption or change process (Backer, Liberman, & Kuehnel, 1986; Parcel, Perry, & Taylor, 1990); when peer supervision, feedback, and support is available (Henggeler, Melton, Brondino, Scherer, & Hanley, 1997); and where computer technologies such as the web and e-mail services are used to support and provide consultative backup to professionals. In organizations where a culture of innovation is supported by management through the provision of resources and attention, a greater success in establishing and implementing new initiatives is predicted (Ash, 1997).

In Germany, marital counseling agencies are primarily financed by the Catholic and Lutheran churches, which have developed their own training programs for counselors, not in cooperation with empirically oriented clinical psychology or with respective university departments. In the Catholic church, training is provided in every diocese; in the Lutheran church, the training is centralized and conducted in Berlin. The training (regardless of the institution) consists of 140 hours of theoretical teaching, 140 hours of group-dynamic meetings, 150 hours of practical client counseling, and 70 hours of supervision. The theoretical approach is psychodynamically oriented with few, if any, cognitive-behavioral elements and is open for a variety of BA-educated professions. In order to change the way counseling is taught in the near future, a strategy is needed to influence and convince key figures (stakeholders) in the various churches as well as the counselors working in the agencies – which are often very reluctant to change, devalue cognitive-behavioral approaches, and oppose using manuals for treatment.

Are Couple/Parent Interventions Widely Available?

As discussed in the previous section, the base rate of trainers/therapists adhering to an empirically based approach in Germany is not known. One could add to the 2,600 counselors approximately 16,000 psychological psychotherapists working in private practice. How many of those are trained in couple therapy is not known. In psychotherapy training, couple therapy is most often not offered, basically because (a) psychotherapy is viewed as individual therapy and (b) insurance companies do not pay for couple therapy.

Even having evidence-based interventions available in principle does not mean that all couples will participate. As Doss, Carhart, Hsueh, and Rahbar (this volume) summarized, only about 25–37% of couples in the US and 42% of couples in Australia seek relationship counseling or marital therapy of any kind before getting divorced. In Germany alone, 200,000 couples got divorced in 2006. Using the US data, 50,000–70,000 should have looked for some form of couple counseling. Couple therapy is also underutilized by non-divorced couples since only 10% seek marital therapy (10% go to clergy for help) despite the high rate of divorce and marital distress. Empirically based estimates for Germany or Switzerland are not available; percentages are most likely not higher. The percentage of couples receiving evidence-based interventions is not known.

Estimates of the utilization of evidence-based treatments can be derived from couple counseling in Germany. There are approximately 900 counseling institutions with about 2,600 counselors in Germany. The mean age of counselors is 45 years; the mean duration of their counseling experience is 11 years. The mean number of sessions per year is about 500 (SD = 243, range 50–1,040), the mean number of sessions per couple is 13 (SD = 6.7). The theoretical number of couples that could be treated per year is 2.600 × 39 (500/13) = 100,000.

All counselors in Germany have university (master's) degrees: Approximately 25% in psychology, 25% in theology, 15% in social work, 20% in teaching, and 15% in other areas. In addition to counselor training cited above, most of them have some form of additional postgraduate training in psychotherapy of varying intensity. The main therapeutic orientations they rely on when treating couples vary considerably (Hahlweg & Klann, 1998): 40% integrative, 30% systems-communication theory, 20% psychodynamic, 20% Gestalt, 17% behavior therapy, and 16% Rogerian. These orientation labels are subjective and add to more than 100% because some counselors reported more than one orientation. One can estimate that at the outmost only about one third of counselors use some form of evidence-based interventions, and only very few apply manualized treatments – one of the prerequisites of an evidence-based treatment.

The situation in the area of universal prevention/premarital education is as follows: In the US and Australia, the percentage of couples receiving some form of universal preventive interventions (relationship education) is about 30% (see Doss et al., this volume). Samples collected in religious organizations have considerably higher participation rates – given that most churches require premarital counseling in order to get married in church. Representative data for Germany and Switzerland is not available.

In 2006, 380,000 couples got married in Germany. How many of those couples attended a premarital education course is unknown. However, the dissemination of the EPL program gives some suggestions about the status of empirically based interventions: Since 1988, approximately 1,600 EPL providers have been trained in Germany. Of those, about 50% are still active. It is unknown how many EPL trainings in total are conducted in Germany. In Munich (50 trainers are active) $N = 20$ EPL groups were conducted in 2006 with $N = 92$ couples (in 2005 $N = 95$ couples). Participation was subsidized in that each couple received €110 from the Catholic church. Given these figures, one can estimate that approximately 1,500 couples per year (< 0.5%) attend an EPL course.

In a study by Lösel, Schmucker, Blanckensteiner, and Weiss (2006), the dissemination of relationship education provided by family centers was investigated. Of the 200,000 events offered to the public per year, only about 1,500 were devoted to relationship enhancement; of those, 65% were self-developed by the provider, and only about 7% had a cognitive-behavioral background. Only 1.4% used some form of broader empirical evaluation, and 16% used client satisfaction measures. These very low participation rates in attending evidence-based interventions are unlikely to change the prevalence rates of couple distress or divorce.

Sanders (2008) estimated the number of parents who are required to participate in universal interventions of the Triple P program for a population level benefit to be detected.

> "In Every Family, a large-scale project focusing on the transition to school, we estimated the number of parents that needed to participate in a Triple P intervention to achieve a 5, 10, or 15% reduction of child behavioral or emotional problems at a population level. Calculations used population prevalence rates from a baseline CATI (Computer Assisted Telephone Interview) survey, which indicated that 23% of children were in the clinical range for emotional and behavioral problems. Based on effectiveness studies conducted as part of Every Family (Sanders et al., 2005), we estimated approximately one third of parents would need to participate in the universal program in order to achieve a 5% reduction in population prevalence rates of children's behavioral and emotional problems."

Having determined the minimum numbers of parents who need to participate, strategies are needed to optimize engagement. Parents' willingness to participate in a parenting program depends on a number of factors including the nature of the program offered, how it is delivered, parents' perceptions of whether the program is relevant and meets their needs, how much time they will need to invest in completing the program, and the payoff they anticipate relative to other uses of their time (Morawska & Sanders, 2006). A number of different strategies can be used to promote engagement including using the mass media to normalize and de-stigmatize participation. Television programs on parenting not only attract large viewing audiences, but there is some evidence that parenting practices improve when parents view others undergoing an evidence-based parenting program. The media can play an important role in raising parents' awareness and willingness to attend a parenting program. Different media messages can be used to demystify what is involved by providing relevant, meaningful, and accurate information for parents. Media messages also provide opportunities to depict parents' experiences of receiving professional support.

Do Strategies Exist That Help to Build Sustainability?

The quality of the couple intervention, the type of skills training service providers receive, and the supportiveness of the post-training workplace environment interact to determine whether service providers change the way they work with couples and parents. To promote practitioner self-efficacy, e.g., in using Triple P, program content and processes are introduced through active skills training methods with a focus on self-directed learning, personal goal setting for skill development, self-evaluation, and problem solving (Sanders, 2008). Professional behavior change is more likely when managers, administrators, and colleagues support the adoption of the innovation and when adequate supervision and support is available (Henggeler et al., 1997). Hence, an effective dissemination process must not only adequately train practitioners in the intervention, but must also engage the participating organizations to ensure that the program is supported. Furthermore, a strategy is needed to manage the sociopolitical environment that inevitably surrounds population level interventions.

Are Continuous Quality Control Measures to Monitor the Ongoing Implementation of the Interventions Built in?

Evidence concerning the impact of public health interventions is concerned with the well-being of entire populations of children and parents. This requires some form of population level auditing, community surveillance, or surveying of couples to assess whether couple distress has decreased, whether there has been an increase in partner's use of positive communication and problem-solving methods and a decrease in dysfunctional relationship practices. Changes in participation rates in couple programs and access to media support should increase.

Prinz and Sanders (2007) used both population level household surveys collected through CATIs that included assessment of constructs that provide population indices of penetration and impact, assessment of practitioners, and evaluation of cost considerations. They also employed aggregate archival data at a county level to evaluate the impact of Triple P as a population level intervention to prevent child maltreatment from records of statutory authorities to assess founded and unfounded cases of child maltreatment, out-of-home placements, and hospitalization accident and injury data.

Recommendations for Dissemination and Policy in the Couple Area

As noted in this chapter, a great deal has been learned about the prevention and alleviation of couple distress in recent years. Based upon such findings, we are now at a point where careful thought and planning can reap fruitful results in a national program to prevent marital distress. In order to develop a comprehensive, national scope prevention program, a number of steps are necessary (Baucom, 1998; Hahlweg, 2004):

Development of a Multilevel Set of Interventions to Assist Couples

In order to reach a broad range of couples who have different needs and who will be receptive to different levels of intervention, a multilevel set of couples' interventions must be developed. For example, Sanders and colleagues (1999) have created a multilevel set of interventions for parenting, which can serve as a conceptual framework for a focus on couples. Adapting from Sanders' terminology, several different levels of intervention can be differentiated according to the intensity of intervention: (a) universal couples' interventions based on a public health model with no direct couple contact; (b) primary care for couples who want to address their own relationship without direct contact; (c) active skills training and education for couples involving direct contact with trained interventionists; and (d) couple therapy or counseling for distressed couples.

Universal Couples' Interventions

Many couples do not wish to focus directly on their marital relationships in a concentrated manner, attending workshops or counseling sessions. Yet, minimal intervention might be of assistance to a wide variety of couples when considered from a public health perspective. In the arena of child behavior problems, Sanders, Montgomery, and Brechman-Toussaint (2000) have demonstrated that a professionally produced television series in an infotainment format is watched by a large number of parents with high levels of consumer satisfaction. A similar set of television segments focusing on the couple, either within a larger series devoted to the family or as a stand-alone series, could reach a large segment of the population. In addition to assisting couples in its own right, such a series might open discussion among partners about their own relationship and make them more motivated to seek additional assistance if it is needed.

Primary Care Focusing on a Couple's Own Relationship

While the above strategy provides general information about marriage including universally relevant themes and information, additional intervention strategies are needed for couples who want to focus on their own relationships in a more detailed manner. Again, the couple intervention field could draw upon the work of Sanders and colleagues, who have produced a series of Tip Sheets with information that parents can request about specific aspects of parenting relevant to their own situations; a series of videotapes elaborating upon these themes is also available (Sanders, Turner, & Markie-Dadds, 1996). A similar strategy can be employed focusing on couples. There is already a wealth of information about marriage and communication skills that has been produced in a variety of formats for couples, including handouts and self-help books for couples that can be employed and adapted for such purposes. The availability of such materials can be advertised through the above television series, newspaper advertisements, television and radio announcements, and brochures in primary health care settings.

In addition to the use of television programs, videotapes, and printed materials, recent advances in technology provide additional opportunities for reaching couples without direct, ongoing intervention. The increasing widespread use of computers provides at least two additional mechanisms for reaching couples. One of the strengths of the computer is its ability to provide access to extremely large databases within the context of one's own home. This can be useful to individuals who are in more remote settings or who for a variety of reasons are not comfortable discussing marital issues with persons outside of the family. One mechanism for providing such information is through the Internet. Thus, a web page with a variety of information about couples, married life, links to other sites, and information about agencies and groups to contact if the individual desires direct contact might reach segments of the population who are unlikely to contact professionals initially.

Another strategy for using the computer to assist couples is through the development of interactive DVDs or web-based programs (see Casey & Halford; Halford & Casey, this volume). Such computer programs could be purchased or accessed by the individual couple and used on their home computers. The current storage capacities of these devices provide great flexibility regarding the types of materials that can be presented, along with interactive strategies. Although not all couples would be comfortable with such a format, a number of couples might actually find it to be preferable. For example, most requests for couple therapy or help with family problems come from women; men are known to seek assistance from the mental health field less frequently than women. Thus, a modality that allows men to stay within their homes might be appealing. Second, a significant number of men are captivated by the technology of computer programs, and thus might be receptive to such a medium.

Active Skills Training and Education from Trained Interventionists

The hallmark of the above interventions is that they involve little or no direct contact between the couple and professionals in the couple field. These strategies need to be supplemented with interventions that allow a couple to work directly with persons trained to assist couples with their marriages. As Halford (1999) has noted, existing programs for couples can be categorized as (a) information-based educational programs that do not involve teaching skills to couples and (b) skill-based education programs. Both basic research and treatment research point to the importance of skill-based programs for couples. The results of skill-based couple programs such as PREP, EPL, or FSPP demonstrate that these interventions have promise in assisting couples. The application of such prevention programs in multiple countries including Germany, US, Australia, and The Netherlands provides a wealth of information and experience upon which to draw in establishing a broad network of active skill-based programs for couples.

Couple Therapy for Distressed Couples

The above strategies are designed to help prevent the development of couple discord or provide assistance as distress is developing. In addition, assistance is needed for couples who are currently distressed. At present, there are several approaches to couple therapy (i.e., cognitive-behavioral, integrative-behavioral, insight-oriented, and emotion-focused couple therapy) that have received empirical support for their effectiveness. The most researched and well-validated approach is a cognitive-behavioral intervention that is consistent with the skill-based prevention programs described above. In order to help couples avoid the multiple complications resulting from divorce for both parents and children, it is important that care continue to be provided for these distressed couples.

Summary

As can be seen, in order to develop a comprehensive program to support and assist couples at different levels of need and with different levels of comfort in seeking assistance, a wide variety of intervention strategies are needed. The first two levels of intervention described above rely upon a variety of media strategies to reach couples who do not wish or need to work directly with a trained interventionist in the marital field. The creative use of a variety of media including television, DVD, printed materials, web pages, and interactive computer programs can greatly extend outreach to couples in the community. In order to successfully develop, coordinate, and disseminate such a variety of offerings, an organizational strategy and structure on the national level is needed.

Creation of an Organization and Structure to Oversee the Development and Dissemination of Couple Interventions

The exact nature of the organizational structure necessary to provide the interventions described above will require a great deal of thought by the various parties involved. However, even at present, at least one major recommendation is appropriate: Any organizational structure that is developed should draw heavily on both public agencies and universities. The actual delivery of prevention/intervention programs is likely to be based within a variety of public agencies, and their involvement from the beginning is essential. These agencies know how they operate, who their personnel are, the populations they serve, and regional factors that will either contribute to or deter effective dissemination. Thus, not only do these agencies have a great deal of first-hand experience in the delivery of services, but it also is critical that they have a sense of involvement and ownership of programs that are developed. Widespread development, dissemination, and success of couple programs are unlikely if agencies experience that the programs are being thrust upon them from the outside.

Equally essential in the organizational efforts is the presence and leadership of university faculty who have had experience in conducting basic research on couples and who have experience in developing and evaluating couple treatment and prevention programs. These scholars can help to ensure that changes proposed to the intervention programs due to cultural factors, regional preferences, etc. do not disrupt the basic integrity of the programs and are consistent with basic research findings. University faculty also are likely to be integral in developing and evaluating the training programs to ensure that those delivering the program meet criteria. Similarly, university faculty likely will be central in conducting the ongoing evaluation of the intervention programs, including the design of the evaluation components, data analysis, and interpretation of findings.

Conclusion

The field of couple therapy and prevention has made great strides over the past decades, and innovations continue to evolve as theoreticians, researchers, trainers, and clinicians employ recent findings to benefit couples and families. In order for the field to benefit maximally from these ongoing findings and recommendations, it is important that coordinated efforts be made, such as those in the recommendations discussed above.

References

Achenbach, T. M., & Resorla, C. A. (2000). *Manual for the ASEBA preschool forms and profiles*. Burlington: University of Vermont.

Amato, P. R. (2001). Children of divorce in the 1990s: An update of the Amato and Keith (1991) meta-analysis. *Journal of Family Psychology, 15*, 355–370.

Arnold, D. S., O'Leary, S. G., Wolff, L. S., & Acker, M. M. (1992). The parenting scale: A measure of dysfunctional parenting in discipline situations. *Psychological Assessment, 4*, 66–83.

Ash, J. (1997). Organisational factors that influence information technology diffusion in academic health science centres. *Journal of the American Information Association, 4*, 102–111.

Backer, T. E., Liberman, R. P., & Kuehnel, T. G. (1986). Dissemination and adoption of innovative psychosocial interventions. *Journal of Consulting and Clinical Psychology, 54*(1), 111–118.

Baucom, D. H. (1998). Maßnahmen zur Prävention von Beziehungsstörungen und Scheidung [Recommendations for the prevention of marital distress and divorce]. In K. Hahlweg, D. H. Baucom, R. Bastine & H. J. Markman (Eds.), *Vorhersage und Prävention von Beziehungsstörungen und Scheidung* [The prediction and prevention of marital distress and divorce: An international perspective] (pp. 52–68). Stuttgart, Germany: Kohlhammer.

Baucom, D. H., Epstein, N. B., LaTaillade, J. J., & Kirby, J. S. (2008). Cognitive behavioral couple therapy. In A. S. Gurman & N. S. Jacobson (Eds.), *Clinical handbook of couple therapy* (4th ed, pp. 31–72). New York: Guilford.

Beach, S. R. H., & Broderick, J. E. (1983). Commitment: A variable in women's response to marital therapy. *American Journal of Family Therapy, 11*, 16–24.
Bradley, B., & Furrow, J. L. (2004). Toward a mini-theory of the blamer softening event: Tracking the moment-by-moment process. *Journal of Marital and Family Therapy, 30*, 1–12.
Burman, B., & Margolin, G. (1992). Analysis of the association between marital relationships and health problems: An interactional perspective. *Psychological Bulletin, 112*, 39–63.
Buss, D. H. (1995). Psychological sex differences: Origins through sexual selection. *American Psychologist, 50*, 164–168.
Cherlin, A. (1992). *Marriage, divorce, and remarriage*. Cambridge, MA: Harvard University Press.
Christensen, A., Atkins, D. C., Berns, S., Wheeler, J., Baucom, D. H., & Simpson, L. E. (2004). Traditional versus integrative behavioral couple therapy for significantly and chronically distressed married couples. *Journal of Consulting and Clinical Psychology, 72*, 76–191.
Christensen, A., Atkins, D. C., Yi, J., Baucom, D. H., & George, W. H. (2006). Couple and individual adjustment for two years following a randomized clinical trial comparing traditional versus integrative behavioral couple therapy. *Journal of Consulting and Clinical Psychology, 74*, 1180–1191.
Coie, J. D., Watt, N., West, S. G., Hawkins, J. D., Asarnow, J. R., Markman, H. J., et al. (1993). The science of prevention: A conceptual framework and some directions for a national research program. *American Psychologist, 48*, 1013–1022.
Cordova, J. V., Jacobson, N. S., & Christensen, A. (1998). Acceptance versus change interventions in behavioral couple therapy: Impact on couples' in-session communication. *Journal of Marital and Family Therapy, 24*, 437–455.
Diekmann, A., & Engelhardt, H. (1995). Die soziale Vererbung des Scheidungsrisikos. Eine empirische Untersuchung der Transmissionshypothese mit dem deutschen Familiensurvey [The social inheritance of divorce: An empirical test of the transmission hypothesis using the German family survey]. *Zeitschrift für Soziologie, 24*, 215–228.
Doss, B. D., Thum, Y. M., Sevier, M., Atkins, D. C., & Christensen, A. (2005). Improving relationships: Mechanisms of change in couple therapy. *Journal of Consulting and Clinical Psychology, 73*, 624–633.
Dunn, R. L., & Schwebel, A. I. (1995). Meta-analytic review of marital therapy outcome research. *Journal of Family Psychology, 9*, 58–68.
Epstein, N., & Baucom, D. H. (2002). *Enhanced cognitive-behavioral therapy for couples. A contextual approach*. Washington, DC: APA.
Flay, B. R., Biglan, A., Boruch, R. F., Castro, F. G., Gottfredson, D., Kellam, S., et al. (2005). Standards of evidence: Criteria for efficacy, effectiveness and dissemination. *Prevention Science, 6*(3), 151–175.
Fowers, B. J., Lyons, E. M., & Montel, K. H. (1996). Positive marital illusions: Self-enhancement or relationship enhancement? *Journal of Family Psychology, 10*, 192–208.
Friedman, H. S., Tucker, J. S., Schwartz, J. E., Tomlinson-Keasey, C., Martin, L. R., Wingard, D. L., et al. (1995). Psychosocial and behavioral predictors of longevity. The aging and death of the "Termites". *American Psychologist, 50*, 69–78.
Gallup, G. Jr. (1990). *The Gallup poll: Public opinion 1990*. Wilmington, DE: Scholarly Resources.
Gattis, K., & Christensen, A. (2004). *Couple therapy, parenting and child adjustment*. Paper presented at the meeting of the Association of Cognitive and Behavioral Therapies, Washington DC, USA.
Giblin, P., Sprenkle, D. H., & Sheehan, R. (1985). Enrichment outcome research: A meta-analysis of premarital, marital and family interventions. *Journal of Marital and Family Therapy, 11*, 257–271.
Glenn, N. D. (1998). The course of marital success and failure in five American 10-year cohorts. *Journal of Marriage and the Family, 60*, 269–282.

Goldman, A., & Greenberg, L. S. (1992). Comparison of integrated systemic and emotionally focused approaches to couples therapy. *Journal of Consulting and Clinical Psychology, 60*, 962–969.

Goodman, M. R., Ford, T., Simmons, H., Gatward, R., & Meltzer, H. (2000). Using the strength and difficulties questionnaire (SDQ) to screen for child psychiatric disorders in a community sample. *British Journal of Psychiatry, 177*, 534–539.

Greenberg, L. S., Ford, C. L., Alden, L., & Johnson, S. M. (1993). In-session change in emotionally focused therapy. *Journal of Consulting and Clinical Psychology, 61*, 78–84.

Hahlweg, K. (2004). Strengthening partnerships and families. In P. L. Chase-Lindale, K. Kiernan & R. J. Friedman (Eds.), *Human development across lives and generations* (pp. 204–238). Cambridge, England: Cambridge University Press.

Hahlweg, K., & Klann, N. (1998). The effectiveness of marital counseling in Germany: Contribution to health services research. *Journal of Family Psychology, 11*, 410–421.

Hahlweg, K., & Markman, H. J. (1988). Effectiveness of behavioral marital therapy. Empirical status of behavioral techniques in preventing and alleviating marital distress. *Journal of Consulting and Clinical Psychology, 56*, 440–447.

Hahlweg, K., Markman, H. J., Thurmaier, F., Engl, J., & Eckert, V. (1998). Prevention of marital distress: Results of a German prospective-longitudinal study. *Journal of Family Psychology, 12*, 543–556.

Hahlweg, K., & Richter, D. (2008). The 11-year long-term effects of the EPL-relationship enhancement program. In N. Heinrichs (Chair), *Couple therapy.* Symposium conducted at the 29th International Congress of Psychology, Berlin, Germany.

Hahlweg, K., Schindler, L., Revenstorf, D., & Brengelmann, J. C. (1984). The Munich marital therapy study. In K. Hahlweg & N. S. Jacobson (Eds.), *Marital interaction: Analysis and modification* (pp. 3–26). New York: Guilford.

Halford, W. K. (1999). *Australian couples in millenium three. A research and development agenda for marriage and relationship education*. Brisbane, Australia: Department of Family and Community Services; Academic Press.

Halford, W. K. (2001). *Brief therapy for couples. Helping partners help themselves*. New York: Guilford.

Halford, W. K., Kelley, A., & Markman, H. J. (1997). The concept of a healthy marriage. In W. K. Halford & H. J. Markman (Eds.), *Clinical handbook of marriage and couples interventions* (pp. 3–12). Chichester, NY: Wiley.

Halford, W. K., Sanders, M. R., & Behrens, B. C. (2001). Can skills training prevent relationship problems in at-risk couples? Four year effects of a behavioural relationship education program. *Journal of Family Psychology, 15*, 750–768.

Henggeler, S. C., Melton, G. B., Brondino, M. J., Schereer, D. G., & Hanely, J. H. (1997). Multisystemic therapy with violent and chronic juvenile offenders and their families: The role of treatment fidelity in successful dissemination. *Journal of Consulting and Clinical Psychology, 65*, 821–833.

Hetherington, E. M., & Elmore, A. M. (2004). The intergenerational transmission of couple instability. In P. L. Chase-Lindsdale, K. Kiernan & R. Friedman (Eds.), *Human development across lives and generations. The potential for change* (pp. 171–203). Cambridge: Cambridge University Press.

Holthworth-Munroe, A., Smutzler, N., Bates, L., & Sandin, E. (1997). Husband violence: Basic facts and clinical implications. In W. K. Halford & H. J. Markman (Eds.), *Clinical handbook of marriage and couples interventions* (pp. 129–156). Chichester, NY: Wiley.

Ireland, J. L., Sanders, M. R., & Markie-Dadds, C. (2003). The impact of parent training on marital functioning: A comparison of two group versions of the Triple P-positive parenting program for parents of children with early-onset conduct problems. *Behavioural and Cognitive Psychotherapy, 31*, 127–142.

Jacobson, N. S., & Christensen, A. (1996). *Integrative couple therapy: Promoting acceptance and change*. New York: Norton.

Jacobson, N. S., Follette, W. C., & Pagel, M. (1986). Predicting who will benefit from behavioral marital therapy. *Journal of Consulting and Clinical Psychology, 54*, 518–522.

Jacobson, N. S., & Margolin, G. (1979). *Marital therapy: Strategies based on social learning and behavior exchange principles*. New York: Brunner/Mazel.

Jacobson, N. S., Schmaling, K. B., & Holtzworth-Munroe, A. (1987). Component analysis of behavioral marital therapy: 2-year follow-up and prediction of relapse. *Journal of Marital and Family Therapy, 13*, 187–195.

Johnson, S. M. (2002). Marital problems. In D. H. Sprenkle (Ed.), *Effectiveness research in marriage and family therapy* (pp. 163–190). Alexandria, VA: American Association for Marriage and Family Therapy.

Johnson, S. M. (2004). *The practice of emotionally focused couple therapy* (2nd ed.). New York: Brunner-Routledge.

Kaiser, A., Hahlweg, K., Fehm-Wolfsdorf, G., & Groth, T. (1998). The efficacy of a compact psychoeducational group training program for married couples. *Journal of Consulting and Clinical Psychology, 66*, 753–760.

Karney, B. R., & Bradbury, T. N. (1995). The longitudinal course of marital quality and stability: A review of theory, method, and research. *Psychological Bulletin, 118*, 3–34.

Kiecolt-Glaser, J. K., & Newton, T. L. (2001). Marriage and health: His and hers. *Psychological Bulletin, 127*, 472–503.

Kiernan, K. (2004). Partnership behaviour across nations and generations: Continuities, discontinuities and inter-relations. In P. L. Chase-Lansdale, K. E. Kiernan & R. J. Friedman (Eds.), *Human development across lives and generations: The potential for change* (pp. 139–170). Cambridge, England: Cambridge University Press.

Klann, N. (2002). *Institutionelle Beratung – ein erfolgreiches Angebot* [Counselling in institutions – an effective offer]. Freiburg, Germany: Lambertus.

Kurdek, L. A. (1993). Predicting marital dissolution: A 5-year prospective longitudinal study of newlywed couples. *Journal of Personality and Social Psychology, 64*, 221–242.

Lösel, F., Schmucker, M., Blanckensteiner, B., & Weiss, M. (2006). *Bestandsaufnahme und Evaluation von Angeboten im Elternbildungsbereich. Abschlussbericht* [*Survey and evaluation of educational measures for parents*], Erlangen-Nürnberg: Universität Erlangen-Nürnberg.

Markman, H. J., Floyd, F., Stanley, S., & Storaasli, R. (1988). Prevention of marital distress: A longitudinal investigation. *Journal of Consulting and Clinical Psychology, 56*, 210–217.

Markman, H. J., Renick, M. J., Floyd, F., Stanley, S., & Clements, M. (1993). Preventing marital distress through communication and conflict management training: A 4- and 5-year follow-up. *Journal of Consulting and Clinical Psychology, 61*, 70–77.

McDonald, P. (1995). *Families in Australia*. Melbourne, Australia: Australian Institute of Family Studies.

Morawska, A., & Sanders, M. R. (2006). Self-administered behavioural family intervention for parents of toddlers. *Journal of Clinical and Consulting Psychology, 74*(1), 10–19.

Parcel, G. S., Perry, C. L., & Taylor, W. C. (1990). Beyond demonstration: Diffusion of health promotion innovations. In N. Bracht (Ed.), *Health promotion at the community level: Sage sourcebooks for the human services series* (Vol. 15, pp. 229–251). Thousand Oaks, CA: Sage Publications.

Prinz, R. J., & Sanders, M. R. (2007). Adopting a population level approach to parenting and family support interventions. *Clinical Psychology Review* (available online 19 January 2007).

Sanders, M. R. (1999). Triple-P positive parenting program: Towards an empirically validated multilevel parenting and family support strategy for the prevention of behavior and emotional problems in children. *Clinical Child and Family Psychology Review, 2*, 71–90.

Sanders, M. R., Montgomery, D., & Brechman-Toussaint, M. (2000). The mass media and child behaviour problems. *Journal of Child Psychology and Psychiatry, 41*, 939–948.

Sanders, M. R., Ralph, A., Thompson, R., Sofronoff, K., Gardiner, P., Bidwell, K., et al. (2005). *Every family: A public health approach to promoting children's wellbeing.* Brisbane, Australia: The University of Queensland.

Sanders, M. R., Turner, K. M. T., & Markie-Dadds, C. (1996). *Triple P tipsheets for primary schoolers.* Brisbane, Australia: Families International Publishing.

Sanders, M. R. (2008). Triple P-positive parenting program as a public health approach to strengthening parenting. *Journal of Family Psychology, 22*, 506–517.

Schindler, L., Hahlweg, K., & Revenstorf, D. (2006). *Partnerschaftsprobleme: Diagnose und Therapie. Handbuch für den Therapeuten* [Relationship problems: Assessment and treatment. Therapist manual] (2nd ed.). Berlin: Springer.

Schmaling, K. B., & Sher, T. G. (Eds.), (2000). *The psychology of couples and illness. Theory, research and practise.* Washington, DC: American Psychological Association.

Shadish, W. R., & Baldwin, S. A. (2003). Meta-analysis of MFT interventions. *Journal of Marital and Family Therapy, 29*, 547–570.

Shadish, W. R., & Baldwin, S. A. (2005). Effects of behavioral marital therapy: A meta-analysis of randomized controlled trials. *Journal of Consulting and Clinical Psychology, 73*, 6–14.

Snyder, D. K. (1981). *Marital satisfaction inventory (MSI) manual.* Los Angeles: Western Psychological Services.

Snyder, D. K., Castellani, A. M., & Whisman, M. A. (2006). Current status and future directions in couple therapy. *Annual Review of Psychology, 57*, 317–344.

Snyder, D. K., Mangrum, L. F., & Wills, R. M. (1993). Predicting couples' response to marital therapy: A comparison of short- and long-term predictors. *Journal of Consulting and Clinical Psychology, 61*, 61–69.

Snyder, D. K., & Wills, R. M. (1989). Behavioral versus insight-oriented marital therapy: Effects on individual and interspousal functioning. *Journal of Consulting and Clinical Psychology, 57*, 39–46.

Snyder, D. K., Wills, R. M., & Grady-Fletcher, A. (1991). Long-term effectiveness of behavioral versus insight-oriented marital therapy: A four-year follow-up study. *Journal of Consulting and Clinical Psychology, 59*, 138–141.

Thurmaier, F., Engl, J., & Hahlweg, K. (1999). Eheglück auf Dauer? Methodik, Inhalte und Effektivität eines präventiven Paarkommunikationstrainings. Ergebnisse nach 5 Jahren [Marital satisfaction forever? Method, content, and effectiveness of a prevention intervention. 5-year results]. *Zeitschrift für Klinische Psychologie, 28*, 64–62.

Van Widenfelt, B., Hosman, C., Schaap, C., & van der Staak, C. (1996). The prevention of relationship distress for couples at risk: A controlled evaluation with nine-month and two-year follow-up results. *Family Relations, 45*, 156–165.

Wetzels, P., Greve, W., Mecklenburg, E., Bilsky, W., & Pfeiffer, C. H. (1995). *Kriminalität im Leben alter Menschen. Eine altersvergleichende Untersuchung von Opfererfahrungen, persönlichem Sicherheitsgefühl und Kriminalitätsfurcht.* Band 105 Schriftenreihe des Bundesministeriums für Familie, Senioren, Frauen und Jugend. Stuttgart, Germany: Kohlhammer.

Whisman, M. A. (1999). Marital dissatisfaction and psychiatric disorders: Results from the National Comorbidity Survey. *Journal of Abnormal Psychology, 108*, 701–706.

Whisman, M. A., McKelvie, M. L., & Chatav, Y. (2005). Couple distress. In M. M. Antony, D. R. Ledley & R. G. Heimberg (Eds.), *Improving outcomes and preventing relapse in cognitive-behavioral therapy* (pp. 380–408). New York: Guilford.

Whisman, M. A., & Snyder, D. K. (1997). Evaluating and improving the efficacy of conjoint couple therapy. In W. K. Halford & H. J. Markman (Eds.), *Clinical handbook of marriage and couples interventions* (pp. 679–693). New York: Wiley.

Zimet, D. M., & Jacob, T. (2001). Influences of marital conflict and child adjustment: Review of theory and research. *Clinical Child and Family Psychology Review, 4*, 319–335.

Kurt Hahlweg
Humboldtstr. 33
38106 Braunschweig
Germany
E-mail: k.hahlweg@tu-braunschweig.de

Models of Intervention

A Unified Protocol for Couple Therapy

Andrew Christensen

University of California, Los Angeles, CA, USA

Abstract

Drawing from the "unified protocol for emotional disorders" by David Barlow, Laura Allen, and colleagues (Allen, McHugh, & Barlow, 2008; Barlow, Allen, & Choate, 2004) and drawing from several evidence-based treatments for couple problems, this chapter proposes a unified protocol for couple therapy. The protocol is based on five central principles: (1) provide a contextualized, dyadic, objective conceptualization of problems, (2) modify emotion-driven dysfunctional and destructive interactional behavior, (3) elicit avoided emotion-based private behavior, (4) foster productive communication, and (5) emphasize strengths and encourage positive behavior. These principles are implemented based on a functional analysis of behavior. The clinical and research implications of this unified protocol for couple therapy are discussed.

The verdict from clinical trials is in – couple therapy works. It improves relationship quality and reduces the likelihood of separation and divorce. Not surprising to most in the field but good news nonetheless. A number of literature reviews (Snyder, Castellani, & Whisman, 2006) and meta-analyses (Shadish & Baldwin, 2003) attest to the efficacy of specific types of couple therapy, such as traditional behavioral couple therapy (TBCT; Jacobson & Margolin, 1979) and emotion-focused couple therapy (EFT; Johnson & Denton, 2002). The effect sizes for couple therapy are as large as or larger than those obtained for individual therapy or medical interventions (Shadish & Baldwin, 2003). Recently Caldwell, Woolley, and Caldwell (2007) estimated the cost-effectiveness of two evidence-based couple therapies, TBCT and EFT, and concluded that both were cost-effective "when paid for by government to reduce public costs of divorce or when paid for by insurers to offset the increased health care expenses associated with divorce" (p. 1).

The existing research provides evidence for the efficacy of several different types of couple therapies such as TBCT (Jacobson & Margolin, 1979), EFT (Johnson & Denton, 2002), cognitive-behavioral couple therapy (CBCT; Baucom, Epstein, & LaTillade, 2002), insight-oriented couple therapy (IOCT; Snyder & Wills, 1989), and integrative behavioral couple therapy (IBCT; Christensen & Jacobson, 2000; Jacobson & Christensen, 1998). TBCT has the most evidence supporting it (in shear number of clinical trials) and was designated a well-established treatment by the APA division 12 task force (Chambless & Hollon, 1998); with four clinical trials in its support, EFT was designated a probably efficacious treatment. The task force has not acted on recent clinical trial data. However, IBCT has three separate clinical trials supporting it. The remaining treatments have one or more studies in support of their efficacy. Shadish and Baldwin (2003) found little evidence for differential effectiveness of the different treatments.

This good news about the efficacy of couple therapy must be tempered by the fact that we know little about why these treatments work. Our knowledge of mechanisms of change is substantially limited. Our best and most reasonable guesses about why treatment might work – that improvement in communication brings about a better relationship – have hit the unkind reality of empirical fact: A number of studies have failed to find any relationship between change in communication and change in satisfaction (Whisman & Snyder, 1997). In fact, some have found just the opposite of what would normally be predicted. Schilling, Baucom, Burnett, Allen, and Ragland (2003) found that increases in wife positive communication were associated with deterioration rather than improvement in relationship functioning, a finding replicated by Baucom, Hahlweg, Atkins, Engl, and Thurmaier (2006). Of course, the problem may not be the idea itself but with our simplistic and naïve operationalizations of communication. In a world where you can "kill with kindness" and "damn with faint praise," it is hardly surprising that simple aggregations of positive expressions may not do justice to the complexities of human communication. Nor is the absence of knowledge about mechanism of change unique to couple therapy. We know little about how most of our evidence-based treatments work.

Where Do We Go from Here?

The important question is what to do with this body of empirical data on the efficacy of couple therapy. How do we make the best use of this evidence to facilitate the treatment of distressed couples? How should it guide future research on couple therapy?

The area of emotional disorders, such as anxiety and mood disorders, may provide a model for moving from the current research database to clinical application. David Barlow, Laura Allen, and their colleagues (Allen, McHugh, & Barlow, 2008; Barlow, Allen, & Choate, 2004) noted several important aspects of the research on emotional disorders: (a) substantial evidence of overlap between the various subtypes of these disorders (comorbidity in diagnosis as well as symptom overlap), (b) similar genetic and environmental risk factors for these disorders, (c) "a plethora of treatment protocols for each of the discreet anxiety and mood disorders" with common and/or overlapping elements, and (d) evidence of broad effects of these treatments (i.e., the impact of treatment is not limited to the target disorder or symptom). They suggested that these bodies of evidence argue for "stepping back from individual DSM-IV diagnostic categories and associated specific psychological protocols and considering a more unified approach ...." In their conception, this unified approach to treatment would "include the anxiety and mood disorders, but also other classes of disorders where emotional dysregulation plays a prominent role." Their unified approach is based on current cognitive-behavioral therapy protocols for emotional disorders, which they argue can be reduced to "three broad principles of change: altering emotion based misappraisals of salient events, preventing avoidance of negative emotionally charged internal or external triggers, and modifying emotion driven behaviors." A functional analytic assessment is conducted which guides the therapist in tailoring these principles to the specific circumstances and idiosyncrasies of the patient's life. Barlow et al. (2004) make the dramatic assertion that "these three basic therapeutic principles can be applied, with relatively minor modifications, to each of the emotional disorders" (p. 222).

There are a number of advantages of the unified protocol approach for research and clinical application. At the research level, it changes the focus from endless comparisons of different treatment packages for different discrete disorders to a focus on principles of change. Critics have bemoaned the effort to validate treatment packages and encouraged a focus on principles of change, which can capture the essential ingredients in these packages (Rosen & Davison, 2003). At the practice level, it allows the clinician to concentrate on fundamental principles and their application rather than becoming certified in a plethora of treatment packages. It also acknowledges what clinicians have argued – that good clinical work requires the sensitive application of principles rather than dispensing techniques from treatment packages (Beutler, 2002).

I will suggest in this chapter that the area of couple therapy could benefit from a "unified protocol" for the treatment of couple problems. Such an approach takes advantage of the commonalities that exist between the various evidence-based treatment packages, focusing on fundamental principles of change rather than treatment packages. Moreover, it alters the tasks of clinical training and dissemination from education and training in brand name packages to the application of principles. In addition, a unified protocol for couple therapy can borrow much from the previous work on a unified protocol for emotional disorders. Couples in distress evidence considerable emotional dysregulation (Snyder, Simpson, & Hughes, 2006). Emotional disorders are characterized by what Barlow, Allen, and colleagues call a "negative affect syndrome" (2004, p. 209); similarly, negative affect during interaction is a hallmark of couples in distress (Gottman, Murray, Swanson, Tyson, & Swanson, 2002). This overlap in the fundamental emotional underpinnings of emotional disorders and relationship distress suggests that treatment interventions might also be similar.

In the remainder of this chapter, I will present a first draft of a unified protocol for couple therapy consisting of five principles of therapeutic action, which are based on the existing evidence-based couple therapies. Where relevant, I will show the linkages between this unified protocol and the unified protocol for emotional disorders. I will also suggest ways in which these principles of change can be researched.

Principles of Change in Couple Therapy

Provide a Contextualized, Dyadic, Objective Conceptualization of Problems

The first principle in the unified protocol for emotional disorders is "altering emotion-based misappraisals of salient events" and its dyadic corollary above should be the first principle of a unified protocol for couple therapy. Perhaps all partners in a relationship are to some extent victims of the "fundamental attribution error" or "correspondence bias" (Gilbert & Malone, 1995) in which they attribute greater causal power to their partner's internal characteristics than is deserved and attribute less causal power to the interpersonal circumstances in which their partners interact, including their own behavior, than is appropriate. This tendency is painfully apparent in distressed couples who often blame the partner for relationship difficulties (Karney & Bradbury, 1995). A first step in most evidence-based approaches to couple therapy is to alter these emotion-based attributions.

In TBCT, CBCT, and IBCT a feedback session is conducted after an initial assessment period wherein the therapist offers an interactional framework for viewing problems that removes the burden of blame and guilt from each partner and places it instead on interactional dynamics. Similarly, in stage one of EFT, the therapist identifies a core, negative interaction cycle and "reframe[s] the problem in terms of the cycle" (Johnson & Denton, 2002, p. 230). Different approaches to couple therapy employ different constructs: EFT focuses on attachment problems; IOCT focuses on family of origin issues; and TBCT focuses on current interactional dynamics. However, they all share an effort to remove blame from each partner and shift the causal focus to more benign, less emotionally charged, and sympathetic factors than partner's inadequacy, ill will, or selfishness. These alternative explanations presumably shift the causal focus depending on their plausibility to the couple. A couple that expects therapy to focus on each one's family of origin may find explanations that exclude their families of origin unconvincing. Thus, sensitive therapists applying the first principle would be flexible in the kinds of explanations they use to shift the causal focus from each partner.

Modify Emotion-Driven, Dysfunctional, and Destructive Interactional Behavior

Similar to the unified protocol for emotional disorders, an important principle of couple therapy is to modify emotion-driven behavior. However, in couple therapy this behavior is interactional and, in the case of physical violence, can be dangerous to the other. An early step in couple therapy is to identify emotion-driven behavior, particularly destructive behavior, and modify it appropriately. There is an ongoing debate about what level of violence can be appropriately modified in couple therapy and what level is inappropriate or even unethical to treat in couple therapy because it cannot be modified appropriately (Simpson, Atkins, Gattis, & Christensen, 2008).

"Emotion-driven, dysfunctional, and destructive interaction behavior" includes a broad variety of behaviors in couples such as physical abuse and sexual coercion at the extreme but also more common occurrences such as verbal abuse, yelling, and interrupting.

Couple therapists have a wide variety of strategies that they use to modify emotion-driven behavior. In the session, TBCT and CBCT therapists often structure interactions with an accompanying set of rules to minimize the likelihood that partners will interrupt each other, over-talk each other, or engage in verbally abusive tactics. In EFT and IBCT, therapists initially talk to each individual partner in turn rather than having partners talk directly to each other, thus preventing dysfunctional interactive behavior. For behavior outside of the session, TBCT, CBCT, and IBCT therapists often suggest "time out" procedures and instruct couples in appropriate use of "time out" so their negative interactions will not escalate into destructive acts. They may create agreements or contracts about what they will do with each other, such as allow "freedom of movement" so a partner can leave the situation, and what they won't do with each other, such as "angry touching" – having any physical contact with the other when they are angry.

Elicit Avoided, Emotion-Based Private Behavior

Partners in couples may avoid emotionally charged aspects or issues in their relationships, such as their growing alienation from each other, the increasing lack of physical contact, a partner's increasing use of alcohol, or a partner's grim medical prognosis. This avoidance may be internal to one or both partners, in that one or both avoid thinking about the issue or avoid emotional reactions to the issue although they have some dim awareness of it. Or the avoidance may be only external, in that they focus on it internally but do not discuss it with the other. This internal or external avoidance of the proverbial "elephant in the room" prevents partners from experiencing shared emotional closeness and support about a difficult issue and prevents them from taking joint, corrective action. It is certainly the duty of couple therapists to bring up these important but emotionally heavy issues, although clinical judgment is necessary to determine the timing of these discussions and clinical skill to deal with them with sufficient finesse. These discussions implement the principle articulated in the unified protocol for emotional disorders of "preventing avoidance of negative emotionally charged internal or external triggers."

Another kind of avoidance occurs when partners are aware – however dimly or acutely – of some vulnerable emotional reaction in themselves and avoid any revelation of their internal emotional experience to the partner, such as worry that the other might leave, fear that the other has lost interest, competition with the other over a child's attention, shame or embarrassment about their own behavior, or feelings of rejection or hurt in response to the partner's actions. All these are vulnerable emotions that partners might avoid revealing to the other. Not only do partners fail to reveal these emotions, they often reveal other, more accessible emotions that they experience – such as anger, annoyance, or irritation at the other's behavior. Instead of any obvious emotional reaction, partners may alternatively withdraw from the other in response to these vulnerable emotions.

It would be neither possible nor necessarily desirable to reveal all of these emotions to a partner. However, when vulnerable emotions like those above are linked to focal difficulties in the couple (e.g., emotional distance between the pair or repeated angry exchanges), revealing these vulnerable emotions may be a valuable part of treatment. Certainly, several evidence-based couple therapies focus on the elicitation of these vulnerable emotions. A major strategy in IBCT is "empathic joining" in which the therapist tries to elicit more vulnerable emotions to create an empathic connection between the two during a problem discussion. A common tactic is to elicit "soft emotions" such as feelings of disappointment, hurt, and rejection that may lie behind the expressed "hard emotions" of anger and blame. An important step in EFT is to "access the unacknowledged emotions underlying the interaction position each partner takes in this cycle." Often these unacknowledged emotions have to do with "disowned attachment needs" and "a sense of shame or unworthiness" (Johnson & Denton, 2002, p. 230). In CBCT, the therapist may "use questions, reflections, and interpretations to draw out primary emotions" and may "discourage an individual's attempts to distract him-/herself from experiencing emotion" (Baucom et al., 2002, p. 51).

In the unified protocol for emotional disorders, "treatment takes place in the context of provoking emotional expression (emotion exposure) . . ." (Allen et al., 2008, p. 229). Similarly, evidence-based couple therapists often deliberately provoke emotional expression. IBCT therapists typically focus on emotionally salient incidents that have happened recently or that occur in the session. EFT therapists often heighten emotion in the session. IOCT therapists often stimulate affect. Of course, the goal is not to stimulate the same negative affect that often goes on within the couple but to stimulate different and more constructive emotions. However, the road to those new emotions may traverse some familiar, negative emotional territory.

Foster Productive Communication

Perhaps the most common problem that couples complain about when coming to therapy is "communication problems." All evidence-based couple therapies are conjoint, talk therapies and thus directly or indirectly address couple communication. These efforts to foster productive communication go beyond the efforts to modify emotion-driven, destructive communication (Principle 2) and beyond the elicitation of greater disclosure of private behavior (Principle 3). They typically focus on discussion of problems and address both expression skills (how partners express their concerns to the other) and listening skills (how partners listen to each other's concerns). TBCT and CBCT include direct training in communication skills and provide specific guidelines for expression (e.g., the use of "I statements") and for listening (e.g., paraphrasing or reflecting your partner's message before stating your own message). IBCT therapists can conduct direct training in communication but often shape better communication indirectly. By engaging in repeated discussions of how partners react to each other's communication, IBCT therapists may bring about changes in communication in a nondirective way (as partners get clearer feedback about the impact of their behavior on the other, they may shift in their communication). EFT therapists also bring about changes in communication directly and indirectly. They encourage enactments in which partners are asked to voice new, more direct, and more vulnerable messages to each other. They also reflect communications that partners make and heighten the emotional meaning of those communications such that partners may have an easier time hearing the other and understanding the meaning of the other's communications. Through these indirect means, partners' communications may change.

What is common across therapies is an effort to change the speaker's message into one that is fuller, richer, and more emotionally revealing. Whether this is done directly with guidelines to "Express your *emotions* or feelings, not just your *ideas*" (Baucom et al., 2002, p. 46, italics in the original) or indirectly by the therapist helping a speaker explore more fully what he or she is trying to say, the emphasis on greater emotional disclosure is there. This emphasis on greater disclosure by the speaker is accompanied by a de-emphasis on communication *about* the partner. Sometimes this de-emphasis is direct, such as guidelines to avoid "you statements" or guidelines to only focus on the partner's specific behavior that lead to a reaction rather than focus on the partner's motives. Other times it comes about indirectly as the therapist seeks elaboration of what the speaker feels him or herself and not of what the speaker thinks about the partner's motives, feelings, etc. Another common feature across therapies is an effort to enhance partners' ability to listen to each other. Sometimes this is done directly, as in guidelines to summarize or reflect your partner's message before stating your own. Other times it is done indirectly as when a therapist shifts a speaker's message from a blaming one into a more vulnerable one that may be easier to hear. Thus, across therapies there is an effort to help speakers become more "self-focused" in their communication and help listeners become more "other focused" in their listening.

It is currently unclear whether direct or indirect strategies are generally more beneficial for shaping constructive communication or whether different types of couples might achieve greater benefit from one or the other strategy. In our recent comparison of TBCT versus IBCT, extensive direct training in communication and problem solving was provided in TBCT, whereas indirect training was provided in IBCT. At the end of treatment, couples in both therapies showed improvement in self-report (Christensen et al., 2004) and observational measures of communication (Sevier, Eldridge, Jones, Doss, & Christensen, 2008) but TBCT couples showed significantly greater improvements in observed communication than IBCT couples. This could suggest a greater benefit of direct training. However, observational assessments at 2 years post-therapy showed no differences between the two treatments – any benefit of TBCT had vanished. The initial superiority in TBCT on communication gains may be due to demand characteristics; in TBCT we trained them how to talk: At the end of therapy under video observation, they did what they were trained to do. This style of communication may not have been representative of what was occurring at home or 2 years after therapy had ended. Furthermore, no differences were found between treatments in self-reported communication two years following therapy (Christensen, Atkins, Yi, Baucom, & George, 2006). In addition, couples reported on the use of the specific communication strategies in which they were trained during TBCT. IBCT couples actually reported using these strategies *more* frequently, although nonsignificantly so, than TBCT couples!

Emphasize Strengths and Encourage Positive Behavior

It is common for evidence-based couple therapies to assess for strengths as well as problems during the assessment phase. TBCT, CBCT, and IBCT specifically call for an assessment of strengths in the relationship and feedback about these strengths during the feedback session. Although not a fundamental part of the initial assessment in EFT, therapists in this approach do ask historical questions such as what attracted partners to each other initially, questions that highlight strengths in the relationship.

Apart from this focus on strengths during the initial evaluation and feedback, evidence-based couple therapies encourage positive behavior throughout treatment. Some treatments engage in deliberate attempts to increase positive behavior. In TBCT, behavior exchange procedures involve the deliberate planning of joint, positive behavior change. Similarly, in CBCT, "guided behavior change" strategies are used to lead each partner into making a commitment to changing their own behavior in positive directions, though in a less rule-governed and linked manner as in behavior exchange. IOCT encourages appreciation between partners.

Other evidence-based couple therapies encourage positive behavior in less direct ways. For example, in IBCT, the therapist focuses on emotionally salient incidents in the lives of couples, whether positive or negative, that illustrate their particular issues that were conceptualized in the formulation. For example, imagine a couple locked in a pattern of criticism/defensiveness, where the husband does not feel he can give negative feedback without the wife becoming defensive and where the wife feels that the only feedback she gets is negative. For this couple, positive incidents would occur when the husband gave the wife positive feedback that made her feel good or when he gave her negative feedback that she could accept. In IBCT, the therapist would debrief these incidents in detail so the couple might achieve a greater understanding of how something potentially problematic went well in their relationship. Both IBCT and EFT try to create in the session positive experiences of closeness or bonding by eliciting "softer, more vulnerable" messages in a demanding or hostile partner which then often lead to an affiliative response by the other.

Implementation of Principles Through a Functional Analysis of Behavior

However critical the preceding five principles are for couple therapy, they must be applied in a particular order to particular problems in a particular way. The details of these applications will likely determine the success of therapy for any specific couple. As with the unified protocol for emotional disorders, I would suggest that a "functional analysis of behavior" is the best conceptual basis from which to assess couples and from which to apply these principles. The evidence-based behavioral treatments, TBCT, CBCT, and IBCT, specifically argue for the importance of a functional analytic assessment as a way of understanding couple problems and guiding treatments. Moreover, EFT and IOCT focus on interactional sequences and the controlling stimuli for those sequences in each partner's behavior, also a kind of functional analytic assessment.

A functional analysis of behavior is simply an effort to identify the antecedent and consequent events that influence, control, or cause a target behavior. As applied to couples, a functional analysis leads one to look at each partner's behavior as the important antecedent and consequent for the other's behavior. For example, in looking at one partner's complaint that the other is withdrawn, one might notice that the partner's accusations serve as a trigger for the other's withdrawal, which then serves as a trigger for the initial partner's further accusations. This behavioral analytic examination of the causal chain of events leading to problem behavior need not focus entirely on public behavior and can include important links to private behavior. For example, an important link in the chain might be the withdrawer's experience that if he/she withdraws, it buys him/her some instant, though temporary, peace.

A functional analysis need not be limited to the immediate, proximal antecedent and consequent events. It can also target more historical events, such as past experiences, or distal factors, such as cultural expectations. For example, IBCT and IOCT look at the family of origin experiences that might have led to current vulnerabilities or response tendencies. Perhaps all evidence-based treatments would examine gender and cultural factors in a couple's relationship that might be contributing to their difficulties.

Because of the complexity of human behavior in relationships and because of the therapist's limited ability to manipulate events and thus check out possible causal relationships, conducting a functional analysis of behavior is hardly a straightforward task. Questionnaires that reveal level of distress, commitment, or steps to divorce are of little help in a functional analysis. Questionnaires that identify problem areas for the couple have some limited usefulness in that they point to the target behaviors of relevance. However, a functional analysis requires interviewing to see how these target behaviors combine into large classes, and the mere identification of target behaviors or response classes tells nothing about the variables which control these behaviors. That requires interviewing, careful observation, and skillful hypothesis generation and validation by the therapist. Certainly, more research is needed to systematize this process. However, given the complex nature of the task, an adequate functional analysis will likely be incomplete after the initial assessment, and therapists should always be open to the possibility that additional factors, not previously considered, are playing a major, controlling role in the couple's distress.

An ongoing functional analysis of behavior is necessary not only to discover previously uncovered but important causal factors, but also to adapt treatment interventions to the peculiarities of the couple. For example, a therapist might obtain strong evidence that the husband avoids his wife in the same way that he avoided his mother throughout childhood. However, if the husband is resistant to any explanation that seems "Freudian" to him or suggests that his current behavior might be influenced by his past behavior, the therapist might not share that particular insight during the feedback session. Similarly, a couple might be disdainful of "touchy-feely" talk and resist training in reflective listening. A sensitive behavioral therapist would try a different way to encourage listening between partners.

Research and Clinical Implications of a Unified Protocol

Research Implications

A unified protocol would focus research activity on the fundamental principles of changes articulated in the protocol. Rather than make comparisons between broad packages of treatment, comparisons that are expensive, potentially contaminated by investigator allegiance, and often limited in their substantive impact on our understanding of the mechanism of change, a unified protocol would lead us toward an examination of whether the putative principles of change actually create change. Also, this focus on principles of change lends itself to research strategies that are less expensive and more accessible than large clinical trials between competing treatment packages.

Examples of research with each of these principles of change might be instructive. The first principle, providing an interactional conceptualization to couples, could be examined by assessing couples' own conceptualization of their problems at the beginning of treatment and after the therapist has provided a feedback session where he or she has introduced an interactional framework for viewing their problems. Does the therapist's formulation alter the couples' conceptualization of their problems? Is change in their conceptualization associated with change in their behavior or their satisfaction with the relationship? The second principle, modifying emotion-driven behavior, could be evaluated by tracking such behavior and examining the impact of a particular intervention on that behavior as well as the impact of changing that behavior on the relationship at large. For example, one could track incidents of explosive yelling, teach "time out" procedures, and see to what extent "time out" reduced the incidence of these yelling episodes and had other salutary effects on the relationship (e.g., positive feelings and actions toward each other). The third principle, eliciting important and avoided private behavior, could be evaluated by having couples track their feelings of closeness and intimacy with each other and examine the impact of a revelatory session in which one or both disclosed vulnerable feelings and thoughts to the other. Direct applications of the fourth principle, fostering productive communication, could be examined rather easily. For example, one could track the extent to which couples use techniques taught in communication training and whether the use of these techniques is associated with improved satisfaction or other measures of relationship functioning. The last principle, emphasizing relationship strengths and encouraging positive behavior, could be examined similarly to the other principles. If couples are taught to track positive behavior, it is fairly straightforward to assess whether some intervention to emphasize or promote positive behavior, such as behavior exchange, actually makes an impact on positive behavior.

Each of these research examples requires regular tracking of behavior or emotion, such as satisfaction, by couples prior to and following the therapeutic introduction of a treatment principle. This kind of AB design, in which a baseline period (A) is followed by an intervention period (B), has its limitations. A change during the B phase could be due to other factors in the couple's life rather than the treatment principle; also the change during the B could be temporary. However, if this kind of design is done over many couples and over wide intervals, the accumulation of evidence should provide clarity on the impact of that particular principle.

The research examples presented all focus on the immediate impact of one principle. What is the impact of trying a variety of principles? Does one need to apply all five to achieve successful treatment of couples? Is the brief application of one principle sufficient for the treatment of some couples? How long and to what level does one need to apply these principles? There is an emerging strategy, adaptive treatment interventions, which can answer these kinds of questions (Lavori & Dawson, 1998). In these approaches, which resemble clinical practice, clients are NOT given a uniform treatment. Instead there are decision rules that determine the dosage and type of treatment based on client presenting characteristics and their initial response to treatment. These kinds of decision rules can be incorporated into a complex clinical trial evaluating the impact of the adaptive treatment strategy.

Before engaging in a complex adaptive treatment design for couple therapy, I believe we need considerable research on the impact of particular principles of change, such as I outline above. I am suggesting that we need a "bottom-up" approach to studying the effectiveness of couple therapy. We examine the impact of specific principles of change and how they vary with different client or relationship characteristics. For example, because of the deleterious effect of strong negative episodes such as violence and verbal abuse, it would be extremely helpful to know what kinds of clients will implement "time out" procedures and which will not. Once we have a stronger body of research on specific principles of change, we can use this knowledge to create a complex, adaptive treatment intervention for couples. I believe this "bottom-up" approach will be much more effective than the current "top-down" approach of clinical trials of treatment packages. These leave us with the not-very-satisfying results of knowing that "something in this complex treatment package works for some couples." Wonder what it is?

The focus of all the research examples here has concerned therapeutic intervention. Since this chapter is on couple therapy, such a focus is hardly surprising. However, it is likely that couples can implement certain of these principles on their own. Because of the cost-effectiveness of self-administered materials such as books, manuals, DVDs, computer programs, and Internet applications for treating couples, development and evaluation of these kinds of materials is certainly desirable. Throughout history couples have undoubtedly made improvements in their relationships without the intervention of professional third parties, such as couple therapists, priests, or rabbis. Likely they will continue to do so. However, their efforts might well be enhanced with inexpensive, easily available, educational materials. Certainly many couples will require individual therapeutic attention, but there is every reason to push the limits of self-help materials.

Clinical Implications

Even the most evidence-based clinical work has always been a mixture of art and science. Given the current limits of our science, it has been much more art than science. With the advent of empirically supported treatments and the manuals that describe them, clinicians feared that science would put them and their clients in the straight jackets of rigid manuals with detailed session-by-session outlines (Moras, 2002). Such fears were clearly exaggerated and many manuals allow for quite flexible treatment delivery. However, the manuals are quite complex, learning them can require considerable training, and the proliferation of evidence-based manuals requires that clinicians become proficient in many treatments and their associated manuals, possibly with certification. Such efforts are required by the existing science – if you don't implement the package as tested, then maybe it will not work. However, these efforts go far beyond the science – there is little information about what components of the package are scientifically justified. In contrast, a focus on principles of change facilitates training and dissemination, making more time available for the application of each principle to the idiosyncrasies of the individual case. It keeps the clinical focus, as well as the research attention, on what is fundamental about the treatment.

Conclusion

In this chapter, I have briefly reviewed the outcome data on couple therapy, highlighting its strengths and limitations and asking, "Where do we go from here." I have argued that a "unified protocol" might be the best direction for us to take in couple therapy. I have proposed an outline of the fundamental principles that would constitute such a unified protocol, borrowing in part from the unified protocol for emotional disorders by Barlow, Allen, and colleagues. I have suggested ways of testing these principles of change. Finally, I have presented the clinical and research advantages of a unified protocol for couple therapy and argued that it would serve as the most useful model in leading us toward the future.

References

Allen, L. B., McHugh, R. K., & Barlow, D. H. (2008). Emotional disorders: A unified protocol. In D. H. Barlow (Ed.), *Clinical handbook of psychological disorders* (4th ed., pp. 216–249). New York: Guilford.

Barlow, D. H., Allen, L. B., & Choate, M. L. (2004). Toward a unified treatment for emotional disorders. *Behavior Therapy, 35*, 205–230.

Baucom, D. H., Epstein, N., & LaTillade, J. J. (2002). Cognitive-behavioral couple therapy. In A. S. Gurman & N. S. Jacobson (Eds.), *Clinical handbook of couple therapy* (pp. 26–59). New York: Guilford.

Baucom, D. H., Hahlweg, K., Atkins, D. C., Engl, J., & Thurmaier, F. (2006). Long-term prediction of marital quality following a relationship education program: Being positive in a constructive way. *Journal of Family Psychology, 20*, 448–455.

Beutler, L. E. (2002). It isn't the size, but the fit. *Clinical Psychology: Science and Practice, 9*, 434–438.

Caldwell, B. E., Woolley, S. R., & Caldwell, C. J. (2007). Preliminary estimates of cost-effectiveness for marital therapy. *Journal of Marital and Family Therapy, 33*, 1–14.

Chambless, D. L., & Hollon, S. D. (1998). Defining empirically supported therapies. *Journal of Consulting and Clinical Psychology, 66*, 7–18.

Christensen, A., Atkins, D. C., Berns, S., Wheeler, J., Baucom, D. H., & Simpson, L. E. (2004). Traditional versus integrative behavioral couple therapy for significantly and chronically distressed married couples. *Journal of Consulting and Clinical Psychology, 72*, 176–191.

Christensen, A., Atkins, D. C., Yi, J., Baucom, D. H., & George, W. H. (2006). Couple and individual adjustment for two years following a randomized clinical trial comparing traditional versus integrative behavioral couple therapy. *Journal of Consulting and Clinical Psychology, 74*, 1180–1191.

Christensen, A., & Jacobson, N. S. (2000). *Reconcilable differences*. New York: Guilford.

Gilbert, D. T., & Malone, P. S. (1995). The correspondence bias. *Psychological Bulletin, 117*, 21–38.

Gottman, J. M., Murray, J. D., Swanson, C. C., Tyson, R., & Swanson, K. R. (2002). *The mathematics of marriage: Dynamic nonlinear models*. Cambridge, MA: MIT Press.

Jacobson, N. S., & Christensen, A. (1998). *Acceptance and change in couple therapy: A therapist's guide to transforming relationships*. New York: Norton.

Jacobson, N. S., & Margolin, G. (1979). *Marital therapy: Strategies based on social learning and behavior exchange principles*. New York: Brunner/Mazel.

Johnson, S. M., & Denton, W. (2002). Emotionally focused couple therapy: Creating secure connections. In A. S. Gurman & N. S. Jacobson (Eds.), *Clinical handbook of couple therapy* (pp. 221–250). New York: Guilford.

Karney, B. R., & Bradbury, T. N. (1995). The longitudinal course of marital quality and stability: A review of theory, method, and research. *Psychological Bulletin, 118*, 3–34.

Lavori, P. W., & Dawson, R. (1998). Developing and comparing treatment strategies: An annotated portfolio of designs. *Psychopharmacology Bulletin, 34*, 13–18.

Moras, K. (2002). A tool to advance the effectiveness and dissemination of empirically supported psychotherapies and the NIMH public health research agenda. *Clinical Psychology: Science and Practice, 9*, 425–430.

Rosen, G. M., & Davison, G. C. (2003). Psychology should list empirically supported principles of change (ESPs) and not credential trademarked therapies or other treatment packages. *Behavior Modification, 27*, 300–312.

Schilling, E. A., Baucom, D. H., Burnett, C. K., Allen, E. A., & Ragland, L. (2003). Altering the course of marriage: The effect of PREP communication skills acquisition on couples' risk of becoming maritally distressed. *Journal of Family Psychology, 17*, 41–53.

Sevier, M., Eldridge, K., Jones, J., Doss, B., & Christensen, A. (2008). Observed communication and associations with satisfaction during traditional and integrative behavioral couple therapy. *Behavior Therapy, 39*, 137–150.

Shadish, W. R., & Baldwin, S. A. (2003). Meta-analysis of MFT interventions. *Journal of Marital and Family Therapy, 9*, 547–570.

Simpson, L. E., Atkins, D. C., Gattis, K. S., & Christensen, A. (2008). Low-level relationship aggression and couple therapy outcomes. *Journal of Family Psychology, 22*, 102–111.

Snyder, D. K., Castellani, A. M., & Whisman, M. A. (2006). Current status and future directions in couple therapy. *Annual Review of Psychology, 57*, 317–344.

Snyder, D. K., Simpson, J. A., & Hughes, J. N. (2006). *Emotion regulation in families: Pathways to dysfunction and health*. Washington, DC: American Psychological Association.

Snyder, D. K., & Wills, R. M. (1989). Behavioral versus insight-oriented marital therapy: Effects on individual and interspousal functioning. *Journal of Consulting and Clinical Psychology, 57*, 39–46.

Whisman, M. A., & Snyder, D. K. (1997). Evaluating and improving the efficacy of conjoint couple therapy. In W. K. Halford & H. J. Markman (Eds.), *Clinical handbook of marriage and couples interventions* (pp. 679–693). New York: Wiley.

Andrew Christensen
UCLA Psychology Department
502 Portola Plaza
Los Angeles, CA 90095-1563
USA
E-mail: Christensen@psych.ucla.edu

Integrative Approaches to Couple Therapy

Implications for Clinical Practice, Training, and Research

Douglas K. Snyder and Molly F. Gasbarrini

Texas A&M University, College Station, TX, USA

Abstract

Although meta-analyses affirm that various treatments for couple distress produce statistically and clinically significant outcomes, research findings also indicate that a large percentage of couples fail to benefit or subsequently deteriorate following current therapies. Based on these findings, we advocate potential advantages of integrative approaches to couple therapy. We distinguish among assimilative, transtheoretical, and pluralistic approaches to integration and describe exemplars of each. Integrative approaches to couple therapy are compared to distillatory or common-factors approaches emphasizing common elements of treatment components, therapist characteristics, and client or relationship attributes. We argue that clinical practice of integrative approaches to couple therapy requires conceptual and clinical decision-making skills transcending those of any one theoretical modality and emphasizing the selection, sequencing, and pacing of diverse interventions in a coherent manner. We conclude with implications of integrative couple-based treatments for future research.

Meta-analyses of couple therapy affirm that various approaches to treating couple distress produce statistically and clinically significant improvement for a substantial proportion of couples, with the average couple receiving therapy being better off at termination than 80% of couples not receiving treatment (Shadish & Baldwin, 2003). However, tempering enthusiasm from this overall conclusion are additional findings that in only 50% of treated couples do both partners show significant improvement in relationship satisfaction, and that 30–60% of treated couples show significant deterioration at 2 years or longer after termination (Snyder, Castellani, & Whisman, 2006). Meta-analyses provide little evidence of differential effectiveness across different theoretical orientations to couple therapy, particularly once other covariates (e.g., reactivity of measures) are controlled. Such findings have fostered two alternative lines of attack to treating couple distress: (a) distillation and emphasis of common factors hypothesized to contribute to beneficial effects across "singular" or "pure" treatment approaches and (b) integrative models incorporating multiple components of diverse treatment approaches.

In this chapter, we advocate potential advantages of integrative approaches to couple therapy. We distinguish among assimilative, transtheoretical, and pluralistic approaches to integration and describe exemplars of each. Integrative approaches to couple therapy are compared to distillatory or common-factors approaches emphasizing common elements of treatment components, therapist characteristics, and client or relationship attributes. We argue that clinical practice of integrative approaches to couple therapy requires conceptual and clinical decision-making skills transcending those of any one theoretical modality and emphasizing the selection, sequencing, and pacing of diverse interventions in a coherent manner. We conclude with implications of integrative couple-based treatments for future research.

Current Status of Couple Therapy: An Overview

Empirical findings from randomized clinical trials support the efficacy of six different couple-based treatments for couple distress – including traditional behavioral, cognitive-behavioral, integrative behavioral, emotionally focused, integrative systemic, and insight-oriented couple therapy approaches (Snyder, Castellani, & Whisman, 2006). These approaches vary along a continuum anchored by behavior-exchange and skills-building interventions on one end, to interventions emphasizing intrapersonal dynamics and enduring relationship patterns on the other end.

Although each of the empirically supported approaches to couple therapy posits specific processes or mechanisms of change, there has been little research explicitly indicating these proposed mechanisms as responsible for observed therapeutic effects. For example, mediation regression analyses of data from traditional behavioral couple therapy (TBCT) have failed to find an association between the magnitude of changes in communication behaviors and gains in relationship satisfaction. Similarly, although cognitive-behavioral couple therapy (CBCT) has been shown to produce positive change in targeted cognitions (e.g., expectancies and attributions), changes in these cognitions have not been linked to couples' gains in satisfaction following this treatment.

More encouraging results have been reported by Doss and colleagues (Doss, Thum, Sevier, Atkins, & Christensen, 2005) using hierarchical growth curve analysis to examine mechanisms of change in Christensen and colleagues' (2004) clinical trial comparing TBCT with integrative behavioral couple therapy (IBCT). Both therapies were effective in increasing emotional acceptance and improving communication behaviors across the course of therapy; however, acceptance increased significantly more for couples in IBCT than for couples in TBCT, whereas couples in TBCT showed larger initial gains in positive communication. Moreover, change in targeted behaviors was a powerful mechanism of change early in therapy whereas, in the second half of therapy, emotional acceptance was more strongly related to changes in relationship satisfaction.

Several studies have examined change processes using task analysis to link proximal outcomes occurring within or between sessions to specific therapeutic events. In an initial pilot study comparing IBCT with TBCT, Cordova, Jacobson, and Christensen (1998) found that couples in IBCT showed relatively more constructive detachment over the course of therapy, and that these changes predicted couples' gains in relationship satisfaction. Three task analytic studies of emotionally focused couple therapy (EFCT) (Greenberg, Ford, Alden, & Johnson, 1993) showed that: (a) couples receiving EFCT demonstrated more shifts from hostility to affiliative behaviors than waiting-list couples; (b) best sessions as identified by couples were characterized by greater depth of experiencing and by more affiliative and autonomous statements than were sessions identified as poor; and (c) intimate, emotionally laden self-disclosure by one partner was more likely to lead to affiliative statements by the other partner than were other randomly selected responses. A more recent task analysis of four EFCT sessions by Bradley and Furrow (2004) found that specific therapist interventions linked to "softening events" (reformulations of partners' hostile or critical comments as expressions of vulnerability) involved intensifying a couple's emotional experience and promoting intrapsychic awareness and interpersonal shifts in attachment-related interactions.

Predictors of Treatment Outcome

Research targeting predictors of couple therapy outcome has overwhelmingly emphasized prognostic rather than prescriptive indicators (Snyder, Castellani, & Whisman, 2006). The former predict response to a particular treatment (or response across treatments, irrespective of specific approach), whereas the latter predict response to one versus another treatment. Although prescriptive indicators are essential to informed selection of specific interventions in tailoring treatment to partner or relationship attributes, empirical findings in this regard are virtually nonexistent.

Studies examining demographic, individual, and relationship prognostic indicators of treatment outcome are more frequent, but their yield has been modest and mixed (Snyder, Castellani, & Whisman, 2006). The most consistent finding (but of limited usefulness in selecting interventions) is that couples having the greatest difficulties in their relationship are less likely to benefit from treatment, with initial levels of relationship distress accounting for up to 46% of the variance in treatment outcome. Lack of commitment and behavioral steps taken toward divorce have been associated with poor treatment response to TBCT in two studies. Snyder, Mangrum, and Wills (1993) found that poorer outcomes from couple therapy were predicted by lower relationship quality, greater negative relationship affect and disengagement, and greater desired change in the relationship.

Integrative Approaches to Couple Therapy

Couple therapists confront a tremendous diversity of presenting issues, marital and family structures, individual dynamics and psychopathology, and psychosocial stressors characterizing couples in distress. Because the functional sources of couples' distress vary so dramatically, the critical mediators or mechanisms of change should also be expected to vary – as should the therapeutic strategies intended to facilitate positive change. Even within the more restricted domain of individual interventions, growing recognition of unique strengths and limitations of competing theoretical approaches has fueled a burgeoning movement toward psychotherapy integration. For example, advocates of various integrative models of psychotherapy have emphasized the strengths of psychodynamic approaches for identifying enduring problematic interpersonal themes, the benefits of experiential techniques for promoting emotional awareness, gains from cognitive interventions targeting dysfunctional beliefs and attributional processes, and advantages of behavioral strategies for promoting new patterns of behavior (Bongar & Beutler, 1995).

Thus, couples will benefit most from a treatment strategy drawing from both conceptual and technical innovations from diverse theoretical models relevant to different components of a couple's struggles. That is, effective treatment is most likely to be rendered when the couple therapist has a solid grounding across diverse theoretical approaches, has acquired a rich repertoire of intervention techniques linked to theory, engages in comprehensive assessment of the marital and family system, and selectively draws on intervention strategies across the theoretical spectrum in a manner consistent with an explicit case formulation (Snyder, Schneider, & Castellani, 2003).

Integrative approaches reduce the risk of haphazard, disjointed, or contradictory interventions resulting from an eclectic borrowing of diverse principles or techniques without regard for their potential inconsistency or adverse interaction. There are numerous approaches to integration that vary in their emphasis on technique versus theory, and their goal of assimilating existing techniques or theoretical constructs into an existing predominant theoretical or conceptual framework versus generating a new incorporative theoretical approach. Below we contrast three of these approaches – assimilative, transtheoretical, and pluralistic – and briefly describe an exemplar of each.

Assimilative Approaches

In assimilative integration, specific interventions or constructs from one or more theoretical approaches are translated and incorporated into some alternative, existing predominant theoretical framework. Assimilative integration can occur at either the technical or theoretical level. Both technical and theoretical integration are distinguished from their eclectic counterparts by the number and explanatory power of linkages among interventions or their theoretical substrates.

Among the first integrative couple therapies to be articulated was Gurman's (2002) depth-behavioral integrative approach drawing on principles of social learning theory, object relations theory, and general systems theory. Gurman emphasizes the critical interrelation of intrapsychic and interpersonal factors in couples' interactions and defines the goal of couple therapy as the loosening and broadening of each spouse's implicit matrix of assumptions, expectations, and requirements of intimate interpersonal contact. This is accomplished through interpretation, cognitive restructuring, and creation of therapeutic tasks to promote each spouse's exposure to those aspects of him- or herself and his or her partner, which are blocked from awareness.

Although Gurman's integrative approach to couple therapy has been consistently assimilative, its relative emphasis on psychodynamic versus behavioral theory as the "home theory" in which to assimilate competing constructs has changed significantly over the past 25 years. For example, Gurman (1992) argued that,

> "... the most appropriate theoretical foundation for an integrative understanding of marital interaction, dynamics, and change is to be found in psychodynamic thinking, especially in a focused use of certain concepts originating in object relations theory" (p. 453).

From this perspective, such behavioral techniques as teaching partners to rely on positive reinforcement for modifying their spouse's behavior may be reconceptualized as "... a direct inhibitor of [partners'] proclivities to engage in projective identification" (Gurman, 1980, p. 90). More recently, however, Gurman's "depth-behavioral" integrative approach emphasizes the centrality of functional behavior analytic theory – overlapping with but distinct from enhanced CBCT and IBCT (Gurman, personal communication, August, 2007).

Transtheoretical Approaches

Transtheoretical integration incorporates specific constructs from diverse theoretical approaches in a synergistic manner as to generate some new meta theory not derivable from the respective original approaches separate from one another. Grawe's (2002) *consistency theory* represents a transtheoretical integrative approach well suited to couple-based interventions. According to consistency theory, incongruence between individual perceptions and goals reduces well-being and increases the risk for the development and maintenance of psychopathology. Hence, therapeutic interventions should strive to reduce the level of incongruence in the long term, while potentially inducing inconsistency in the short term to promote changes more likely to lead to healthy self-regulation and enduring consistency.

Based on empirical findings from the psychotherapy literature, Grawe (1997) extracted five broad classes of therapeutic change mechanisms: (1) the therapeutic bond, (2) the problem activation, (3) the resource activation, (d) the mastery and coping, and (5) the motivational clarification. For example, problem-focused interventions are viewed as inducing short-term increases in inconsistency by directing clients' attention toward information inconsistent with underlying emotions or cognitions regarding the problem to encourage accommodative changes in maladaptive regulation patterns to ensure a higher long-term level of consistency. Concurrent resource activation serves to strengthen the healthy patterns of clients' functioning while also increasing tolerance for short-term increases in inconsistency and related stress involved in changing the more problematic patterns.

Couple therapy guided by consistency theory may incorporate individual, concurrent, or conjoint sessions based on a case conceptualization resulting from assessment of partners' respective emotional, cognitive, and behavioral resources and their expression in the couple relationship (Grawe-Gerber, Chapter 4, this volume). In principle, all empirically validated treatment procedures can be used in therapy, provided their use is justified by the specific needs of the individual or couple to whom the treatment plan is tailored. However, the distinction between this approach and pluralistic approaches (described below) lies in the integrative function of consistency theory in guiding the selection and timing of interventions.

Pluralistic Approaches

Pluralism recognizes the validity of multiple systems of epistemology, theory, and practice and draws on these as intact units (as distinct from eclecticism), although not necessarily concurrently or from a transtheoretical perspective. Pluralism is similar to constructs of "empirical pragmatism," "systematic treatment selection," and "prescriptive eclecticism" characterized

> "... by drawing on effective methods from across theoretical camps (eclecticism), by matching those methods to particular cases on the basis of psychological science and clinical wisdom (prescriptionism), and by adhering to an explicit and orderly model of treatment selection ..." (Norcross & Beutler, 2000, p. 248).

Because a pluralistic approach is less constrained than theoretically integrative approaches forced to reconcile competing constructs, it potentially offers greater opportunity to accommodate diverse theoretical perspectives.

Snyder (1999) advocated a pluralistic approach to couple therapy conceptualizing therapeutic tasks as progressing sequentially along a hierarchy comprising six levels of intervention from the most fundamental interventions promoting a collaborative alliance to more challenging interventions addressing developmental sources of relationship distress. Because couple therapy often proceeds in nonlinear fashion, the model depicts flexibility

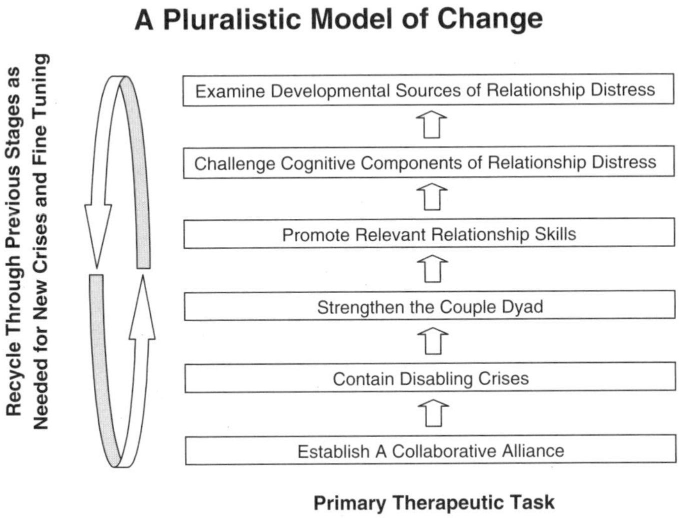

Figure 1. Snyder's (1999) sequential, pluralistic approach to couple therapy.

of returning to earlier therapeutic tasks as dictated by individual or relationship difficulties (see Figure 1).

The most fundamental step in couple therapy involves developing a collaborative alliance between partners and between each partner and the therapist by establishing an atmosphere of therapist competence as well as therapeutic safety around issues of confidentiality and verbal or physical aggression. Subsequent interventions may need to target disabling relationship crises such as substance use, psychopathology, illness or death of a family member, or similar concerns that, until resolved, preclude development of new relationship skills and progress toward emotional intimacy. Because some couples initially present with overwhelming negativity, the therapist may need to instigate behavior change directly before assisting the couple to develop behavior-exchange and communication skills of their own. Along with promoting general relationship skills, the couple therapist may need to assist partners in acquiring a prerequisite knowledge base and competence in specific domains such as sexuality, parenting, finances, or time management.

A common impediment to behavior change involves misconceptions and other interpretive errors that individuals may have regarding both their own and their partners' behavior; interventions targeting partners' relationship beliefs, expectancies, and attributions aim to eliminate or restructure cognitive processes interfering with behavior change efforts. However, not all psychological processes relevant to couples' interactions lend themselves to traditional cognitive interventions. Of particular importance are partners' developmental relationship experiences resulting in enduring interpersonal vulnerabilities and related defensive strategies interfering with emotional intimacy, many of which operate beyond partners' conscious awareness. Hence, when couple distress persists despite system-restructuring, skills-building, and cognitive interventions, then interpretation of maladaptive relationship patterns evolving from developmental processes comprises an essential treatment component (Snyder & Mitchell, 2008).

This pluralistic approach presumes that couples will vary in the extent to which they require interventions at any level of the treatment hierarchy, but also presumes that higher-order interventions (e.g., cognitive- or insight-oriented techniques targeting intrapersonal processes) would ordinarily not be implemented unless lower-order interventions (e.g., crisis intervention, relationship strengthening, or skills-building techniques targeting interpersonal processes) had already proven insufficient. Similar to Grawe's transtheoretical approach, any empirically validated procedures could be incorporated within this pluralistic approach – including common factors distilled from diverse therapeutic approaches presumed to relate to treatment processes or outcome.

Integration Versus Distillation: The Common-Factors Approach

The common-factors approach argues that shared mechanisms of change cutting across the diverse couple therapies account for the absence of significant differences in their overall effectiveness. Sprenkle and Blow (2004) cited five types or classes of common factors characterizing psychotherapy in general, and three specific to couple or family therapy. Common factors viewed as generic to psychotherapy include: (a) client characteristics (e.g., learning style, perseverance, and compliance with instructions or assignments), (b) therapist characteristics (e.g., abilities to foster a therapeutic alliance and to match activity level to clients' expectations or preferences), (c) characteristics of the therapeutic relationship (e.g., emotional connectedness and congruence between the therapist's and client's specific expectations or goals), (d) expectancy or placebo effects, and (e) nonspecific interventions promoting emotional experiencing, cognitive mastery, and behavioral regulation. Those common factors viewed by Sprenkle and Blow as specific to couple or family therapies include: (a) emphasis on the interpersonal context in which specific problems occur, (b) inclusion of multiple members of the extended family system in direct treatment, and (c) fostering an expanded therapeutic alliance across partners or multiple members of the family as a whole. More recently, Christensen (Chapter 2, this volume) has proposed an alternative formulation of common factors underlying empirically supported treatments for couple distress. To date, however, there has been little research documenting specific treatment effects attributable to proposed common factors – nor systematic efforts in designing couple treatment approaches intended to maximize common-factors' therapeutic impact.

Among client characteristics potentially contributing to similar outcomes across treatment approaches, there has been increasing emphasis in recent years on the role of emotion regulation in health and dysfunction (Snyder, Simpson, & Hughes, 2006). Deficits in emotion regulation may lead to either the overcontrol or undercontrol of affect, with the latter typically receiving the greater attention in the clinical literature. Indeed, analysis of affect-related symptoms in the current Diagnostic and Statistical Manual of Mental Disorders (DSM-IV-TR) reveals symptoms of both overcontrol (e.g., constricted or flat affect; emotional coldness or detachment) and undercontrol (e.g., inappropriate, labile, or intense affect) related to a broad spectrum of emotional and behavioral disorders other than specific mood disorders (e.g., posttraumatic stress disorder, schizophrenia, organic brain syndromes, diverse substance abuse disorders, and most personality disorders).

One widely recognized model of emotion regulation (Gross, 2001) distinguishes between antecedent-focused emotion-regulation strategies (e.g., situation selection and modification, attentional deployment, and stimulus interpretation) and response-focused strategies promoting either increases or reductions in experiential, physiological, and behavioral emotion response tendencies. This model readily lends itself to translation into specific couple-based interventions for general couple distress or specific disorders (e.g., disease-related pain; see Keefe, Porter, & Labban, 2006) targeting both individual and relational processes. A common-factors perspective suggests that diverse couple-based treatments may yield similar outcomes to the extent that different specific techniques within each approach therapeutically impact relevant emotion-regulation processes.

Empirical findings regarding the efficacy of specific theoretical approaches to couple therapy – and the review of alternative integrative approaches as well as a common-factors perspective – offer several implications for clinical practice, training, and research.

Implications of Integrative Approaches for Clinical Practice and Training

- *Effective treatment of couples often requires therapists to conceptualize and practice integratively across diverse theoretical orientations.*

Couple therapy often requires thinking outside the parameters of any one theoretical orientation – in part because theoretical approaches vary in their attention to cognitive, affective, and behavioral components of intrapersonal and interpersonal functioning. The more difficult the couple, the greater the need may be to draw on increasingly diverse intervention strategies to address multiple individual and relationship problems. Training programs need to focus explicitly on instructing developing therapists in the principles and strategies of integrative practice – ensuring a technical understanding of specific therapeutic techniques, the theoretical context in which these evolved, and their demonstrated efficacy for particular problems in specific populations.

- *Effective treatment of individuals and couples requires comprehensive assessment of intrapersonal and interpersonal functioning throughout affective, behavioral, and cognitive domains across multiple levels of the family and socio-ecological system.*

Couples presenting with primary complaints of relationship difficulties often fail to recognize, understand, or acknowledge the role of individual problems in their interpersonal distress. Similarly, individuals seeking treatment for their own emotional or health problems may neglect or minimize the interaction of these concerns with interpersonal functioning in their intimate or broader social relationships. Hence, both individual and couple therapists need to assess clients' individual and relationship strengths and vulnerabilities as well as broader elements of the extended family and social systems – drawing on well-validated self-report and observational techniques.

- *Therapy will be most effective when individuals and couples are matched to treatments for which they possess prerequisite attributes and are excluded from treatments for which they are particularly ill suited.*

In order for assessment to influence treatment, individual differences in intrapersonal and interpersonal functioning need to be linked to alternative models and modalities of intervention. Clinicians need to be as attentive to exclusionary characteristics influencing treatment selection as they are to inclusionary criteria. Moreover, they need to be sufficiently trained both in theory and research methods to be discerning consumers of the literature in evaluating diverse treatment modalities.

- *Differences in urgency of individual and relationship issues and their progression during therapy require an organizational conceptual framework for selecting, sequencing, and pacing interventions.*

Although virtually all approaches to couple therapy possess an implicit progression of individual treatment components, couples with interactive individual and relationship difficulties demand special attention to the selection, sequencing, and pacing of specific interventions. Treatment of particularly difficult couples often requires alternating attention between partners and their relationship with each other or other family members in promoting growth in one individual or relationship and then working with other members to promote their adaptation to this change.

Until a comprehensive integrative theoretical model emerges, we advocate integration from a sequential, pluralistic approach. From this perspective, moderators influencing both the selection and the pacing of interventions would include (a) partners' commitment to conjoint therapy and views toward their own roles in relationship problems, (b) acute psychosocial stressors or individual crises precluding sustained attention to relationship issues, (c) family organization regarding patterns of influence and emotional attachment, (d) partners' effectiveness in enlisting support but limiting intrusion from individuals outside their relationship, (e) intensity and pervasiveness of hostility, (f) levels and resiliency of emotional warmth and positive regard, (g) communication skills involving emotional expressiveness, listening, and decision making, (h) additional relationship skills in such domains as parenting, money management, and physical intimacy, (i) disruption of relationship functioning by unrealistic assumptions or standards, faulty attributions, or related cognitive processes, and (j) recurrent maladaptive relationship patterns rooted in early developmental experiences or operating beyond immediate awareness.

Implications of Integrative Approaches for Clinical Research

- *Couple therapy needs to move beyond existing therapies to examine integrative approaches: including indicators for selecting and sequencing specific treatment components, alternative integrative models, and moderators of therapeutic effectiveness.*

Efforts to decompose couple-based interventions into their smallest transportable components should lead to research on the most effective ways of reassembling these in a manner uniquely tailored to couples' variation in individual and relationship functioning. Each intervention incorporated into an integrative approach needs to be considered with respect to its necessity, sufficiency, and interactive effects. Issues of necessity involve delineating those individual and couple characteristics for which a given intervention or set of interventions is essential for reducing distress or promoting well-being. By comparison, issues of sufficiency involve delineating those constellations of individual and relationship functioning for which a given intervention or set of interventions are enough to produce some desired therapeutic outcome. Research on intervention interactions also needs to identify combinations of techniques that produce either positive or negative synergistic effects. Because some treatment components may be interactively inconsistent, contradictory, neutralizing, or harmful, research also needs to identify when specific combinations or sequences of treatment interventions produce deleterious effects.

- *Studies of treatment outcome need to be complemented by research on treatment processes, focusing particularly on "common factors" related to client, therapist, and treatment characteristics.*

Research on couple therapy process should begin with efforts to articulate both common factors in couple-based interventions and specific components that distinguish one approach from another. To the extent that diverse treatment approaches share common attributes, this may facilitate shifting from one therapeutic modality to another to capture unique techniques specific to that approach when working with difficult couples. Because some techniques may require a set of interventions linked together in a specific constellation or sequence to be effective, research on articulating therapeutic components should identify the smallest unit of intervention that can be transported across approaches while retaining its efficacy. Research on variations in treatment process across individual and relationship factors should be integrated with studies of how specific intervention components and their variations are linked to within- and between-session responses of each of the participants. That is, process research interfaces with outcome research by emphasizing more immediate, proximal effects of therapist interventions on partners' behavior and partners' effects on the therapist and each other.

Research on such therapeutic event-related processes also needs to attend to changes in these linkages across the course of treatment. For example, the effects of interpreting developmental components of interpersonal distress may be very different if conducted early in therapy than later in treatment once collaborative alliances and constructive communication skills are more firmly established. Consequently, stages of couple therapy need to be defined not only by the composition or structure of clinical interventions, but also by their proximal effects on partners' responses and the therapeutic process.

- *The conceptualization of treatment outcome should extend beyond reduction of couple distress to include indicators of individual and relationship functioning across a broad spectrum.*

Most studies of couple therapy have included measures of partners' individual functioning targeting emotional/behavioral disorders, and a few (e.g., Christensen et al., 2004) have assessed well-being of partners' children. Largely absent have been measures targeting such positive elements as joy, hopefulness, or generosity. Moreover, despite widespread recognition that clinically favorable outcomes can include terminating an unhealthy marriage, few if any studies have incorporated measures of "success" that reflect constructive processes culminating in partners' decision to end their marriage and move on separately.

- *Clinicians and researchers need to pursue more effective collaboration in identifying critical questions related to integrative couple treatments: designing and conducting relevant research, and disseminating and incorporating findings germane to clinical practice.*

Researchers need to be knowledgeable regarding both clinical and pragmatic issues of couple therapy in today's practice environment. This requires learning from practitioners what clinical and logistical issues present the greatest challenges in working with difficult couples – particularly from an integrative perspective. Researchers also bear responsibility for disseminating their findings in a format relevant to practitioners. This entails attending to multiple styles and media of communication including detailed treatment manuals, case-study publications, and clinical practice guidelines for selecting and sequencing specific treatment components linked to particular individual or relationship characteristics.

Clinicians need to contribute to the scientific enterprise by collaborating with researchers in articulating issues critical to conducting couple therapy and by participating in the research process. The latter may involve willingness to administer structured treatments according to a research protocol in a community setting, assessing couples before and after "treatment-as-usual" in a treatment-comparison condition, or facilitating integrative approaches by providing videotaped treatment sessions for task analyses linking therapist and client behaviors to within-session processes and outcomes. Clinicians also bear responsibility for remaining abreast of both theoretical and empirical advances in couple treatment, reading both the clinical and the research literature, and discerning between new treatment approaches that are fashionable or cleverly marketed and those that are empirically supported.

Similar to couple interventions promoting the respective strengths of each partner, so too the field of couple therapy will advance when clinicians and researchers collaboratively encourage each other's respective professional pursuits in working with couples in a more theoretically integrative and clinically effective manner.

References

Bongar, B., & Beutler, L. E. (1995). *Comprehensive textbook of psychotherapy: Theory and practice.* New York: Oxford University Press.

Bradley, B., & Furrow, J. L. (2004). Toward a mini-theory of the blamer softening event: Tracking the moment-by-moment process. *Journal of Marital and Family Therapy, 30*, 1–12.

Christensen, A. (this volume). A "unified protocol" for couple therapy. In K. Hahlweg, M. Grawe-Gerber & D. H. Baucom (Eds.), *Enhancing couples: The shape of couple therapy to come.* Göttingen: Hogrefe.

Christensen, A., Atkins, D. C., Berns, S., Wheeler, J., Baucom, D. H., & Simpson, L. E. (2004). Traditional versus integrative behavioral couple therapy for significantly and chronically distressed married couples. *Journal of Consulting and Clinical Psychology, 72*, 76–191.

Cordova, J. V., Jacobson, N. S., & Christensen, A. (1998). Acceptance versus change interventions in behavioral couple therapy: Impact on couples' in-session communication. *Journal of Marital and Family Therapy, 24*, 437–455.

Doss, B. D., Thum, Y. M., Sevier, M., Atkins, D. C., & Christensen, A. (2005). Improving relationships: Mechanisms of change in couple therapy. *Journal of Consulting and Clinical Psychology, 73*, 624–633.

Grawe, K. (1997). Research-informed psychotherapy. *Psychotherapy Research, 7*, 1–19.

Grawe, K. (2002, June). *Consistency theory: A neuroscientific view of symptom formation and therapeutic change.* Paper presented at the annual meeting of the Society of Psychotherapy Research, Santa Barbara, CA.

Grawe-Gerber, M. (this volume). Would a comprehensive psychological model for working with couples improve dissemination of evidence-based treatments of couple problems? A clinician and trainer's point of view. In K. Hahlweg, M. Grawe-Gerber & D. H. Baucom (Eds.), *Enhancing couples: The shape of couple therapy to come.* Göttingen: Hogrefe.

Greenberg, L. S., Ford, C. L., Alden, L., & Johnson, S. M. (1993). In-session change in emotionally focused therapy. *Journal of Consulting and Clinical Psychology, 61*, 78–84.

Gross, J. J. (2001). Emotion regulation in adulthood: Timing is everything. *Current Directions in Psychological Science, 10*, 214–219.

Gurman, A. S. (1980). Behavioral marriage therapy in the 1980's: The challenge of integration. *American Journal of Family Therapy, 8*, 86–96.

Gurman, A. S. (1992). Integrative marital therapy: A time-sensitive model for working with couples. In S. H. Budman & M. F. Hoyt (Eds.), *The first session in brief therapy* (pp. 186–203). New York: Guilford Press.

Gurman, A. S. (2002). Brief integrative marital therapy: A depth-behavioral approach. In A. S. Gurman & N. S. Jacobson (Eds.), *Clinical handbook of couple therapy* (3rd ed., pp. 180–220). New York: Guilford Press.

Keefe, F. J., Porter, L. S., & Labban, J. (2006). Emotion regulation processes in disease-related pain: A couples-based perspective. In D. K. Snyder, J. A. Simpson & J. N. Hughes (Eds.), *Emotion regulation in couples and families: Pathways to dysfunction and health* (pp. 207–229). Washington, DC: American Psychological Association.

Norcross, J. C., & Beutler, L. E. (2000). A prescriptive eclectic approach to psychotherapy training. *Journal of Psychotherapy Integration, 10*, 247–261.

Shadish, W. R., & Baldwin, S. A. (2003). Meta-analysis of MFT interventions. *Journal of Marital and Family Therapy, 29*, 547–570.

Snyder, D. K. (1999). Affective reconstruction in the context of a pluralistic approach to couple therapy. *Clinical Psychology: Science and Practice, 6*, 348–365.

Snyder, D. K., Castellani, A. M., & Whisman, M. A. (2006). Current status and future directions in couple therapy. *Annual Review of Psychology, 57*, 317–344.

Snyder, D. K., Mangrum, L. F., & Wills, R. M. (1993). Predicting couples' response to marital therapy: A comparison of short- and long-term predictors. *Journal of Consulting and Clinical Psychology, 61*, 61–69.

Snyder, D. K., & Mitchell, A. E. (2008). Affective-reconstructive couple therapy. In A. S. Gurman (Ed.), *Clinical handbook of couple therapy* (4th ed., pp. 353–382). New York: Guilford Press.

Snyder, D. K., Schneider, W. J., & Castellani, A. M. (2003). Tailoring couple therapy to individual differences: A conceptual approach. In D. K. Snyder & M. A. Whisman (Eds.), *Treating difficult couples: Helping clients with coexisting mental and relationship disorders* (pp. 27–51). New York: Guilford Press.

Snyder, D. K., Simpson, J. A., & Hughes, J. N. (Eds.). (2006). *Emotion regulation in couples and families: Pathways to dysfunction and health*. Washington, DC: American Psychological Association.

Sprenkle, D. H., & Blow, A. J. (2004). Common factors and our sacred models. *Journal of Marital and Family Therapy, 30*, 113–129.

Douglas K. Snyder
Department of Psychology -- MS 4235
Texas A&M University
College Station, TX 77843-4235
USA
E-mail: d-snyder@tamu.edu

Would a Comprehensive Psychological Model for Working with Couples Improve Dissemination of Evidence-Based Treatments of Couple Problems?

A Clinician and Trainer's Point of View

Mariann Grawe-Gerber

Klaus Grawe Institute for Psychological Therapy, Zurich, Switzerland

Abstract

There is an increased interest in evidence-based couple therapy (EBCT) to look for common change factors that make the different treatments work rather than doing more comparative research. We suggest to take the field even a step further by making use of the findings of scientific psychology, psychotherapy research, and the neurosciences, such as Grawe's general change mechanisms and his consistency theory for developing case formulations and treatment plans. Such a comprehensive research-based theory could serve as a model for integrating different empirically based treatment procedures. We also argue that it is not patient oriented to mainly train clinicians in only one treatment modality. Training in research-informed psychotherapy would imply that more future clinicians would also become more familiar with EBCT and would then also be able to treat patients with individual and relationship problems in a more systematic and theory-based way.

Couple therapy, individual therapy, family therapy, and child therapy are at first glance basically nothing but treatment modalities. The terms only tell you who will be present during the therapy session. Different schools of psychotherapy have developed their own belief systems, theories, models, and corresponding procedures and interventions to work within these treatment modalities.

Gurman and Jacobson's *Clinical handbook of couple therapy* (Gurman, 2002) illustrates these different *schools of couple therapy* extensively. Within cognitive-behavioral therapy (CBT), couple therapy has been innovatively developed and well researched. For a more detailed account of the history of behavioral couple therapy (BCT) and cognitive-behavioral couple therapy (CBCT), see Baucom, Epstein, LaTaillade, and Kirby (2002). Newer expanded models emerged from it, such as integrative behavioral couple therapy by Christensen and Jacobson (1995). Research on the developed couple therapy procedures and consideration of research in other areas of psychology, such as relationship functioning, cognition, and emotion, led to more and more sophisticated concepts and models.

Not only in individual psychotherapy but also in couple therapy, CBT is the school of psychotherapy that integrates more than others the results of empirical research in psychology and psychotherapy and carefully investigates newly developed treatment procedures.

An enormous amount of pioneering, sophisticated work has been done in couple therapy and prevention to enhance relationship functioning. These efforts have led to the recognition of certain evidence-based forms of couple therapy as empirically validated treatment forms in the US. The guide to beneficial psychotherapy on the homepage of APA's Division 12, published by the Dissemination Committee of Empirically Validated Treatments, states that for marital problems behavioral marital therapy has been well established as a beneficial treatment for marital distress and that some evidence also suggests that emotionally focused couple therapy (EFCT) and insight-oriented marital therapy (IOMT) are useful treatments of marital distress.

Couple Therapy Is Expanding

The area of couple therapy is expanding quickly and its exponents are increasingly incorporating research from other treatment modalities and other disciplines in psychology, such as research on attachment theory (Bowlby, 1988), which is empirically very well supported, and research on relationship functioning and distress. In general there are many studies demonstrating the enormous impact of an individual's close relationships on psychological and physical well-being, stress and illness, and *vice versa*. Individual intrapsychological processes are being more and more taken into account and couple therapists are looking for psychological theories that help them develop a better understanding of the relationship between individual and interactional processes.

For example, in addition to paying attention to dysfunctional couple interaction patterns and their accompanying cognitions, Greenberg and Johnson's (1988) concept of EFCT centers on the connection between individual emotion regulation and interactional conflicts. Their research efforts concentrate on therapeutic procedures to change emotion regulation processes in the partners that have led to dysfunctional relationship patterns. Goldman and Greenberg (2006) proposed more process research on how EFCT changes individual and interpersonal emotional processes in couples.

Also, the fact that individual and relationship problems often occur together and that the quality of intimate relationships has a strong influence on individual, mental, and physical health is increasingly being recognized and studied. Zimmermann's and Heinrichs' (2008) "side by side" program is an example of a new intervention program for engaging partners in the treatment of an individual's physical health problem, in this case breast cancer. Empirical research has shown that couple therapy has an effect not only on the relationship functioning but also on the individual pathology. For a review of empirically supported interventions to address the couple's interactions to influence individual psychological problems or psychopathology, see Baucom, Shoam, Mueser, Daiuto, and Stickle (1998).

New Developments in Couple Therapy and Psychotherapy Research

To this day, there is empirical support for several different treatments for couples with relationship problems (for a summary, see Snyder & Gasbarrini, in this volume) and most likely there are more to come. Even though they differ in their approach to couple dysfunctioning and in their treatment procedures, they are similarly effective. However, it remains unclear what the reasons for this phenomenon are.

According to Grawe (1997) psychotherapy research can be divided into four phases on the basis of the fundamental question addressed. The first phase he calls *the legitimation phase*, addressing the basic question: Is psychotherapy effective? In couple therapy research, during the last 20 years, a large number of studies have demonstrated efficacy and effectiveness of marital therapy and prevention programs to relationship distress and divorce as, for example, Hahlweg's longitudinal study of a premarital prevention program which after 11 years showed that the prevention program lowered the divorce rate by about 50% (Hahlweg & Richter, 2008).

In the second phase, different forms of psychotherapy are being compared to find out which one is better than the other. Grawe calls this phase *the competition phase*. In couple therapy research, Snyder and Wills (1989), for example, compared insight-oriented couple therapy with BCT. Then the field of psychotherapy research moved on to the question of which form of psychotherapy should be prescribed for whom, *the prescription phase*. The first three research questions are limited to studying treatment procedures that already exist. They are conservative in the sense that they are not directed at improving psychotherapeutic procedures.

Since it is well established that certain forms of individual psychotherapy are effective and a catalog of treatments that are recognized as evidence based by APA's Division 12 is available, the focus in individual psychotherapy research during the last 20 years moved into a fourth phase, turning more to the question of how therapy works: *the psychotherapy process research phase*. The notion is that if there were a better understanding of the underlying change processes, the effectiveness of the treatments could be increased.

The problem, nevertheless, remains that different forms of treatment for individual disorders have turned out to be similarly effective. However, the benefits of these different therapy procedures can not clearly be linked to their specific ingredients. There is strong evidence that psychotherapeutic techniques do not have specific effects. This has been very difficult to accept by the proponents of the different schools of therapy and theoretical orientations and has caused heated debates up to this day. It has become an issue in psychotherapy research whether ingredients of change can be identified, and if so, how their influence can become enhanced in psychotherapeutic processes (Lambert, Bergin, & Garfield, 2003). The same phenomenon of course has become apparent in couple therapy. It works, but we do not know why the different empirically validated treatments are effective.

In couple therapy, we can now invest in more research into possible links between the ingredients of these efficacious treatments and therapy outcome. However, it is unlikely that these attempts will be successful since little evidence has been found in empirical psychotherapy research over the years that treatment outcome is related to specific ingredients of the treatment (Lambert, 2003). The history of psychotherapy is full of examples of treatments that are beneficial to the patients but whose psychological explanations for the benefits have failed to be verified (Kazdin, 2007).

The situation within couple therapy today is very similar to what happened in psychotherapy research in general. In couple therapy, the field is also moving into the fourth phase, the process research phase.

Looking for Principles of Change in Couple Therapy

Christensen (in this volume) is suggesting to look for *principles of change* within evidence-based couple therapy (EBCT) instead of "staying the course" and developing new treatment package and then compare it to others to find out which one is more effective.

Christensen distills five general principles of change from the analysis of the fundamental treatment principles of the existing EBCT. In order to be able to come up with a treatment plan that applies these principles for a specific couple, an understanding of the problems, that is a *case conceptualization*, has to be developed. Christensen suggests using the method of a *functional analysis of behavior* as a conceptual basis for applying his five general change principles. The ingredients of the different EBCTs make up the components of these principles of change. Instead of several different treatment packages a unified protocol for EBCT would then be formulated. This, of course, would have very important consequences for clinical practice, training, and research.

General Change Mechanisms in Psychotherapy

Why not take it even a step further and look to psychotherapy research during the last years, where the same problem became apparent in individual therapy? The question of how psychotherapy works has been a main focus of psychotherapy research for many years. Literally thousands of studies have been conducted investigating the influence of hundreds of variables on therapeutic outcome (Lambert, 2003). Orlinsky found several significant variables influencing therapeutic change processes and described a *generic model of psychotherapy* (Orlinsky, Grawe, & Parks, 1994). This model was very influential and led to an increased interest in eclectic and integrative approaches. Since then, empirical psychotherapy process research is finding more and more evidence that change achieved by therapeutic procedures and interventions seems to be more influenced by general principles and factors common in different therapy approaches rather than specific methods and techniques.

After years of studying thousands of findings for his meta-analysis and extracting such common factors, Grawe, Donati, and Bernauer (1994) concluded that the empirically established effects of different forms of treatments can be attributed to *four general change mechanisms*: *problem actuation, resource activation, mastery,* and *clarification of meanings*, and to the therapeutic relationship (Grawe, 1995).

Problem actuation means that the therapist creates therapeutic situations in which the patient immediately experiences his problem, using the assumption that only what the patient actually experiences can be changed. The couple therapy setting is a good example for problem actuation since the dysfunctional interactions and their related emotions are activated by the fact that they actually take place, are experienced by the partners during the couple session, and can be addressed and modified. Resource activation addresses the patient's strengths, abilities, and motivational readiness. For example, including the spouse in the patient's treatment to support the therapeutic process is the activation of an interpersonal resource in the patient's life (Grawe & Grawe-Gerber, 1999; Gassmann & Grawe, 2006; Smith & Grawe, 2001). The third mechanism of change (mastery) refers to increasing the patient's ability to cope with difficulties and to learn new behaviors in order to gain more confidence and a better repertoire of abilities to master problematic situations and experiences. Clarification of meanings, the fourth change mechanism, focuses on motivational conflicts. The therapist works toward developing an understanding of emotional difficulties and therapeutic procedures to clarify and resolve them.

Focusing Interpersonal Aspects of Symptomatic Behaviors

Disorder-specific research has contributed so much to the understanding of the disorder-specific dynamics that other important aspects of the psychological problems of a patient, such as the interpersonal dimension, have been neglected and are mostly not included in case formulations and treatment planning.

All patients live in a relationship context that has a big influence on them, and they influence their nearest and dearest just as much. The separation of treatment and training into individual, couple, family, and child therapeutic treatment modalities is not patient oriented. It developed within psychotherapy, and it is strongly influenced by psychodynamic thinking about problems. Patients are sent to individual therapists and if they turn out to have relationship problems they might be referred to a couple or family therapist, or the individual therapist might try an eclectic or integrative approach. Many therapists even believe they should not see the couple or the family when treating an individual patient. Research studies on the therapy goals of outpatient psychotherapy patients, carried out by Grosse Holtforth and Grawe, however, demonstrated that 75% of patients who seek therapy in an outpatient clinic would like to achieve interpersonal goals, this being especially true for depressed patients and less so for patients with anxiety problems (Grosse Holtforth, 2001; Grosse Holtforth & Grawe, 2002). The finding that the majority of patients report treatment goals in respect to relationship problems corresponds with research related to attachment styles which found that about 80% of all psychotherapy patients who seek treatment in outpatient clinics have insecure attachment patterns. Problematic relationship experiences, especially with parents in early childhood, seem to lead to interpersonal problems and psychopathological symptoms, such as depression.

It is becoming more and more evident that treatments only directed at the symptoms are for many patients not only too restricted in respect to their treatment goals but also too restricted from a scientific perspective. This might also explain why the long-term effect of psychotherapy for depression seems to be limited (Grawe, 2007).

The Interplay Between Relationship Functioning and Psychological and/or Physical Problems

In their review of empirical studies of the association between relationship functioning and mental and physical health, Whisman and Uebelacker (2003) found compelling empirical evidence concerning the high comorbidity between couple distress and behavioral, emotional, and physical disorders in one or both individuals and concluded that

> "the existing research suggests that people who are unhappy with their intimate relationships and have poor relationship functioning are not only more likely to have mental or physical health problems, they are also less likely to respond to treatment for such a problem" (p. 13).

If research in scientific psychology, such as research in attachment patterns, shows evidence of a strong relationship between attachment experiences and resulting problematic behavior and mental disorders such as depression, then the interpersonal perspective in problem formulation and treatment planning will be indispensable. Figure 1 shows the six perspectives to be adopted by the clinician for treatment planning independently of his school's therapeutic orientation. Psychological disorders can develop in very different intrapsychological and interpersonal contexts, and these contexts can contribute to maintain the disorders.

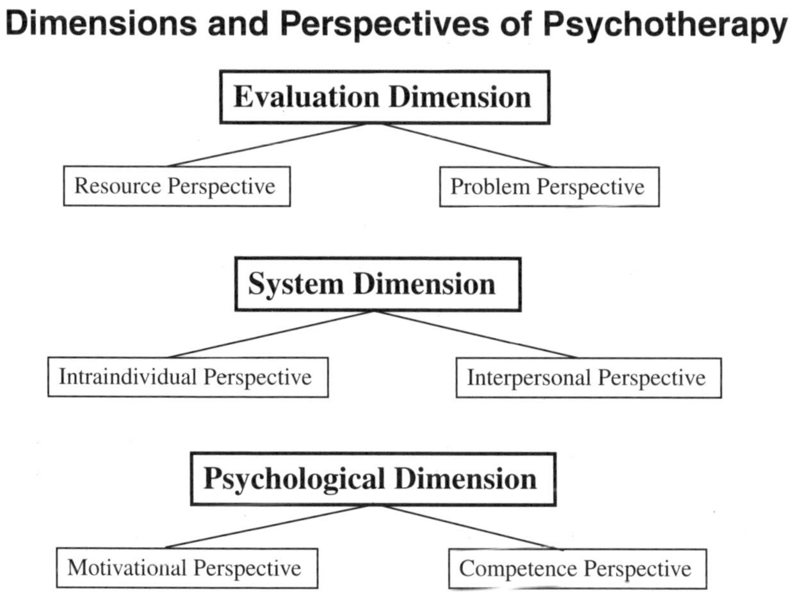

Figure 1. The six perspectives to be adopted by the clinician for treatment planning.

The field of couple therapy is expanding, and more and more sophisticated techniques are being developed and studied to address both perspectives in the therapeutic procedures and interventions. An additional very important development in couple therapy is the increased focus on recognizing and understanding the important role of emotion regulation in the interplay of interactional behavior and intrapsychological processes as presented in the book *Emotion regulation in couples and families* by Snyder, Simpson, and Hughes (2006).

A treatment modality-oriented psychotherapy neglects the fact that focusing either on intrapsychological or on interactional processes and dynamics is not patient oriented and not empirically based. In real life, these two perspectives are equally relevant for understanding and treating psychological problems.

Even though it has been shown by many studies that marital distress demonstrates high comorbidity with individual disorders such as depression, anxiety, and substance abuse, the decision to treat an individual exhibiting comorbid individual and relationship problems in either individual therapy, couple therapy, or a combination of the two is often determined by the therapist's training rather than by the patient's specific problems and resources. However, the question remains: How clinicians develop an understanding of the patient's problem to help them decide whether or not couple therapy is indicated and then develop a treatment plan? What is in fact the situation for the practicing therapist?

Treatment of Individual and Relationship Problems in Everyday Practice

Orlinsky and Ronnestad (2005), in their study of the professional development of psychotherapists, found in respect to treatment modalities that

> "by far the largest proportion of therapists conduct only individual therapy, yet they do not have the happiest work experience. Fewer than half (48%) showed evidence of an Effective Practice and a third had Distressed or Disengaged Practice. Therapists who used a combination of individual with both couple and family therapy most typically reported their work as Effective Practice and rarely as Distressing Practice" (p. 95).

A large number of therapists treat individuals and couples. Many experienced clinicians adopt a personal eclectic approach. Even if they are empirically oriented and try to stay informed about new research results, they also will rely on their personal experience of what they think works. They lack an integrative theoretical framework to conceptualize the problems and the resources in order to develop a treatment plan. Even the most evidence-based clinical work has always been a mixture of art and science. The increasing number of empirically supported treatments and manuals has professionalized the practice of psychotherapy. Clinicians have to become experienced in many different disorder-specific treatments. The belief is that only if adherence to the manual is very good, the treatment will be effective.

Becoming More Patient Oriented and Effective by Integrating Different Perspectives in the Conceptualization of the Problem

However, even the most effective empirically based treatments work only for about two-thirds of the patients. As discussed above, there seems to be a whole list of reasons why not to restrict our attempts at further increasing the efficacy of our treatments to the refinement of disorder-specific procedures. We should also deliberately focus our attention on factors that have nothing to do with the disorder itself, such as the therapeutic relationship, the resources of the patient, his conflictual motivational predispositions, and the general intrapsychological and interpersonal contexts of the problems. These factors also have a sound empirical basis as potent therapeutic influences. They determine the therapeutic outcome to a considerable degree and should therefore be explicitly addressed by our theoretical conceptions.

Snyder, Schneider, and Castellani (2003) argue that

> "no single treatment modality or theoretical approach fully addresses the broad spectrum of individual and relationship dysfunction that difficult couples may

> present. Hence, working with difficult couples requires therapists working with difficult couples to tailor interventions to individual differences by practicing integratively across diverse theoretical orientations, specific intervention modalities, and levels of individual and family functioning" (p. 2).

To improve their effectiveness, the clinicians should therefore also be familiar with the most recent theoretical, clinical, and empirical advances in psychology and psychotherapy research. What is needed is an integrative comprehensive theoretical framework for a patient-oriented and individually tailored problem conceptualization and integrative therapy planning. The intrapsychological, interpersonal, and physical functionings of the patients have to be assessed within a theoretical framework derived from scientific psychology and psychotherapy research and put together in a case conceptualization from which a treatment plan taking into account the general mechanisms of change derived from psychotherapy process research (Grawe, 1997) can be developed.

Research-Informed Integration of Treatment Modalities and Therapeutic Procedures

Snyder and Gasbarrini (in this volume) also argue that without an overarching conceptual framework for integrating specific techniques from diverse theoretical approaches and tailoring these to individual and couple differences, therapeutic interventions are likely to be disjointed, contradictory, and ultimately ineffective. The authors favor what they call a pluralistic approach. This is an approach to psychotherapy integration based on Norcross and Beutler (2000) that makes use of different orientations and systematically selects different empirically based treatment forms depending on the patient's problems and the clinician's inclinations. It is not a comprehensive theory but rather a more systematic way of making use of different theoretical orientations. It remains within the therapy school-oriented way of thinking and it is not based on a scientific psychological concept for integrating the different treatment approaches and interventions. For integration, it relies on the clinician's experience and personal approach.

The author would like to argue that psychotherapists should not only look to different schools of therapy for their theory of human psychological functioning, change processes, and to their personal wisdom, but also to scientific psychology, psychotherapy research, and the developments in the neurosciences. What do today's empirical psychology and neuroscience have to tell us about psychological functioning that could help explain the origin and maintenance of mental disorders? According to the findings of empirical psychotherapy research, how could or should therapists intervene in mental processes in order to set them on a better and healthier track? A model of psychological functioning should make it clear to us at which points the different therapeutic procedures come into play in order to achieve their goals.

Grawe's Consistency Theory as a Generic Model for a Research-Informed Psychotherapy

Grawe's consistency theory (2003) allows for a comprehensive understanding of psychological problems and symptoms from an intrapersonal and an interpersonal perspective. Consistency theory is based on the current state of modern scientific psychology, psychotherapy research, and the neurosciences. It is a model that aims at connecting a conception of mental functioning with a conception of therapeutic change. Consistency theory can only briefly be summarized here. It is presented in detail by Grawe (2004).

Every human being is always trying to satisfy his basic psychological needs. According to Epstein's Cognitive-experiential self-theory (1990) the most relevant ones for psychological functioning and well-being are experiencing pleasure and avoiding pain, and enhancing and protecting self-esteem, to secure close relationships and intimacy with others, and to feel in control and well oriented. In order to fulfill these needs we behave in certain ways to achieve our goals. However, if an individual gets hurt while trying to fulfill basic psychologically vital needs, he will start to protect himself, and he begins to avoid harmful and negative experiences and disappointments. Our mental activity and patterns of psychological functioning are regulated by behavioral goals that serve the satisfaction of needs (approach goals) and behavior toward avoidance of painful emotions and experiences (avoidance goals).

Consistency theory assumes that inconsistency in mental functioning, that is motivational conflicts resulting from trying to satisfy important needs while at the same time trying to avoid negative painful experiences, leads to mental instability and is a main source for psychopathology. Psychological problems and symptoms are maladaptive patterns to reduce inconsistency while at the same time making the satisfaction of the basic needs more difficult to achieve.

For a case conceptualization according to this model, the therapist analyzes the patient's sources of incongruence and then develops an individual treatment plan to reduce avoidance behavior, to help the patient to strengthen his approach behavior in order to be able to satisfy the above-mentioned basic psychological needs, and to reduce psychopathology or psychological problems. In each case it should be examined which sources of inconsistency are especially relevant. For the analysis of incongruence and the planning of different interventions to reduce incongruence, see Figure 2.

The patient's sources of incongruence indicate the most promising starting points for therapeutic interventions. Quite often, a combination of different therapeutic procedures will be the most promising, because different sources of inconsistency have to be taken into account simultaneously.

For most of these inconsistency producing difficulties, there are already effective interventions. Up to now, they have been grouped into different schools of therapy. This is why many therapists work predominantly only with certain interventions and disregard other potential sources of inconsistency. A future truly scientific psychotherapy should take all sources of inconsistency into consideration. From this theoretical point of view

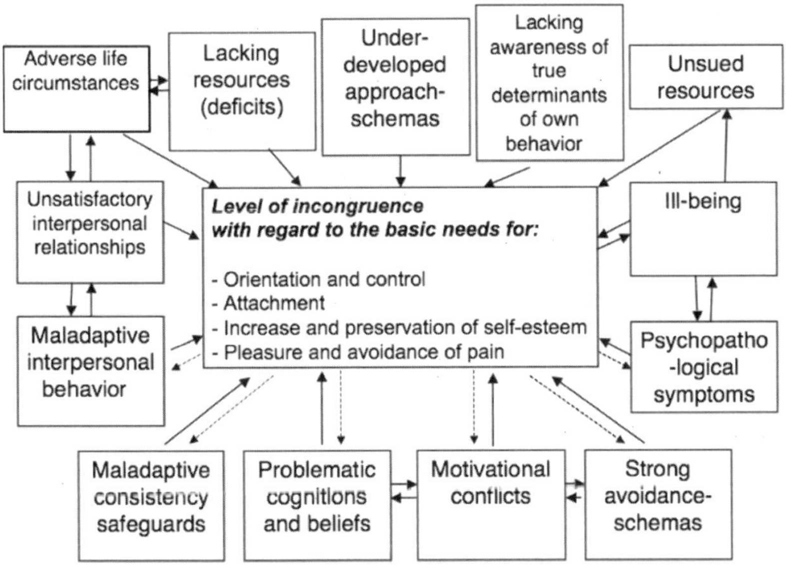

Figure 2. Analysis of sources of incongruence and treatment planning.

indications emerge for working in a couple setting, in an individual setting, or in a combination of the two, depending on the conceptualization of the presenting problems rather than on therapists training or preferences.

Research-informed psychotherapy, also called neuropsychotherapy (Grawe, 2007), is not a new school of therapy but a paradigmatic or generic model for all empirically oriented psychotherapists. A case conceptualization according to consistency theory makes use of empirically validated guidelines for the clinician to integrate different methods and to decide on his proceedings with an individual patient and/or a couple in order to be successful with instigating change and the achievement of treatment goals.

Figure 3 shows the combination of the interpersonal and intrapsychological perspectives with the four general change mechanisms: problem actuation, resource activation, mastery, and clarification of meaning for treatment planning. Which treatment modality or which combination of modalities is indicated depends on the analysis of the patient's sources of incongruence. For the question whether or not to work within the couple treatment modality these different questions have to be answered.

Examples are: In which *setting* can the problematic behavior best be activated and then be modified or changed? Does one of the partners have to clarify a motivational conflict? If so, in which setting can this clarification process best be initiated and worked through? Is there a problem with the lack of competences in the patient or with the couple? If so, a unified protocol for couple therapy, such as Christensen's, would then come into use if

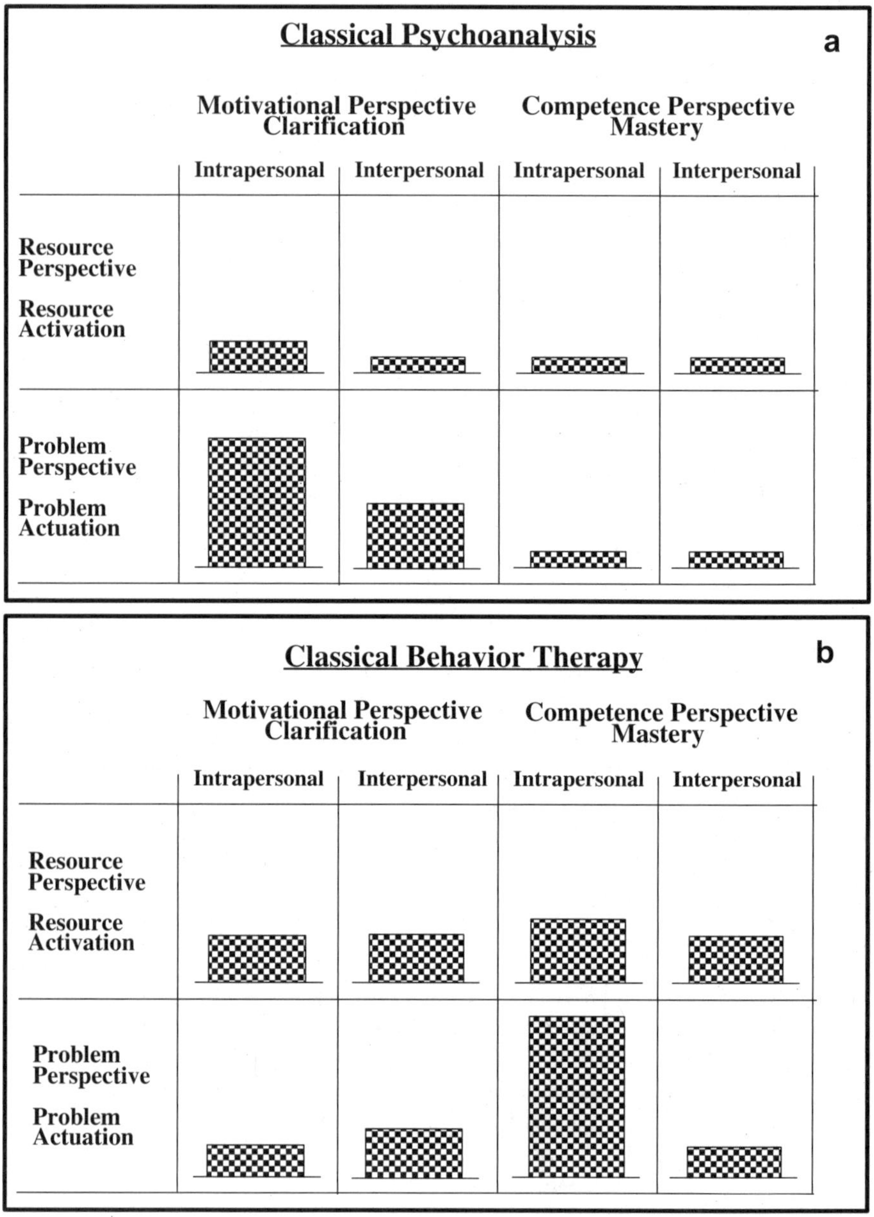

Figure 3. The combination of the interpersonal and intrapsychological perspectives with the four general change mechanisms: problem actuation, resource activation, mastery, and clarification of meaning for treatment planning.

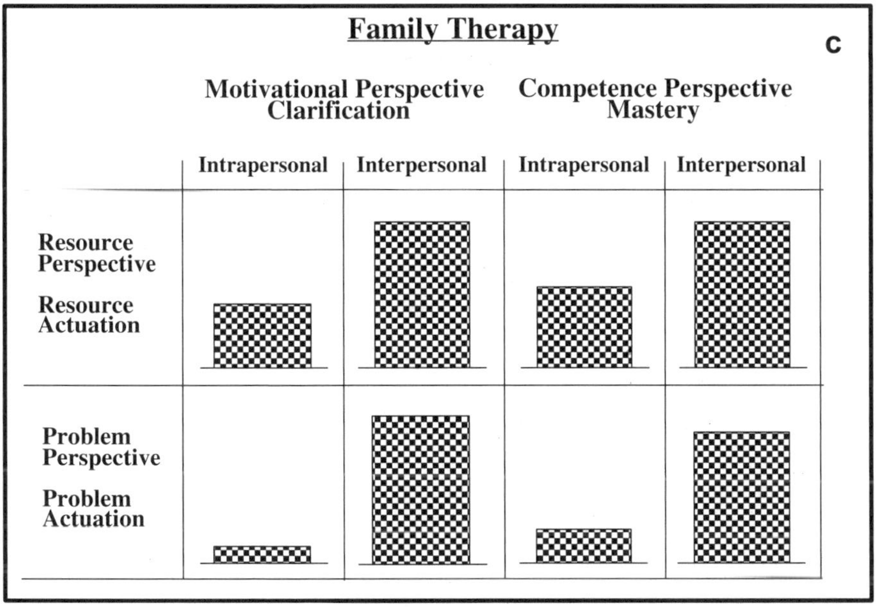
Family Therapy
c
Motivational Perspective
Clarification
Competence Perspective
Mastery
Intrapersonal
Interpersonal
Intrapersonal
Interpersonal
Resource Perspective
Resource Actuation
Problem Perspective
Problem Actuation

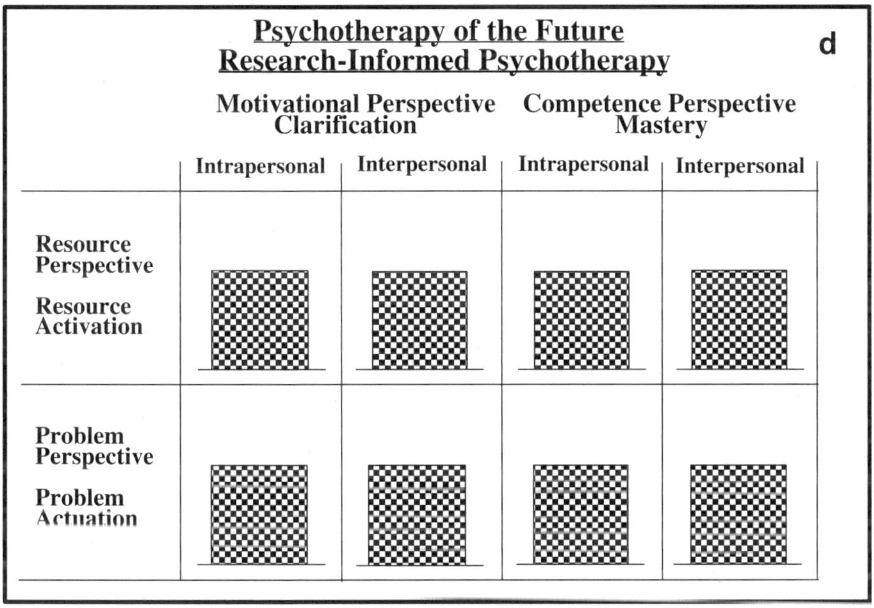
Psychotherapy of the Future
Research-Informed Psychotherapy
d
Motivational Perspective
Clarification
Competence Perspective
Mastery
Intrapersonal
Interpersonal
Intrapersonal
Interpersonal
Resource Perspective
Resource Activation
Problem Perspective
Problem Actuation

couple therapy were indicated and the therapist had to look for evidence-based treatment procedures within the field of couple therapy.

The well-established confirmation of the efficacy and effectiveness of psychotherapy has led evidence-based treatments to become more available to patients and health insurance companies to become more willing to pay for them. There is a lot of engaged activity and discussion on the dissemination of evidence-based treatments for individual patients as presented, for example, in the paper on evidence-based best practice in psychology by the APA Presidential Task Force in the American Psychologist in 2006.

Since CBCT has become more and more empirically supported and recognized as evidence based, why then is there a problem with the dissemination of the know-how and treatment packages CBCT has to offer?

Intervention programs that achieve the status of recognition of being registered officially as an empirically based intervention or treatment program should be easily accessible for clients and patients. Excellent manuals and textbooks for clinicians have been written by couple therapy researchers. The presented treatment programs have been developed at the universities, where researchers look for specific kinds of patients, and clinicians are then trained in a narrowly defined manualized therapeutic procedure, to which they have to adhere carefully and are supervised. This is one of the reasons why the impact of empirically validated couple therapy on the general public so far has been limited. In order to bring couple therapy to the couples who might benefit from it rather than recruiting certain couples for a specific study, a better knowledge of couples' help-seeking behavior and the availability of information about evidence-based treatment packages for them is necessary. Doss (in this volume) presents a summary of the empirical research and literature available on couples' help-seeking behaviors.

Implications for Training

However, we also need to look at who gets trained in these effective couple treatment programs. In psychotherapy training, the assumption that working with a couple, a family, or a child requires different competences and skills than working with individual patients leads to a lack of skills to work in different treatment modalities of trained clinicians. In most training programs, no clear criteria have been developed as to when individual and when couple or family therapy or a combination might be indicated.

If in real life most practitioners work with patients who are involved in intimate relationships that play an important role in the development and maintenance of psychological disorders, then training in psychotherapy should always include learning to be able to work within different treatment modalities. Many more clinicians would then feel more confident to work with couples when indicated. This would improve the impact of couple therapy in psychotherapy.

To improve effectiveness of psychotherapy, a scientific approach to training needs is to be adopted. A research-informed psychotherapy training would teach a scientific model for case conceptualizations and treatment planning. The trainees would then be able to

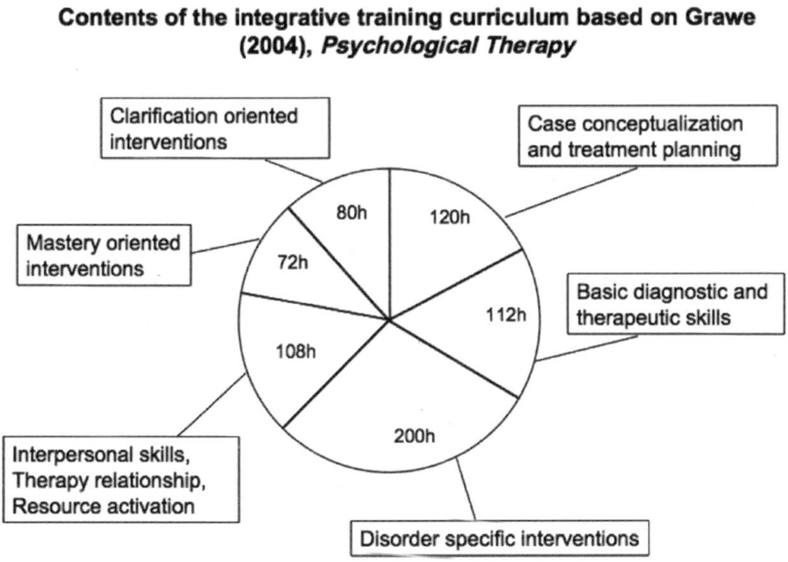

Figure 4. A model of training in research-informed psychotherapy.

systematically draw from psychotherapy research (e.g., Grawe's general change mechanisms) and from different treatments and procedures of different orientations for their interventions.

Improving training not only improves the effectiveness of psychotherapy, it also makes evidence-based treatments available to more patients.

In the last 15 years such a research-informed psychotherapy training model has been developed by Grawe, Grawe-Gerber, and Heiniger at Bern University and at the Klaus-Grawe-Institut in Zürich, Switzerland. The curriculum is based on consistency theory and the analysis of incongruence, the interpersonal and intrapsychological perspectives, and the general change mechanisms. Within that model, evidence-based treatment procedures are taught and practiced. For a presentation of this training model, see Figure 4.

Trainees are taught for each individual patient and couple to focus on relationship functioning under the resource and problem perspective as well as on intrapsychological functioning. The decision on the treatment modality then depends on the questions in which setting the patient's resources and problems can best be activated and in which treatment modality or combination of modalities can necessary motivational clarification processes and/or the learning new competences best be initiated.

Dissemination of EBCT would then be improved not only by taking it to the couples in need for it, but also by taking it to the clinicians. We as clinicians and trainers should let go of the artificial separation of the individual from his interpersonal context and include his partners, parents, children, and families and the way they interact with him and each other into our professional understanding.

References

Baucom, D. H., Epstein, N. B., LaTaillade, J. J., & Kirby, J. S. (2002). Cognitive behavioral couple therapy. In A. S. Gurman (Ed.), *Clinical handbook of couple therapy* (4th ed.). New York: Guilford Press.

Baucom, D. H., Shoam, V., Mueser, K. T., Daiuto, A. D., & Stickle, T. R. (1998). Empirically supported couple and family interventions for marital distress and adult mental health problems. *Journal of Consulting and Clinical Psychology, 66*(1), 53–88.

Bowlby, J. (1988). *A secure base: Parent-child attachment and healthy human development.* New York: Basic.

Christensen, A., & Jacobson, N. S. (1995). Integrative behavioral couple therapy. In N. S. Jacobson & A. S. Gurman (Eds.), *Clinical handbook of couple therapy.* New York: Guilford.

Epstein, S. (1990). Cognitive-experiential self-theory. In L. A. Pervin (Ed.), *Handbook of personality: Theory and research* (pp. 165–192). New York: Guilford.

Gassmann, D., & Grawe, K. (2006). General change mechanisms: The relation between problem activation and resource activation in successful and unsuccessful therapeutic interactions. *Clinical Psychology and Psychotherapy, 13*, 1–11.

Goldman, R. N., & Greenberg, L. S. (2006). Promoting emotional expression and emotion regulation in couples. In D. K. Snyder, J. A. Simpson & J. N. Hughes (Eds.), *Emotion regulation in couples and families – Pathways to dysfunction and health* (pp. 231–248). Washington, DC: American Psychological Association.

Grawe, K. (1995). Grundriss einer Allgemeinen Psychotherapie [Layout of a general psychotherapy]. *Psychotherapeut, 40*, 130–145.

Grawe, K. (1997). Research-informed psychotherapy. *Psychotherapy Research, 7*, 1–19.

Grawe, K. (2004). *Psychological therapy.* Kirkland, WA: Hogrefe & Huber Publishers.

Grawe, K. (2007). *Neuropsychotherapy.* London: Lawrence Erlbaum Associates.

Grawe, K., Donati, R., & Bernauer, F. (1994). *Psychotherapie im Wandel: Von der Konfession zur Profession* [Changes in psychotherapy: From confession to profession]. Göttingen, Germany: Hogrefe.

Grawe, K., & Grawe-Gerber, M. (1999). Ressourcenaktivierung. Ein primäres Wirkprinzip der Psychotherapie [Resource activation: A primary effective factor in psychotherapy]. *Psychotherapeut, 44*, 63–73.

Greenberg, L. S., & Johnson, S. M. (1988). *Emotionally focused therapy for couples*. New York: Guilford Press.

Grosse Holtforth, M. (2001). Was möchten Patienten in ihrer Therapie erreichen? – Die Erfassung und Kategorisierung von Therapiezielen mit dem Berner Inventar für Therapieziele (BIT) [What do clients wish to achieve during therapy? The assessment of therapeutic goals using the Bern inventory for therapeutic goals (BIT)]. *Verhaltenstherapie und Psychosoziale Praxis, 33*, 241–258.

Grosse Holtforth, M., & Grawe, K. (2002). Bern inventory of treatment goals (BIT), Part 1: Development and first application of a taxomony of treatment goal themes (BIT-T). *Psychotherapy Research, 12*, 79–99.

Gurman, A. S. (2002). *Clinical handbook of couple therapy* (3rd ed.). New York: Guilford Press.

Hahlweg, K., & Richter, D. (2008). *The 11-year long-term effects of the EPL-relationship enhancement program.* Paper presented at the XXIX International Congress of Psychology, Berlin, Germany.

Kazdin, A. E. (2007). Mediators and mechanisms of change in psychotherapy research. *Annual Review of Clinical Psychology, 3*, 1–27.

Lambert, M. J. (2003). *Bergin and Garfield's handbook of psychotherapy and behavior change* (5th ed.). New York: Wiley.

Lambert, M. J., Bergin, A. E., & Garfield, S. L. (2003). Introduction and historical overview. In M. J. Lambert (Ed.), *Bergin and Garfield's handbook of psychotherapy and behavior change* (5th ed.). New York: Wiley.

Norcross, J. C., & Beutler, L. E. (2000). A prescriptive eclectic approach to psychotherapy training. *Journal of Psychotherapy Integration, 10*, 247–261.

Orlinsky, D., Grawe, K., & Parks, B. (1994). Process and outcome in psychotherapy. In A. E. Bergin & S. L. Garfield (Eds.), *Handbook of psychotherapy and behavior change* (4th ed., pp. 270–376). New York: Wiley.

Orlinsky, D. E., & Ronnestad, M. H. (2005). *How psychotherapists develop: A study of therapeutic work and professional growth.* Washington, DC: American Psychological Association.

Smith, E., & Grawe, K. (2001). Die funktionale Rolle von Ressourcenaktivierung für Psychotherapie [The functional role of resource activation for therapeutic changes]. In H. Schemmel & J. Schaller (Eds.), *Ressourcen: Ein Hand- und Lesebuch zur therapeutischen Arbeit* (pp. 111–122). Tübingen, Germany: DGVT Verlag.

Snyder, D. K., Schneider, W. J., & Castellani, A. M. (2003). Tailoring couple therapy to individual differences: A conceptual approach. In D. K. Snyder & M. A. Whisman (Eds.), *Treating difficult couples: Helping clients with coexisting mental and relationship disorders* (pp. 27–51). New York: Guilford Press.

Snyder, D. K., Simpson, J. A., & Hughes, J. N. (Eds.). (2006). Emotion regulation in couples and families: Pathways to dysfunction and health. Washington, DC: American Psychological Association.

Snyder, D. K., & Wills, R. M. (1989). Behavioral versus insight-oriented marital therapy: Effects on individual and interspousal functioning. *Journal of Consulting and Clinical Psychology, 57*(1), 39–46.

Whisman, M. A., & Uebelacker, L. A. (2003). Comorbidity of relationship distress and mental and physical health problems. In D. K. Snyder & M. A. Whisman (Eds.), *Treating difficult couples: Helping clients with coexisting mental and relationship disorders*. New York: Guilford.

Zimmermann, T., & Heinrichs, N. (2008). *Seite an Seite – eine gynäkologische Krebserkrankung in der Partnerschaft gemeinsam betwältigen* [Side by side: Jointly mastering gynecological cancer within a partnership]. Göttingen, Germany: Hogrefe.

Mariann Grawe-Gerber
Klaus Grawe Institute for Psychological Therapy
Grossmünsterplatz 1
8032 Zurich
Switzerland
E-mail: mgrawe@ifpt.ch

Couple-Based Interventions to Assist Partners with Psychological and Medical Problems

Donald H. Baucom, Jennifer S. Kirby, and Jasmine T. Kelly

University of North Carolina, Chapel Hill, NC, USA

Abstract

A great deal of couple-based treatment research has been conducted in multiple countries since the early 1970s. Most of these investigations have focused on altering couple functioning in order to benefit the couple's relationship *per se*, whether attempting to alleviate relationship distress, prevent the development of relationship discord, or enhance already healthy relationships. In addition, the couple's relationship can be a valuable resource in helping the partners work together as a team when one person experiences a significant individual problem, whether it involves individual psychopathology or a health problem. This chapter describes how therapists can employ what they know about relationship functioning to assist couples who are experiencing one of these individual difficulties. The following three types of couple-based interventions are described. *Partner-assisted interventions* do not focus on the couple's relationship *per se* but rather employ the partner as a coach or surrogate therapist to help the other individual make important changes focal to the psychological or health concern. *Disorder-specific interventions* emphasize changing the couple's relationship but only in those domains that are focal to the health or psychological concern. Finally, *couple therapy* can be employed if the couple is experiencing relationship distress that becomes a broad source of stress on the vulnerable individual. Examples regarding how to employ these couple-based interventions for specific types of psychopathology and health concerns are provided. Broadening the use of couple principles to these populations can greatly expand the range of services provided by therapists to couples in need over the lifespan of their relationship.

In the 1960s and 1970s, psychologists and other mental health professionals began developing a new approach to working with couples based on social learning or behavioral principles. The explicit goal of these cognitive-behavioral interventions was to improve or optimize the *couple's relationship*. In this chapter, we will focus on ways in which couple-based interventions can be used with a very different, yet important, goal in mind – to improve the *well-being of one of the partners* who is experiencing either psychological distress or medical difficulties. As it is not obvious why a couple-based intervention might be the treatment of choice for individual difficulties, we will provide a conceptual and empirical basis for offering these types of interventions. From a practical standpoint, clinicians need to know how to offer these couple-based treatments for individual problems, and the majority of the chapter is devoted to clarifying different ways that such interventions can be delivered. Finally, we discuss the challenges and opportunities for the future as we develop a broader set of couple-based interventions to assist with individual difficulties.

Why Offer Couple-Based Interventions for Individual Psychological or Medical Difficulties?

As Epstein and Baucom (2002) have noted, there is a close, reciprocal interaction among (a) couple functioning, (b) individual functioning, and (c) the couple's environment. The most obvious implication of this statement is that in order to develop the healthiest relationship, it also is important to make certain that each partner as an individual is functioning as adaptively as possible and the couple relates to their environment in constructive ways. In addition, there is another very important implication that perhaps is less obvious and is the focus of this chapter: *Individuals are likely to function most adaptively both psychologically and physically if they are involved in healthy relationships that contribute to and help shape the individual's environment. Thus, couple-based interventions can be employed not only to improve the quality of the relationship but also to improve the functioning of individual partners or patients* (in the current discussion, we will use the term *patient* to designate the individual member of the couple with psychological or medical complications). In many instances, these couple-based interventions focused on helping the patient will have a different emphasis from marriage counseling or couple therapy that emphasizes strengthening the relationship, but all of these interventions have in common that they intervene with the couple as a unit employing cognitive-behavioral intervention strategies.

Consistent with the above general assertion that individual well-being is influenced by the person's close relationships, there is a great deal of evidence that both individual psychological well-being (Snyder & Whisman, 2003) and physical well-being/response to disease (Schmaling & Sher, 2000) are greatly influenced by intimate relationships. For example, being in a marriage or committed relationship that provides high levels of social support is related to less individual psychopathology (Snyder & Whisman, 2003), whereas a critical, hostile family environment predicts negative outcomes for individuals with a wide range of psychopathology (Butzlaff & Hooley, 1998). Likewise from a physical perspective, women with breast cancer report greater emotional adjustment to their illness if their husbands are highly supportive, particularly if the latter provide good emotional support (Neuling & Winefield, 1988). Furthermore, findings also indicate that among individuals with congestive heart failure, the quality of their marriages significantly predicts their mortality 4 years later, even after the level of physical disease has been taken into account (Coyne et al., 2001).

Given the strong reciprocal association between individual and couple functioning, it then becomes a question of how best to use a couple's relationship to facilitate an individual's well-being. This is a question posed not only by mental health professionals, but also by spouses and partners in both happy and unhappy relationships. Often partners who care about the patient remark, "I want to be of help, but I don't know what to do. Can you help me understand how I can be of assistance? I care about [patient] so much, and I'm afraid I'm either doing the wrong thing or not being as helpful as I want to be. But I really don't know what is best to do." For example, the partner of someone with depression might ask whether it is better to let the person lie in bed or encourage/force the depressed person to get up and become engaged with daily activities. Understandably, such concern and questions come from partners in happy relationships, not just from partners in distressed marriages. Such questions do not focus on "How do I make our relationship better?"; instead, these questions address the following concern: "How do I as a partner help the patient get better, or how do we use our relationship to assist the patient who is suffering in some way?" Therefore it is important to develop interventions in which the couple can work together to assist one partner who has psychological or medical complications, whether the couple is happy with their relationship or distressed.

Recently, our research team, as well as other investigators, has developed a variety of couple-based interventions to assist one partner who is experiencing such psychological (Snyder & Whisman, 2003) or medical concerns (Schmaling & Sher, 2000). Whereas the content of these interventions differs greatly depending upon the specific disorder that is being addressed, these couple-based approaches can be classified into three different categories that vary according to how broadly the couple's relationship is addressed in the intervention: (a) partner-assisted interventions, (b) disorder-specific interventions, and (c) couple therapy. These three strategies are based on a body of empirical findings that indicate that in many instances, for individuals with psychological and medical difficulties to function at an optimal level, those persons need (a) to make specific behavioral changes and (b) operate in a positive/noncritical emotional climate. The following three types of couple-based interventions are intended to use the couple's relationship to help achieve these two goals.

Partner-Assisted Interventions

The first of these three approaches that uses the couple's relationship to assist the individual is referred to as *partner-assisted interventions*. This approach focuses specifically on behavior changes that the individual patient needs to make and how the partner can help the patient make these changes, hence the term *partner-assisted*. This approach does not emphasize changing the couple's relationship in any fundamental or meaningful way.

Instead, the partner is assuming the role of a substitute or surrogate therapist in some ways, or a coach and cheerleader in helping the patient make important changes. For example, agoraphobia is an anxiety disorder in which the individual broadly experiences the world as dangerous, resulting in an individual restricting his or her environment to what feels safe. The individual believes that venturing out from safe settings will result in some extremely negative consequence such as a panic attack, a heart attack, or losing control in some other frightening way. Thus, the person with agoraphobia might be unwilling to go more than a few miles from home, avoid crowded places, or even be restricted to his or her own house or specific rooms that in some way feel safe. There is a great deal of research that indicates that for someone to overcome agoraphobia, it is critical to confront the feared situations and stay in the situation without withdrawing until the anxiety decreases, experiencing that the anticipated negative consequences did not occur (Barlow, Gorman, Shear, & Woods, 2000). This treatment principle, referred to as exposure, serves as the basis for the treatment of all anxiety disorders, which in one form or another all involve an experience of danger, unpredictability, and/or some expected, yet unrealistic negative consequence. In essence, the treatment involves confronting the fearful situation and learning that nothing bad happens after all.

A partner-assisted approach to agoraphobia would involve including the partner in an appropriate way in these exposure outings that focus on the patient's feared situations. As we describe in more detail elsewhere (Baucom, Stanton, & Epstein, 2003), this typically would involve the couple: (a) discussing the plans for a specific exposure outing prior to the exposure, (b) planning and carrying out how they will respond together if the patient becomes extremely anxious during the exposure outing, and (c) once the exposure outing is finished, debriefing regarding what was helpful and unhelpful from each partner during the exposure experience. In order for the patient to develop a sense of efficacy and self-confidence to confront these feared situations alone, the partner's role in these exposure outings would be decreased over time.

There are several factors to recognize in considering this partner-assisted exposure. Most importantly, this intervention does not focus upon the couple's relationship in any fundamental way. Instead, the patient needs to go on exposure outings, and the partner is being of assistance in helping to make them successful; in essence, the partner serves as a coach or substitute therapist, given that in other contexts, these exposure outings are conducted at times between a patient and a therapist. Also, this role for the partner typically is for a time limited basis, during the active treatment of agoraphobia. That is, treatment for agoraphobia involves very specific exposure outings that occur over a defined period of time, once these exposure outings are completed, the partner's role in formal exposure outings terminates as well. Thus, partner-assisted interventions typically are time limited in contrast to other strategies described below. These characteristics typify a partner-assisted approach to treating individual psychological difficulties or medical conditions. The interventions are time limited and do not attempt to alter the couple's relationship in any broad fashion.

Partner-assisted interventions also can have utility in the treatment of some medical conditions. The appropriateness of this type of couple-based intervention depends upon whether treatment or rehabilitation for a medical condition emphasizes specific health behavior changes on the part of the patient. If so, then it is appropriate to think in terms of how the partner can assist with these changes. If, however, specific health behavior changes are not central to the treatment of the medical condition, then partner-assisted interventions are not emphasized, although other forms of couple-based interventions as described below might still be of value. As an example of a medical condition calling for health behavior changes, consider osteoarthritis which is a condition that often afflicts the elderly, with accompanying significant pain in the limbs. Effective behavioral interventions for osteoarthritis include teaching the patient strategies for coping with the pain, including relaxation, meditation, and distraction from the pain, as well as alternating activities with rest (rest-activity cycles) to promote moderate exercise without excessive strain to the patient. Recently, along with Keefe and colleagues, we have developed partner-assisted interventions to facilitate these health behavior changes for individuals with osteoarthritis (Keefe et al., 1996, 1999, 2004). These interventions include, for example, the couple going on outings in which they schedule moderate activity and build in a rest period prior to the patient experiencing pain. Similarly, both partners might learn to meditate together, enjoying the relationship aspects of this joint activity, at the same time decreasing the partner's pain. The findings from these partner-assisted interventions for osteoarthritis have been promising and demonstrate the importance of teaching the partner about how to be helpful in the treatment of this painful disease. More specifically, the results indicated that if the couple was treated together and the partner learned how to be of assistance in managing pain, then the better the marriage, the *better* the long-term adjustment of the patient in dealing with pain. However, if the patient was treated individually and the partner did not know how to be of assistance, then the better the marriage, the *worse* the long-term adjustment for the patient (Keefe et al., 1999). These findings seem to confirm that well-intended partners in a good relationship can inadvertently behave in maladaptive ways when trying to be of help if they are not trained in how to best assist the patient.

As another example of partner-assisted interventions for medical conditions, in collaboration with Sher, Baucom helped to develop a multifaceted couple-based intervention for coronary artery disease (Sher & Baucom, 2001). Treatment of this medical condition often involves increases in physical exercise, medication compliance, and dietary changes. Consistent with the overall logic described above, we proposed that these health changes might be easier and more persistent if the couple works together to help the patient follow-through with these potentially difficult changes. The various strategies employed included partner-assisted approaches in which the couple might decide together on a schedule for the patient to take medication, or the partner might provide gentle reminders without taking over responsibility for medication. Similarly, the couple might shop together at the grocery store to select heart healthy, appealing food choices, later served in appropriate portion sizes. Again, the sole focus of these partner-assisted interventions is to help the patient make appropriate health behavior changes without attempting to create notable changes in the couple's relationship.

Often partner-assisted interventions are used in combination with other types of couple-based interventions described below to contribute a multifaceted approach to treating individual psychological and medical concerns, and in such instances it is difficult to tease apart their unique contributions. However, both as the sole treatment (see Baucom, Shoham, Mueser, Daiuto, & Stickle, 1998 for a review) and as part of a multifaceted set of interventions, partner-assisted interventions appear to hold great promise.

Disorder-Specific Interventions

In partner-assisted interventions, the partner is used as a coach or surrogate therapist to help the patient make particular changes that have been identified as critical for addressing specific psychological and medical conditions. The same changes would be expected of the individual patient even if the partner were not included in the intervention, and including the partner is seen as a way to include an important person in the patient's life to help structure the patient's environment and reinforce appropriate patient behavior changes. The couple's relationship is not the central focus of the intervention, and the partner's role in such interventions ends as the patient terminates active treatment.

A disorder-specific intervention builds upon this approach but involves different strategies. More specifically, these interventions do focus upon creating fundamental changes in the couple's relationship that will persist long term, but only in the domains that are focal to the patient's disorder, hence the name *disorder-specific* interventions. In these interventions, the therapist helps the couple identify ways that they can use or alter their relationship to encourage changes that the individual patient needs to make to address psychological or medical difficulties. As described below, these interventions also can involve the partners providing mutual support to each other.

As an example, once again consider the role of partners in treating anxiety disorders, such as agoraphobia or obsessive-compulsive disorder (OCD). As described above, through the use of exposure outings, an individual with agoraphobia learns that the world is not as dangerous as anticipated; therefore, the patient can become involved in situations and settings that previously were avoided because they lead to disabling anxiety. One important use of a disorder-specific couple intervention in this context is to help couples create an everyday life style that helps to encourage and maintain the patient's new-found ability to interact with the outside world. This might involve, for example, significant shifts in the patient's and partner's household roles and responsibilities. When the agoraphobia was most severe, the nonagoraphobic partner might have done most of the grocery shopping and transportation of the children because of the distress created when the person with agoraphobia engaged in these tasks. Although inadvertent, the partner's assumption of these roles actually encouraged or helped to maintain the agoraphobic avoidance and escape from frightening situations. Therefore, in a disorder-specific intervention, the therapist would work with the couple to redistribute responsibilities such that the agoraphobic individual would interact with the outside world on a regular basis, such as doing the grocery shopping and transporting the children away from home. Similarly, the couple would be encouraged to develop new social activities that maintain engagement with the outside world as well, including visiting friends and family on a regular basis or taking vacations far beyond where the agoraphobic was able to go in the past. In essence, the couple is building the concept of exposure into the fabric of their relationship on a continual basis in a way that feels natural and sustainable. Consistent with the perspective that it is valuable to teach the couple healthy ways to alter their relationship in the context of agoraphobia, Arnow, Taylor, Agras, and Telch (1985) demonstrated that if couples were taught to communicate and make effective joint decisions regarding the agoraphobia, the patient responded more positively to treatment compared to intervention without this couple-based disorder-specific approach.

OCD is another anxiety disorder in which an individual typically engages in repetitive acts in order to reduce anxiety or distress. For example, an individual who fears germs or becoming contaminated might spend hours a day compulsively washing clothes or cleaning his/her hands so often that the outer layer of his/her skin deteriorates. Engaging in these repetitive acts provides short-term alleviation of anxiety, but the relief is only temporary. Unfortunately, the anxiety returns and the cleaning rituals must be repeated, leading to significant disruption in daily life as well as ongoing distress. For treatment to be successful in the above scenario, the individual would need to be exposed to dirt and potential germs without being allowed to engage in excessive cleaning or hand washing, thus learning that excessive cleaning is not necessary. Prior to treatment and in order to help the person with OCD to avoid distress, a partner might inadvertently help to create an "obsessive-compulsive environment," although the opposite is needed for the patient to improve. For example, in order to avoid "contaminating" their apartment, one wife agreed with her OCD husband that she would only place her books, purchases, or other items that she brought into the apartment in a specified room in a "contamination area" that was one meter square. In that way, the remainder of the apartment would remain contamination free, and the contamination zone would be cleaned excessively each day after she left the apartment. Without intending to do so, the wife was contributing to his ritualistic obsessive-compulsive behaviors and building an "obsessive-compulsive" environment in which they lived.

After explaining the nature of OCD and the principle of exposure and response prevention to the couple, the therapist taught them to use couple-based disorder-specific interventions in the treatment of OCD. This included the wife bringing items into the home and placing them in appropriate rooms, as any couple might do. The husband was forbidden to decontaminate or clean when she left items in various rooms. In this and many other ways, the couple created a life style in which the husband was confronted with potential germs on an ongoing basis without being allowed to clean excessively. The well-established principle of treatment for anxiety disorders, exposure, was incorporated into the couple's life on an ongoing basis and in a natural fashion (see Baucom et al., 2003 for a fuller discussion of couple-based interventions for OCD and agoraphobia). Although this intervention altered the couple's relationship, it did so only in areas that were focal or specific to OCD; for example, the couple was not discussing in-law difficulties that were unrelated to OCD. Such disorder-specific interventions can be critical in the treatment of psychological disorders, regardless of whether the couple is in a happy or an unhappy relationship.

Similar disorder-specific interventions can likely have great utility in the treatment of a variety of medical conditions. For example, in the couple-based treatment for coronary artery disease created by Sher and colleagues, extensive use was made of disorder-specific interventions to help the patient engage in physical exercise on a regular basis. After teaching effective communication and problem-solving skills, each couple was asked to decide how they would incorporate physical exercise into their ongoing life style. Couples decided upon any of several strategies that would meet their particular needs and preferences. Couples in which both partners enjoyed exercise and had a similar level of fitness and ability might decide to exercise together on a regular basis, perhaps playing tennis together, running, or bicycling as a couple. If both partners wanted to exercise regularly but had different interests or ability levels, they might exercise separately but still build time into their schedules for both persons to get appropriate exercise as part of their daily routines. Finally, if the nonpatient partner did not plan to exercise, the couple would devise a strategy to provide ample time and encouragement for the patient to exercise on a regular basis. Thus, exercise was to be a regular part of the couple's life style, with each couple individualizing how this would best be accomplished.

The findings to date from this intervention study demonstrate the utility of a couple-based intervention that included both partner-assisted and disorder-specific strategies (Sher, 2005). Overall, the findings indicated that if the couple was in a happy marriage, then both the individual treatment and the couple-based intervention were equally effective in reducing cardiac risk. However, if the couple was in a distressed marriage, then the patient benefited significantly more from the couple-based intervention. Sher interpreted these findings to mean that if the relationship was distressed, then having both partners present was necessary to help them work together effectively as a team in order to assist the patient in making necessary behavioral changes to reduce his/her cardiac risk. On the other hand, if the couple was in a satisfied relationship, both interventions were helpful in that either the partner was present to learn about necessary changes or the patient would come home and explain the changes to the partner who would then be available to assist the partner carry out what was necessary to reduce his/her risk (Sher, 2005). Although these findings merit replication in another investigation, the results suggest that couple-based interventions may be particularly helpful for some couples, whereas individual interventions may suffice for other individuals. At present, we do not have enough information to identify clearly the circumstances under which couple-based versus individual interventions will be differentially effective.

Disorder-specific interventions also can be of utility in medical conditions that do not emphasize specific health behavior changes such as exercise and diet. For example, in recent years investigators have developed interventions to help couples in which the female partner is diagnosed with breast cancer. Unlike coronary artery disease in which exercise and dietary change are essential components of treatment, no such central health-related behavior changes have been identified for breast cancer. Instead, the emphasis in working with couples with breast cancer involves helping them learn to support each other effectively. These strategies involve both emotional support, as well as practical support such as making decisions about medical procedures, rearranging roles and responsibilities while the woman is in treatment, making good financial decisions to pay for treatment, and so forth. Scott, Halford, and Ward (2004) conducted the first large-scale intervention study to work with couples facing breast cancer, employing disorder-specific interventions in a treatment entitled CanCope in Australia. Their findings demonstrated the superiority of the couple-based intervention over individual treatment and treatment-as-usual. More specifically, CanCope produced significant improvements in couples' supportive communication, reduced psychological distress and coping effort, and improved sexual adjustment. Overall, the focus on couple coping rather than individual coping was more effective in facilitating adaptation to cancer.

These encouraging findings also set the stage for additional couple-based interventions for breast cancer in other countries, including the US (Baucom, Porter, Gremore, Kirby, & Keefe, 2006) and Germany (Heinrichs & Zimmermann, 2008). Whereas much of this work is still in progress, we have reported the results from a pilot study entitled CanThrive conducted in the US (Baucom et al., 2006). In this intervention, couples in which the female had early stage breast cancer received six disorder-specific sessions that addressed the following topics: (a) the importance of approaching breast cancer as a couple, (b) making effective joint decisions about breast cancer, (c) supporting each other emotionally through difficult experiences, (d) addressing changes in body image and sexuality, (e) noticing the good during the trauma of breast cancer, and (f) moving forward into the future. The results from this study suggest that compared to couples receiving routine care as offered in a large university-based cancer center, both women and men receiving CanThrive experienced improved functioning on individual psychological variables as well as relationship functioning at posttest and 1-year follow-up. In addition, compared to women receiving routine care, women receiving CanThrive showed fewer medical symptoms at both time periods.

Looking at the pattern of findings across disorder-specific interventions for both coronary artery disease and breast cancer, it appears that these types of strategies can be of assistance both when specific health behavior changes are needed (such as diet and exercise for coronary patients), as well as when effective emotional and practical support is of central importance (such as in the treatment of breast cancer). Whereas both partner-assisted and disorder-specific interventions focus solely on the individual patient's psychological or medical condition from a couple's perspective, there also are times when a broader focus on the couple's overall relationship is indicated as well during the treatment of an individual psychological or medical condition.

Couple Therapy

Broad-based couple therapy or marriage counseling approaches, such as cognitive-behavioral couple therapy (CBCT), are intended to assist couples experiencing relationship difficulties in a variety of domains. These same interventions can be of assistance to maritally distressed couples, who in addition to their relationship concerns, have one partner with individual psychological or medical complications. In these instances, couple therapy can be helpful in at least two ways. First, it can be difficult or impossible to implement the types of partner-assisted or disorder-specific interventions described above if the two partners are interacting in a negative/hostile manner or are distant and disengaged. For example, having the partners go together on an exposure outing for agoraphobia and supporting each other might be unrealistic if they generally are angry and unmotivated to help each other. Likewise, providing emotional support or making oneself vulnerable to disclose fears of death during the treatment of breast cancer will be compromised if the couple's relationship feels threatening. Therefore in order to conduct a variety of couple-based interventions focal to the patient's disorder as described earlier in this chapter, it might be necessary to help the couple establish overall goodwill between the two partners along with a collaborative mind-set in their relationship. Stated differently, improving the overall quality of the relationship may have indirect effects on the psychological or medical condition by making it possible to conduct effective partner-assisted and disorder-specific interventions.

Second, couple therapy such as CBCT may have a direct effect on some of these disorders as well. Whereas the role of stress in the development and treatment of different medical conditions appears to be more variable, most psychological disorders are understandable within a diathesis-stress model. That is, individuals might have a biological vulnerability to specific psychological disorders such as anxiety disorders or depression. These disorders are likely to be precipitated or exacerbated when such an individual experiences a high level of stress. Relationship discord or marital distress can be viewed as a broad, chronic stressor on an individual. Consequently, it is not surprising that many psychiatric disorders seem to be precipitated following significant interpersonal stressors (Snyder & Whisman, 2003). Likewise, a large body of literature focusing on a variety of psychiatric conditions demonstrates that an individual's long-term psychiatric outlook or prognosis is worse if that individual lives in a critical/hostile family environment (Butzlaff & Hooley, 1998).

At times a poor marriage or committed relationship may not only be a broad, diffuse stressor that creates a negative environment, but the relationship may be a specific stressor or the substantive issue that has contributed to an individual disorder. For example, the experience of loss is central to the development of depression. Therefore, the loss of a loving relationship along with the dreams and expectations of what a marriage or committed relationship might be, could be the central concern in an individual's clinical depression (Beach, 2000). Consistent with this notion that couple therapy might be of assistance when marital distress and depression co-occur, two treatment studies have indicated that behavioral couple therapy in this context helps to alleviate depression as well as improve relationship functioning (Beach & O'Leary, 1992; Jacobson, Dobson, Fruzzetti, Schmaling, & Salusky, 1991; Jacobson, Fruzzetti, Dobson, Whisman, & Hops, 1993).

Therefore a major reason to focus upon relationship distress is to provide an optimal interpersonal environment with minimal discord and maximal positive experiences for the individual confronting significant psychological or medical complications. As noted above, even if the stress of an unhealthy intimate relationship is not directly involved in the precipitation, exacerbation, or alleviation of a medical or psychological condition, attending to relationship discord can still help to set the stage for the optimal delivery of a variety of partner-assisted and disorder-specific interventions.

Summary

Although the field is still young with regard to the development and implementation of couple-based interventions for individual psychopathology and medical conditions, there is growing evidence that such strategies can be of help across a wide range of individual concerns. Partner-assisted and disorder-specific couple-based interventions use the partner and the relationship to target *specific* changes that an individual needs to make or ways that one or both partners can support the other person during these difficult experiences. Supplementing these targeted domains that are specific to a given disorder, a broad-based couple therapy can also be implemented to assist couples suffering from relationship distress at the same time, thus helping to alleviate a chronic stressor on the individual patient. A thoughtful combination of targeted changes within the context of an overall supportive interpersonal environment provides the optimal conditions for individuals addressing psychological and medical difficulties.

What Expertise Is Needed to Create and Implement These Interventions?

As witnessed by the recent increase in research on the association between couple and individual functioning as well as the development of couple-based clinical interventions for individual distress, an increasing number of mental health professionals are recognizing the utility of the types of couple-based strategies outlined in this chapter. Yet even if convinced that such treatments might be helpful, many professionals can feel overwhelmed by the task of developing or implementing such strategies. Although demanding, effective couple-based treatment to assist in individual psychological or medical problems can be developed and implemented if several domains of expertise are developed.

First, a therapist must have a strong grounding in intimate interpersonal relationships, including knowledge of fundamental relationship principles and how to intervene with couples to promote relationship change, such as through the use of CBCT principles for relationship distress or education. When one partner develops significant psychological difficulties or a medical condition, the fundamental principles of relationship functioning do not change. A couple is still a couple; thus, well-trained couple therapists are essential in the delivery of these interventions. Second, a firm understanding of the individual psychopathology or medical condition is needed, again with knowledge of the effective treatments that exist, typically as they have been applied in the form of individual therapy. For example, it is essential to understand the phenomenon of OCD, with its wide range of cognitive, behavioral, and emotional components. Relatedly, the clinician must understand the value of exposure and response prevention in the treatment of OCD. Third, the clinician must understand how this particular disorder affects the partner and the relationship, for example how a partner can inadvertently exacerbate the OCD by giving in to the patient's demands for excessive cleanliness. Finally, the clinician must learn how to integrate the above factors (general couple functioning, the nature of the individual disorder and its related treatments, and how the disorder affects the partner and the relationship) in order to utilize the couple's relationship to promote the specific changes needed to address the individual's disorder.

Whereas this might sound like an impossible task, well-trained couple therapists and researchers in the mental health field often have or can develop these areas of expertise. At the same time, it is not necessary that one individual have full expertise in all of these domains. Routinely we collaborate with other therapists and researchers who have knowledge beyond our own areas of expertise in order to develop these couple-based interventions. Thus, we work with professionals in a variety of disciplines to understand cardiovascular difficulties, arthritis, cancer, anxiety disorders, and eating disorders. Our experience has been that bringing together such a multidisciplinary team can create a "healthy marriage" in the service of assisting couples experiencing psychological and medical difficulties. For many couple therapists this will involve moving beyond one's "comfort zone," but doing so provides an opportunity to contribute one's expertise in relationship functioning to an ever wider range of life circumstances that couples frequently confront.

Where Do We Go from Here?

First and foremost, a great deal of treatment development and evaluation is needed for couples experiencing the types of psychological and medical complications discussed throughout this chapter. Whereas such interventions might seem reasonable and at times essential, there is only a small body of empirical research on the efficacy of these couple-based interventions compared to our knowledge of the efficacy of individual psychotherapy for various disorders. Therefore, the first task is to develop a thoughtful set of couple-based interventions that are grounded in empirically supported couple therapy as well as efficacious individual treatments for these disorders.

Second, it will be important to provide a thoughtful analysis of which disorders are likely to be assisted most greatly by couple-based interventions. For example, we refer to breast cancer as a "relational cancer" for at least two reasons. First, basic research indicates that when a woman experiences breast cancer, it typically affects her, her partner, and their relationship (Baucom, Porter, Kirby, Gremore, & Keefe, 2005). Whereas this is true of most cancers, it is likely to be particularly true of breast cancer in which the affected body part is central to body image, a sense of femininity, and sexual functioning. In addition, not only does breast cancer affect the woman's intimate relationship, but it also appears that her relationship with her partner impacts her response to breast cancer.

As noted earlier, many women report that the support from their partner is one of the most important factors in their adaptation to breast cancer (Neuling & Winefield, 1988). Based upon these findings, breast cancer is an example of what appears to be a good candidate for a couple-based intervention. Because it is unrealistic to develop thoughtful couple-based intervention strategies for each type of psychological and medical condition any time in the near future, investigators and clinicians must use empirical findings and their clinical experience to prioritize which individual disorders merit the time and resources needed to develop couple-based interventions.

Third, it will be important to isolate which couples will benefit maximally from a couple-based intervention versus an individual-level intervention for one partner's psychological or medical complications. We would not presume that couple-based interventions are the treatment of choice for every couple with every disorder. Instead, it will be important to match the type of intervention to a particular individual's and couple's circumstances. For example, Fredman (this volume) has demonstrated that a family-based cognitive-behavioral intervention is superior to individual interventions for bipolar disorder when the family demonstrates emotional involvement with the patient in inappropriate ways. Thus, the resources needed to provide this intervention can then be targeted to specific families in need.

In summary, we believe that the agenda for the next decade regarding couple functioning and individual psychological/medical disorders is clear. Couple-based interventions have applicability far beyond the treatment of relationship discord and relationship education. Our success in these more traditional areas of intervention provides optimism that we can integrate our understanding of relationship functioning with our knowledge of individual psychopathology and/or medical problems to derive effective couple-based interventions for these concerns. As couple therapists and researchers, our goal is to be of assistance to couples and both partners over the full course of their relationship, whatever difficulties they encounter along the way. Couple-based interventions for individual psychological and medical difficulties are an important part of that commitment to couples, and developing and evaluating the efficacy of these interventions is our next and most important step along this path.

References

Arnow, B. A., Taylor, C. B., Agras, W. S., & Telch, M. J. (1985). Enhancing agoraphobia treatment outcome by changing couple communication patterns. *Behavior Therapy, 16*(5), 452–467.

Barlow, D. H., Gorman, J. M., Shear, K. M., & Woods, S. W. (2000). Cognitive-behavior therapy, imipramine, or their combination for panic disorder: A randomized controlled trial. *Journal of the American Medical Association, 283*(19), 2529–2536.

Baucom, D. H., Porter, L. S., Gremore, T. M., Kirby, J. S., & Keefe, F. J. (2006, October). *Enhancing survivorship for couples facing breast cancer: A pilot study of a couple-based cognitive-behavioral intervention*. Paper presented at the NCI Cancer Survivorship Conference Bi-Annual Meeting, Bethesda, MD.

Baucom, D. H., Porter, L. S., Kirby, J. S., Gremore, T. M., & Keefe, F. J. (2005). Psychosocial issues confronting young women with breast cancer. *Breast Disease, 22*, 1–11.

Baucom, D. H., Shoham, V., Mueser, K. T., Daiuto, A. D., & Stickle, T. R. (1998). Empirically supported couples and family therapies for adult problems. *Journal of Consulting and Clinical Psychology, 66*, 53–88.

Baucom, D. H., Stanton, S., & Epstein, N. (2003). Anxiety. In D. K. Snyder & M. Whisman (Eds.), *Treating difficult couples* (pp. 57–87). New York: Guilford.

Beach, S. R. H. (Ed.). (2000). *Marital and family processes in depression: A scientific foundation for clinical practice*. Washington, DC: American Psychological Association.

Beach, S. R. H., & O'Leary, K. D. (1992). Treating depression in the context of marital discord: Outcome and predictors of response of marital therapy versus cognitive therapy. *Behavior Therapy, 23*(4), 507–528.

Butzlaff, R. L., & Hooley, J. M. (1998). Expressed emotion and psychiatric relapse: A meta-analysis. *Archives of General Psychiatry, 55*, 547–552.

Coyne, J. C., Rohrbaugh, M. J., Shoham, V., Sonnega, J. S., Nicklas, J. M., & Cranford, J. A. (2001). Prognostic importance of marital quality for survival of congestive heart failure. *American Journal of Cardiology, 88*, 526–529.

Epstein, N., & Baucom, D. H. (2002). *Enhanced cognitive-behavioral therapy for couples*. Washington, DC: American Psychological Association.

Heinrichs, N., & Zimmermann, T. (2008). *Seite an Seite. Krebs gemeinsam bewältigen: Ein partnerschaftliches Unterstützungsprogramm für Brust- und Gynäkologische Krebserkrankungen*. Göttingen: Hogrefe.

Jacobson, N. S., Dobson, K. S., Fruzzetti, A. E., Schmaling, K. B., & Salusky, S. (1991). Marital therapy as a treatment for depression. *Journal of Consulting and Clinical Psychology, 59*(4), 547–557.

Jacobson, N. S., Fruzzetti, A. E., Dobson, K. S., Whisman, M., & Hops, H. (1993). Couple therapy as a treatment for depression: II. The effects of relationship quality and therapy on depressive relapse. *Journal of Consulting and Clinical Psychology, 61*, 516–519.

Keefe, F. J., Blumenthal, J., Baucom, D. H., Affleck, G., Waugh, R., Caldwell, D., et al. (2004). Effects of spouse-assisted coping skills training and exercise training in patients with osteoarthritic knee pain: A randomized controlled study. *Pain, 110*(3), 539–549.

Keefe, F. J., Caldwell, D. S., Baucom, D. H., Salley, A., Robinson, E., Timmons, K., et al. (1996). Spouse-assisted coping skills training in the management of osteoarthritic knee pain. *Arthritis Care and Research, 9*, 279–291.

Keefe, F. J., Caldwell, D. S., Baucom, D. H., Salley, A., Robinson, E., Timmons, K., et al. (1999). Spouse-assisted coping skills training in the management of knee pain in osteoarthritis: Long-term follow-up results. *Arthritis Care and Research, 12*, 101–111.

Neuling, S. J., & Winefield, H. R. (1988). Social support and recovery after surgery for breast cancer: Frequency and correlates of supportive behaviours by family friends and surgeon. *Social Science and Medicine, 27*, 385–392.

Schmaling, K. B., & Sher, T. G. (2000). *The psychology of couples and illness: Theory, research and practice*. Washington, DC: American Psychological Association.

Scott, J. L., Halford, W. K., & Ward, B. (2004). United we stand? The effects of a couple-coping intervention on adjustment to breast or gynecological cancer. *Journal of Consulting and Clinical Psychology, 72*(6), 1122–1135.

Sher, T. G. (2005, September). *Couples, illness, and coronary artery disease*. Paper presented at the European Association for Behavioral and Cognitive Therapy, Athens, Greece

Sher, T. G., & Baucom, D. H. (2001). Mending a broken heart: A couples approach to cardiac risk reduction. *Applied and Preventive Psychology, 10*, 125–133.
Snyder, D. K., & Whisman, M. A. (Eds.). (2003). *Treating difficult couples*. New York: Guilford Press.

Donald H. Baucom
Richard Simpson Distinguished Professor of Psychology
University of North Carolina
Davie Hall CB #3270
Chapel Hill, NC 27599-3270
USA
E-mail: don_baucom@unc.edu

What Makes Couples-Based Interventions Work?

A Centuries' Debate with Few Answers to Offer

Nina Heinrichs[1] and Tanja Zimmermann[2]

[1]University of Bielefeld, Germany
[2]University of Braunschweig, Germany

Abstract

Despite a large amount of research in the area of couple therapy and the knowledge that there are several couples-based interventions which work, there has been only little application of evidence-based interventions for couples in therapeutic practice. Many therapists are trained primarily in individual therapy. Although it is well known that partners are also impaired by mental and physical disorders of their significant others, partners or children are only rarely included in treatment. There are differences in each of these therapy modalities (individual vs. couple or child vs. adult) but little is known about the mechanisms of change that help understand how they work. Thus, we analyzed the extent to which the four principles of change (mastery, clarification, problem actuation, and resource activation) identified by Grawe were used in two different couples-based interventions where the woman was faced with gynecological cancer. Side by Side is a couples' intervention program which is compared to a partner-assisted brief educational program for ill woman. Side by Side is expecting to make better use of clarification of feelings, resource activation, and motivational clarification, whereas the educational interventions should work through the therapeutic alliance and acquisition of skills. The results showed that Side by Side is working better than the educational intervention in supporting women in coping with cancer. All common factors were significantly more distinct in Side by Side. The common factors mediated relationship outcome. It seems beneficial to compare mechanisms of change across treatment modalities in order to move forward from the "splintering perspective" to a "family perspective" including the individual, the partner, and the child.

There has been a significant amount of work being conducted in the area of couples' interventions. In 2006, there were more than 1,100 scientific publications relating to couples compared to far less than a 100 in 1970. Thus, more than 35 years of research is behind of us – and *what do we really know about couples-based interventions*? The only thing we really know is that there are several couples-based interventions which work. If couples participate in these interventions, they will feel better (i.e., less distressed) and they are, for example, less likely to divorce. This knowledge has, however, rarely been transported to the public. Many individuals live in relationships but very few attend a relationship enhancement course such as the *Prevention and Relationship Enhancement Program* (Markman, Renick, Floyd, Stanley, & Clements, 1993) or *Ein Partnerschaftliches Lernprogramm* (Thurmaier, Engl, Eckert, & Hahlweg, 1992), although these programs have specifically been shown to *prevent* the likelihood of a breakup by supporting couples to learn how to stand together in rough times. There are certainly a number of reasons for the low uptake, among them the low publicity of evidence-based interventions for couples, the lack of susceptibility in couples in love for the potential loss of this intense and thrilling feeling despite the well-known divorce rate, and the low rate of professionals who are appropriately trained in delivering couples-based interventions. Many professionals are primarily trained in individual psychotherapy: They deliver – at best – evidence-based programs to overcome excessive anxiety or intensive mood problems such as depression by working with the very person who is suffering from these problems. Although it is well known that the partner is also significantly impaired by psychological or physical problems of his or her significant other, the benefit of including the partner into individual treatment has only been investigated more recently. Similarly, the inclusion of children or even only the consideration of children (as another "significant other" who may suffer from mom's or dad's individual problems or their couple's distress) in treatment has been more or less ignored. Thus, psychotherapy has traditionally been an individual-focused approach which at times even explicitly excluding a family perspective (e.g., in Germany where a health insurance will pay for individual treatment only, the inclusion of a family member is possible up to a maximum of one-fourth of the treatment time but not more independent of the problem the individual is encountering). This artificial separation of an individual from his social context is also supported by the structure of training that is delivered to the next generation of psychotherapists. Psychologists who want to study psychotherapy need to decide for a certain "track" of training, adult or child, individual or couple, but they cannot be trained in both simultaneously.

What is the reason for this *splintering*? It is primarily based on the assumption that treating an individual is different from treating a couple and that treating a child is different from treating an adult, and therefore different competencies need to be delivered in training. Although this statement has been approved of repeatedly, and it almost seems so inherently logical that everyone has an inclination to approve, we would like to challenge this assumption. The format of treatment, the content of treatment, and the setting of treatment are certainly different across these domains of services, but how about what makes these treatments work?

Mechanisms of Change: Why Is Identifying Mechanisms of Change Important?

Mechanisms of change are those concepts that are supposed to produce therapeutic change (i.e., they tell us about how or why a specific intervention works). Identifying these mechanisms of change in each of these treatment modalities (individual or couple, and adult or child) will help us understand in what ways these different aspects of mental health services vary (or do not vary) in *how* they work. It will enhance training individuals in the competencies that are necessary to deliver treatments in these modalities. For example, if a therapist who is very competent in building up a positive relationship with an adult client (known as "therapeutic alliance" or "therapeutic relationship"), would s/he also be able to build up a positive relationship with a client's partner? Could s/he also relate well to a child? Child treatment is usually considered to be more different from individual or couple treatment with adults than either one of those is to the other.

Moreover, mechanisms of change could help us in identifying the underlying principles of *negative* change that may cut across techniques, treatment types, settings, or modalities. Examples for negative change are premature termination of exposure in individual treatment which can leave patients more anxious than before treatment (Lilienfeld, 2007) or beginning an affair during couple's treatment. Doss, Thum, Sevier, Atkins, and Christensen (2005, p. 624) write

> "Knowledge of mechanisms of change can inform combinations and modifications of existing therapies, speeding progress toward more effective treatments."

Although these authors may not have intended to extend the meaning of this sentence across treatment modalities, we would argue that exactly this is the largest benefit of knowing about mechanisms of change: They can inform us about combinations of individual with couples' approaches (or *vice versa*), and about when and how to include a child (or *vice versa* from a child treatment perspective: When and how to include the parent). Identifying mechanisms of change across these modalities may therefore be a centerpiece of coming to terms with the disadvantageous splintering that is making an individual human being who is by nature vitally social completely asocial. Unfortunately, we know very little about *why* interventions work despite an overwhelming body of evidence that they work.

Common Factors as a Part of Mechanisms of Change

Common factors are one set of mechanisms of change that have been the focus of research for a long time. Conceptually, common factors "are those dimensions of the treatment setting (therapist, therapy, and client) that are not specific to any particular technique or theory" (Blow & Sprenkle, 2001, p. 385; Lambert & Bergin, 1994). Thus, they are core ingredients of change which are independent of the underlying intervention models or intervention techniques. The most prominent common factor is the *therapeutic alliance*. However, there are a number of other common factors that might be (more) relevant to change.

Common Factors in Individual, Couple, and Child Treatment

There have been several calls for research on mechanisms of therapeutic change based on the fact that there is hardly any "breakthrough" or "cutting-edge research" completed that would illuminate what actually produces change (Kazdin, 2006). In fact, even most recent publications state that "the processes and mechanisms underlying therapeutic change are still largely unknown" (Johansson & Hoglend, 2007).

In general, studies focus on identifying *mediators* of change; i.e., variables which *produce* the outcome of a certain intervention. Although the concept of causality is not unequivocal, the criteria for demonstrating it are not (Johansson & Hoglend, 2007). Many of these mediators of change relate to the primary focus of the intervention. For example, in the treatment of obsessive-compulsive disorder with exposure and response prevention (or any other exposure-based treatment for anxiety disorders) the change in the primary negative emotion (i.e., anxiety or disgust) through exposure has been identified as a mediator of change (Cougle, Wolitzky-Taylor, Lee, & Telch, 2007). To a certain extent this seems tautological because the mediator of change is equivalent to the primary targeted outcome (less anxiety in anxiety disorders). Nevertheless, this mediator and others identified in individual treatment studies may have something in common despite being very specific to the disorder addressed: They might produce change because the intervention provided patients with skills to cope with their primary negative emotions, such as mindfulness or acceptance. Thus, it is rather the *acquisition of skills* that is producing the change and not the reduction in fear or tension. In dismantling the effective components of psychosocial interventions for cancer populations, Graves (2003) identified *concrete skills* to be among the centerpieces of successful and effective interventions. Likewise, in parenting interventions for alleviating conduct problems in children, changes in *parenting skills* are a key mechanism of change. For example, the change in positive parenting behavior mediates change in child problem behavior (Gardner, Burton, & Klimes, 2006). In the treatment of anxious children, skills-based approaches have been advocated for a long time assuming that the acquisition of coping skills for these children is essential for overcoming their excessive fears (Kendall et al., 1997). In couples-based interventions, changes in *communication* and *problem-solving skills* have been repeatedly pointed out as a primary mechanism of change in behavioral couple interventions. Although the change in communication as a mediator of intervention outcome has not always been consistently associated with change in marital satisfaction, more recent results demonstrate that these associations do exist but may not always be easily detected (e.g., because they might occur differentially dependent upon the time point and the type of intervention; Doss et al., 2005; Snyder, Castellani, & Whisman, 2006). Thus, independent of the intervention modality (working with an individual adult, a couple, or working with parent-child dyads or triads), skills acquisition seems to be across the board an important mediator of change. This has already been realized by Grawe (1997): While other researchers are still persistent in the debate of which approach researchers and clinicians should be paying more attention to, the common factor approach in which the *intervention model-independent factors* are considered of primary importance for treatment outcome (see, e.g., Blow, Sprenkle, & Davis, 2007; Sprenkle & Blow, 2004) or the intervention model approach in which the *specific ingredient of the intervention itself* matters the most (see, e.g., Sexton, Ridley, & Kleiner, 2004), Grawe and colleagues (Gassmann & Grawe, 2006; Grawe, 1994, 2004; Grawe & Grawe-Gerber, 1999) identified four principles of change that might help overcome the lack of integration between intervention-*dependent* and intervention-*independent* mechanisms of change (see Figure 1).

Mastery refers to the individual's

> "concrete experience of learning to cope with situations experienced (...) as very difficult or anxiety provoking. (...) Therapists need a detailed, disorder-specific understanding of the specific determinants of their patient's problems and concrete skills for an appropriate translation of this understanding if they are to help their patients develop mastery" (Grawe, 1997, p. 4).

Clarification refers to illuminating the meaning of an emotional experience.

> "When the threatening meaning of a particular situation for particular goals is clarified or when the importance of these goals is revised by making explicit the implicit meanings involved, (...) the patient's feelings may change dramatically." (Grawe, 1997, p. 4).

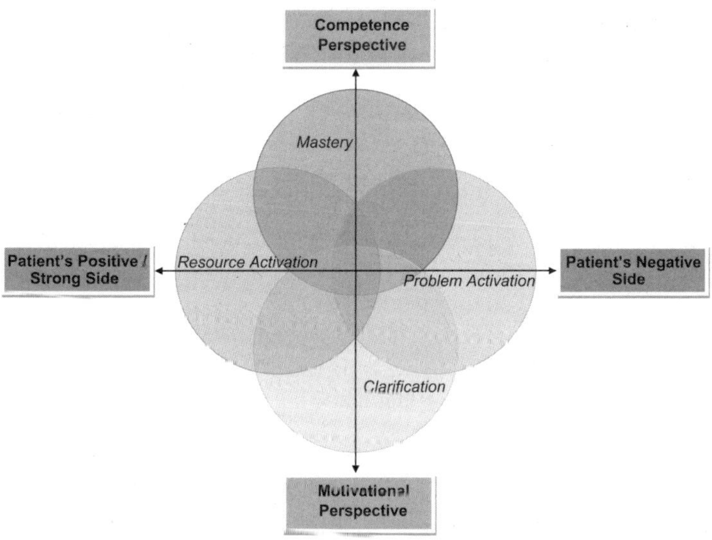

Figure 1. The four change principles (modified after Grawe, 1997).

Problem actuation refers to the activation of actual and current difficulties. It is based on the assumption that problems can be addressed best while they are experienced. Including the partner in interventions to relieve marital distress is a good example for how this mechanism of change can be introduced through a therapeutic setting.

Resource activation refers to the fact that what the client is bringing along to treatment is very important and should be systematically attended to by therapists.

Across individual, couples, and child interventions, different approaches have been undertaken to look at mechanisms of change and common factors specifically making it difficult to directly compare results across these approaches. Most research has been conducted in the area of individual treatment, followed by couples-based interventions and little is known about the mechanisms of change in child treatment.

It seems that the field of marital therapy in particular has basically been overtaken by the research agenda on common factors from individual treatment. However, it still rather reminds of a battlefield about who is right rather than a field of academic research if we look at recent publications in the marital field (Sexton et al., 2004; Sprenkle & Blow, 2004). Many of the articles on mechanisms of change in couple therapy are theoretical in nature and do not attempt to specifically test the mechanisms of change they believe to be most important; instead, they infer from reviews or meta-analyses stating the absence (or presence) of better outcomes for one or the other intervention about the causal (in-) significance of common factors which is not appropriate (Kazdin, 2005).

Grawe (1994, 1997) provided a framework of change in which he outlined four common factors of change which are hypothesized to occur on an intra- *and interpersonal* level. This framework is derived from an extensive review of the treatment literature and several process studies on individual treatment. His framework includes the significance of relational aspects and is not merely taken over from individual therapy, although his change principles have neither been derived from couples-based interventions nor have they been actively applied to them either. Grawe (1997) argued that interventions will be most effective if these common factors would be used *systematically* (on a regular basis, planned but adaptive to the treatment process and phase). He assumed that therapists employ them more or less instead of dichotomously.

To our knowledge, the four principles of change have never been investigated in couples-based intervention. Blow and Sprenkle (2001) attempted to transport Lambert's four-factor model (Lambert, 1992) derived from the individual treatment literature to marital and family therapy and they added three factors that were unique to couples-based interventions: relational conceptualization, the expanded direct treatment system, and the expanded therapeutic alliance. *Relational conceptualization* refers to keeping "the whole system in view when relating to any individual client (…) regardless of the number of clients present in the therapy room" (p. 387). The *expanded direct treatment system* refers to the fact "that persons who may affect treatment are also considered even if they are not physically present" (p. 387) and *the expanded therapeutic alliance* involves that in couples-based interventions an alliance needs to be built up with two individuals. Blow and Sprenkle (2001) then asked a panel of experts to achieve a consensus regarding common factors in marital and family therapy. Relationship factors were considered more important than client factors and model or technique factors were mostly viewed as equally important. The authors conclude that "much of the work of MFTs (Marriage and Family Therapies) do overlap with psychotherapy generally" (p. 399). They recommend more research on common factors in couple- and family-based interventions. This study clearly indicates the difference in the breadth and integrative power of the two different conceptualizations of common factors (four change principles vs. seven common factors) and how they operate according to these research groups.

The following sections will focus on the attempt to address the lack of empirical data regarding common factors in couples-based interventions by investigating if the change principles derived by Grawe (1994, 1997) could be transported and applied to a couples-based intervention delivered to couples where the woman has recently faced with a diagnosis of breast or gynecological cancer.

Understanding Common Factors of a Couples-Based Intervention for Women with Gynecological Cancer and Their Partners

Gynecological cancers (including breast, ovarian, and cervix cancers) are the most commonly occurring cancers among women. They are the leading causes of cancer death among women in Germany. However, advances in early detection and medical treatment of breast cancer have improved survival, such that 81% of women will meet the 5-year survival criterion validating them as "cured" if their cancer had been detected early. A woman who receives such a diagnosis is suddenly faced with an enormous threat to her physical and psychological well-being, her role in the family, and her economic situation. She ultimately fears for her life, as many other cancer patients do when they hear about their diagnosis. However, specific to gynecological cancers is that the cancer occurs in those body parts most intimately associated with womanhood. This may lead to additional problems with body image, feelings of femininity, sexual functioning, and intimate relationships in *both* men and women. With many females surviving the cancer, couples need to work through these issues, which may be an emotional roller coaster. When women with cancer are in intimate relationships, they do express a great need for their partner's support (Helgeson & Cohen, 1996), yet most psychosocial support offers for these women are based on either an individual approach or a group approach in which the woman is seen together with other women diagnosed with cancer (Zimmermann, Heinrichs, & Baucom, 2007). Recently, Shands, Lewis, Sinsheimer, and Cochrane (2006) reported that there are four primary areas for female breast cancer couples in which they would like to have some help: (1) dealing with tension in the relationship, (2) needing to be together as a couple, (3) wondering about the children, and (4) managing the threat of cancer. As it becomes very clear from these topics, the individual problem is not limited to the individual but causes concerns and problems which relate to the entire family, the women, her partner, and the children. Noteworthy, including the partner to cope with cancer is different from treating marital dissatisfied couples. The primary outcome variable is not necessarily marital satisfaction as many of these couples are not marital distressed to begin with. Nevertheless, it might be beneficial to look at what is necessary to help these "couples in despair" to jointly cope with the disease.

Intervention

According to the four primary areas for female breast cancer couples in which they would like some help, we developed a brief intervention for couples dealing with a gynecological cancer diagnosis which is addressing each of these topics. The intervention ("Side by Side"; Heinrichs & Zimmermann, 2008) is focused on communication processes. Communication is the single best predictor of relationship functioning (Karney & Bradbury, 1995) and thus, it seems to be the most relevant mediator of change to consider (intervention-dependent mechanism of change). The intervention supports women and their partners to provide each other with emotional (e.g., empathetic listening) and practical support (e.g., organizing transportation to and from the hospital during chemotherapy) by learning to communicate about their needs and by enhancing dyadic coping. Coping is viewed as a genuine dyadic phenomenon. The concept of dyadic coping as employed in the present intervention is based on Bodenmann (2000) who defined it "as a process on the dyadic level in which the coping reactions of one partner take into account the stress signals of the other partner (. . .)." (Bodenmann, Ledermann, Blattner, & Galluzzo, 2006, p. 496).

Communication skills and dyadic coping skills reflect the centerpiece of the intervention and it is proposed that learning or enhancing these skills will make couples more competent in addressing the cancer-related problems. Maladaptive interpersonal interactions, such as avoiding cancer-related conversations or criticizing the partner for their emotional reaction, have been identified as predictors of poor adjustment even if the relationship is functioning well outside of the cancer experience. As such, couples may grow together standing up to face cancer side by side. In fact, women with breast cancer find the more benefit, the more they talk about their cancer (Cordova, Cunningham, Carlson, & Andrykowski, 2001). Thus, *Side by Side* teaches individual and relationship skills for partners as they address the female's gynecological cancer and its effects on both individuals and the couple. The intervention components included in *Side by Side* are all adapted from empirically supported cognitive behavioral interventions and maintain a focus on the couple (for the detailed manual, see Heinrichs & Zimmermann, 2008).

The couples-based intervention is compared with a brief educational program for women with cancer in which the partner is present. However, *no active skills training* is found in this program. Thus, it is an approach based on providing couples with medical information relating to the specific disease the women is suffering from. Therapists are instructed to be warm, empathetic, and understanding without conveying active coping skills. This way, the intervention is tested against another active ingredient and controlling for the power of the therapist-client relationship factor (someone who is there in this stressful time listening to the woman's distress).

Table 1. The MPQ to assess common factors (Heinrichs et al., 2006)

Item	Theoretically underlying common factor	Matching item*
I was happy with the therapist's competence	Therapeutic alliance	–
I have now the feeling that I better understand myself and my problems	Motivational clarification	12
My skills and strengths were explicitly addressed and enhanced	Resource activation	5
I am pleased with the therapist's engagement	Therapeutic alliance	–
What was done in the program was at times affecting me strongly	Problem actuation	17
Through the program the different options for coping with my problems became clear to me	Mastery	11
The program helped me to perceive my positive (strong) sides	Resource activation	–
I feel better up to the situations now than I have had up to now	Mastery	18
Through the program links became clear that I had not seen so far	Motivational clarification	16
I was emotionally strongly involved	Problem actuation	15

*The MPQ is based on the Patient Session Questionnaire (Braun, 2003). The matching item is the equivalent item in the original process measure. The therapeutic alliance is not assessed in the process measure.

Assessment of Common Factors

Common factors were assessed with the Modified Patient Questionnaire (MPQ; Heinrichs, Stehr, & Zimmermann, 2006, see Table 1), which is based on the Berner Patient Session Questionnaire (BPSQ; Braun, 2003). The BPSQ is an intersession instrument which the patients complete after each therapy session to evaluate the process of treatment. The short form includes 18 items and its reliabilities vary between 0.94 (therapeutic affiliation, 7 items), 0.92 (resource activation, 7 items), and 0.72 (problem actuation, 4 items) (Braun, 2003). The MPQ includes two items per common factor from the BPSQ which theoretically best represented the common factor. We made slight changes to selected items to allow for the change from a process to a state measure (post-intervention assessment only: instead of referring to the session we refer to the entire intervention), and we added two items to assess the quality of therapeutic relationship. Each partner completed the questionnaire independently and each participating couple completed the measure independent of whether they were randomized to the couples-based intervention or the partner-assisted educational program. The current sample size is $N = 36$ with $n = 20$ and $n = 16$ randomized to Side by Side and education only, respectively. The internal consistency for females and males varies between 0.72 (resource activation – males) and 0.89 (therapeutic relationship – males).

This design allows for making specific predictions about the differential extent to which each intervention is *a priori* assumed to systematically make use of the four principles of change. It seems reasonable to assume that the problem will be activated equally in both types of interventions because talking about the cancer experience will be central to both approaches. However, since problem actuation is usually inferred from emotional activation and because the Side by Side intervention explicitly employs strategies to activate emotions in sessions, there should be still preponderance in the couples-based intervention. In contrast, the principle of coping (mastery) may be equally relevant to both interventions because providing medical information is a generally efficacious approach to help cancer patients cope with the disease (Zimmermann et al., 2007), particularly in the short term, i.e., within 3 months after the diagnosis. Interestingly, it has never been reported if partners of cancer patients also benefit from a pure delivery of medical information. In anyway, the couples-based intervention could have the potential to activate a sense of mastery beyond the level achieved in the educational intervention. Clarification of feelings is theoretically assumed to be a centerpiece of the couples-based but not the educational intervention. And finally, resource activation should almost be inherently more distinct in the couples intervention than in the medical information condition because the partner as the primary resource of women with cancer is actively included in the treatment. In sum, the couples-based intervention is expecting to make better use of three of the common factors, namely: (1) clarification of feelings, (2) resource activation, and (3) motivational clarification and the educational intervention would work through (a) the therapeutic alliance and (b) the acquisition of skills (knowledge about the disease and how to deal with side effects, etc.).

Results

In general, about 55% of female and 63% of male partners in the Side by Side condition stated their relationship improved significantly post-intervention. In comparison, 13% of women and 21% of male partners in the information delivery intervention stated their relationship improved significantly post-intervention. These differences in frequencies are statistically significant for both genders, indicating that Side by Side is more efficacious than the information-based intervention in improving the relationship. In addition, women in the Side by Side condition demonstrated a significantly larger decrease in distress around the cancer diagnoses 3 months after the diagnosis than women in the control condition who even showed a slight increase in their distress level (current controlled effect size: 0.53). Thus, the couples-based intervention is working better than the information-based

Table 2. Means and *SD*s on the MPQ to assess common factors

	Female (cancer patient)		Male (patient's partner)	
Common factor	Side by Side	Information	Side by Side	Information
Therapeutic relationship	*6.4 (0.7)*	*5.7 (0.9)**	*6.4 (0.5)*	*5.7 (1.0)**
Clarification	5.1 (1.3)	4.0 (1.5)**	5.3 (0.7)	4.3 (1.0)**
Resource activation	5.2 (1.2)	4.2 (1.3)**	5.4 (0.6)	4.2 (1.0)**
Problem actuation	5.6 (0.9)	4.6 (1.3)**	5.5 (0.8)	4.5 (1.1)**
Mastery/coping	4.8 (1.0)	4.1 (1.4)ns	5.1 (0.6)	4.1 (0.8)**

Note. Mean scores can vary between 1 and 7, the larger the value the more the common factor took shape. Complete data are currently available from $N = 31$ male partners and $N = 33$ female patients. $^{*}p < .05$, $^{**}p < 0.1$.

intervention for supporting women in coping with their cancer disease. But what makes it work better?

Table 2 illustrates means and standard deviations (*SD*) on the common factors divided by intervention type. As expected, significant differences occurred between interventions across change principles, however, contrary to our expectation these differences were observed across *all common factors*. The only significant gender difference occurred in skills acquisition which was significantly different for partners (more skills acquisition in the couples-based intervention compared to the educational intervention), but not for their female spouses. In addition, *all* these *common factors* were strongly related to the subjective rating of *improvements in relationship quality* (Spearman r between 0.48 and 0.59). However, they were not strongly correlated with the gain in individual distress around the cancer diagnosis in females. Only the extent of *problem actuation* occurred to be related to this *improvement in individual functioning* ($r = 0.30$, $p < .06$).

To determine if these common factors act as a mechanism of change, a series of regression analyses were performed. When *improvement of relationship quality* was the outcome variable, there was (1) a main effect of group membership with the couples-based intervention predicting more improvement, (2) group membership significantly predict each common factor, and (3) each common factor predict relationship outcome. Furthermore, the effect of group membership on outcome disappeared when each common factor was included in the model, which implies that the common factors fully mediated relationship outcome. However, if all predictors were entered simultaneously, neither group membership nor any common factor reached the significance level.

Finally, looking at three therapists who had at least seen five couples, a clear difference occurred in how well they made use of the four change principles despite having gone through the same training procedure for the couples-based intervention (a three-day workshop). The variation is not explained by therapeutic orientation (behavioral vs. client centered) or by prior expertise in working with couples (yes or no). Furthermore, the differences are almost visible on every single common factor.

What to Take Home and What to Chew on from (Not Only) This Study

The present study demonstrates that the four change principles derived from Grawe can be applied to couples-based intervention as well as to individual psychotherapy. The two interventions compared in this study indeed make differentially strong use of the four change principles in line with the content and skills delivered in each program but dependent on the primary outcome variable (individual vs. dyadic improvement). Solely the therapeutic alliance did – contrary to the expectation – also differ between both programs which might reflect that medical education, even if delivered very attentively and empathetically and in a couple's setting, is not sufficient to reach the same level of therapeutic alliance. The therapeutic alliance is assessing the couple's satisfaction with the therapists' engagement and competence. Maybe psychologists are just not sufficiently competent or believable if they deliver medical information which in turn reduces the alliance. It could also mean that couples may not be able to differentiate on these dimensions of change (Halo effect): A therapist is either good or not so good in all of these areas.

The findings are interesting and worth to explore further, however, looking at common factors in general might be more helpful, if done experimentally. The interpretation of results from the present study and from many other studies looking at common factors is difficult because many alternative explanations can be put in place and would need to be controlled to come to final conclusions. This is also the reason why the literature so far has not been very helpful in understanding what actually causes change in efficacious treatment. It is at times not only rather guided by theoretical standpoints and opinions than by empirical data but it is far away from being experimental. Even with the present study which was designed to assess common factors and intervention model factors *a priori* and which is based on a sound theoretical framework of change, it remains questionable how much insight it really provides. Thus, *only* straightforward experimental research on common factors will move the field forward at the current point in time.

There might be good and not so good therapists. If a therapist is reaching a good outcome, the person is making more use of the principles of change and the therapeutic alliance than a therapist with a worse outcome. Does this mean being a good therapist is in the individual, it is dispositional and therefore carries across situations? Common factors are correlated (in this study, they share between 10% and 30% of variance). So maybe this finding is artificial. However, there is still a significant proportion of non-shared variance between common factors, supporting that it is not necessarily the same therapist behavior that activates these change principles. Theoretically, we know what therapist behaviors are related to which common factor. Experimentally manipulating these behaviors across therapists could help in identifying their causal role. Can therapists learn to be good therapists? If we define a good therapist as one who is making use of the four principles of change, then we could conclude that therapists should learn a wide variety of strategies which are all appropriate to enhance the four principles of change no matter with whom they work – independent if the client is an individual person, a couple, or a family.

Where Do We Need to Go?

We do not understand the mechanisms of change in any kind of psychotherapy with some isolated exceptions – and this lack of knowledge is independent of the modality in which the intervention is delivered. Thus, we also do not know how to optimize change in already efficacious treatments. Kazdin (2005, p. 187) states this very precisely:

> "How does a given factor produce the change if it is causally involved? (...) What are the connections between these factors and actual symptom change? (...) and which factors can be modified to improve treatment outcome?"

We need more *interaction between child and adult interventionists, between individual and couple therapists*. Investigating commonalities in how these approaches work does not inherently imply that intervention models are ignored. In fact, the four change principles allow each intervention model to locate itself based upon eight points in a two-dimensional (intra- and interpersonal) cube. However, any intervention model should make precise prediction as to where it is anchoring itself and then test these predictions empirically. Looking at commonalities across individual treatment, couple- and family-based treatment will help shape psychotherapist to deliver services in the social context of a human being, and it will thus help to join what has artificially been divided – the individual, the partner, and the child – in other words the family.

References

Blow, A. J., & Sprenkle, D. H. (2001). Common factors across theories of marriage and family therapy: A modified Delphi study. *Journal of Marital and Family Therapy, 27*, 385–401.

Blow, A. J., Sprenkle, D. H., & Davis, S. D. (2007). Is who delivers the treatment more important than the treatment itself? The role of the therapist in common factors. *Journal of Marital and Family Therapy, 33*(3), 298–317.

Bodenmann, G. (2000). *Stress und Coping bei Paaren* [Stress and Coping in Couples]. Göttingen: Hogrefe.

Bodenmann, G., Ledermann, T., Blattner, D., & Galluzzo, C. (2006). Associations among everyday stress, critical life events, and sexual problems. *Journal of Nervous and Mental Disease, 194*(7), 494–501.

Braun, U. (2003). *Was ein Patientenstundenbogen erzählt ... Eine Studie zum Prädiktorwert von Post-Session-Stundenbogen für den Therapieerfolg* [What a patient session questionnaire tells ... A study of post-session-questionnaire as a predictor for therapeutic success]. Dissertation. Universität Bern.

Cordova, M. J., Cunningham, L. L. C., Carlson, C. R., & Andrykowski, M. A. (2001). Posttraumatic growth following breast cancer: A controlled comparison study. *Health Psychology, 20*, 176–185.

Cougle, J. R., Wolitzky-Taylor, K. B., Lee, H.-J., & Telch, M. (2007). Mechanisms of change in ERP treatment of compulsive hand washing: Does primary threat make a difference? *Behaviour Research and Therapy, 45*(7), 1449–1459.

Doss, B. D., Thum, Y. M., Sevier, M., Atkins, D., & Christensen, A. (2005). Improving relationships. Mechanisms of change in couple therapy. *Journal of Consulting and Clinical Psychology, 73*(4), 624–633.

Gardner, F., Burton, J., & Klimes, I. (2006). Randomized controlled trial of aprenting intervention in the voluntary sector for reducing child conduct problems: Outcomes and mechanisms of change. *Journal of Child Psychology and Psychiatry, 47*(11), 1123–1132.

Gassmann, D., & Grawe, K. (2006). General change mechanisms: The relation of problem activation to resource activation in successful and unsuccessful therapeutic interactions. *Clinical Psychology & Psychotherapy, 13*, 1–11.

Graves, K. D. (2003). Social cognitive theory and cancer patients' quality of life: A meta-analysis of psychosocial intervention components. *Health Psychology, 22*(2), 210–219.

Grawe, K. (1994). Psychotherapie ohne Grenzen – von den Therapieschulen zur allgemeinen Psychotherapie [Psychotherapy with no Limits – From schools of psychotherapy to common psychotherapy]. *Verhaltenstherapie und psychosoziale Praxis, 26*, 357–370.

Grawe, K. (1997). Research-informed psychotherapy. *Psychotherapy Research, 7*(1), 1–19.

Grawe, K. (2004). *Psychological therapy.* Ashland, OH: Hogrefe & Huber.

Grawe, K., & Grawe-Gerber, M. (1999). Ressourcenaktivierung. Ein primäres Wirkprinzip der Psychotherapie [Resource activation. A primary active principle of psychotherapy]. *Psychotherapeut, 44*, 63–73.

Heinrichs, N., Stehr, M., & Zimmermann, T. (2006). Der Modifizierte Patientenfragebogen [The modified patient questionnaire]. *Unpublizierter Fragebogen* [Unpublished questionnaire]. TU Braunschweig.

Heinrichs, N., & Zimmermann, T. (2008). *Bewältigung einer gynäkologischen Krebserkrankung in der Partnerschaft. Ein psychoonkologisches Behandlungsprogramm für Paare.* [Mastery of a gynecological cancer disease in partnership. A psychooncological treatment program for couples]. Göttingen: Hogrefe.

Helgeson, V. S., & Cohen, S. (1996). Social support and adjustment to cancer: Reconciling descriptive, correlational, and intervention research. *Health Psychology, 15*(2), 135–148.

Johansson, P., & Hoglend, P. (2007). Identifying mechanisms of change in psychotherapy: Mediators of treatment outcome. *Clinical Psychology & Psychotherapy, 14*, 1–9.

Karney, B. R., & Bradbury, T. N. (1995). The longitudinal course of marital quality and stability: A review of theory, methods, and research. *Psychological Bulletin, 118*(1), 3–34.

Kazdin, A. E. (2005). Treatment outcomes, common factors, and continued neglect of mechanisms of change. *Clinical Psychology: Science and Practice, 12*(2), 184–188.

Kazdin, A. E. (2006). Mechanisms of change in psychotherapy: Advances, breakthroughs, and cutting-edge research (do not yet exist). In R. R. Bootzin & P. E. McKnight (Eds.), *Strengthening research methodology: Psychological measurement and evaluation* (pp. 77–101). Washington: APA.

Kendall, P. C., Flannery Schroeder, E., Panichelli Mindel, S. M., Southam Gerow, M., Henin, A., & Warman, M. (1997). Therapy for youths with anxiety disorders: A second randomized clinical trial. *Journal of Consulting and Clinical Psychology, 65*, 366–380.

Lambert, J. (1992). Psychotherapy outcome research: Implications for integrative and eclectic therapists. In J. C. Norcross & M. R. Goldfried (Eds.), *Handbook of psychotherapy integration* (pp. 99–129). New York: Basic.

Lambert, M. J., & Bergin, A. E. (1994). The effectiveness of psychotherapy. In A. E. B. S. L. Garfield (Ed.), *Handbook of psychotherapy and behavior change* (pp. 157–211). New York: John Wiley.

Lilienfeld, S. O. (2007). Psychological treatments that cause harm. *Perspectives on Psychological Science, 2*(1), 53–70.

Markman, H. J., Renick, M. J., Floyd, F. J., Stanley, S. M., & Clements, M. (1993). Preventing marital distress through communication and conflict management training: A 4- and 5-year follow-up.

Special section: Couples and couple therapy. *Journal of Consulting and Clinical Psychology, 61*(1), 70–77.

Sexton, H., Ridley, C. R., & Kleiner, A. J. (2004). Beyond common factors: Multilevel-process models of therapeutic change in marriage and the family therapy. *Journal of Marital and Family Therapy, 30*, 131–149.

Shands, M. E., Lewis, F. M., Sinsheimer, J., & Cochrane, B. B. (2006). Core concerns of couples living with early stage breast cancer. *Psycho-Oncology, 15*, 1055–1064.

Snyder, D. K., Castellani, A. M., & Whisman, M. A. (2006). Current status and future directions in couple therapy. *Annual Review of Psychology, 57*, 1–28.

Sprenkle, D. H., & Blow, A. J. (2004). Common factors are not islands – they work through models: A response to Sexton, Ridley, and Kleiner. *Journal of Marital and Family Therapy, 30*, 151–157.

Thurmaier, F., Engl, J., Eckert, V., & Hahlweg, K. (1992). Prävention von Ehe - und Partnerschaftsstörungen EPL (Ehevorbereitung – ein partnerschaftliches Lernprogramm) [Prevention of relationship disorders EPL (Marriage Preparation – a Partnership Learning Program)]. *Verhaltenstherapie, 2*, 116–124.

Zimmermann, T., Heinrichs, N., & Baucom, D. H. (2007). Does one size fit all? Moderators in psychosocial interventions for breast cancer patients. A meta-analysis. *Annals of Behavioral Medicine, 34*, 225–239.

Nina Heinrichs
Department of Psychology
P.O. Box 100131
33501 Bielefeld
Germany
E-mail: nina.heinrichs@uni-bielefeld.de

Models of Prevention

Taking It to the People

Using Technology to Enhance the Impact of Couple Relationship Education

W. Kim Halford[1] and Leanne M. Casey[2]

[1]University of Queensland, St. Lucia, Australia
[2]Griffith University, Mt. Gravatt, Australia

Abstract

There is established efficacy of couple relationship education (CRE) in assisting at least some couples to maintain a mutually satisfying relationship (Halford, in press). However, the impact of CRE on the prevalence of couple relationship problems is modest at best, primarily because of the low reach of evidence-based programs. The low reach is partly due to difficulties in getting evidence-based programs adopted into delivery systems, and partly because of the modest uptake of CRE in the target population of couples. Information technologies provide new options for enhancing couples' access to evidence-based CRE. Such technologies can provide an evidence-based approach to CRE that can be easily adopted to enhance accessibility for couples. In this chapter we analyze the challenges to extending reach, particularly reach to couples most likely to benefit from CRE, and describe an exemplar program in which information technology is designed to enhance the reach and impact of CRE by combining web-based assessment and flexible delivery of skills-based training.

The Concept of Impact and Couple Relationship Education

In public health terms, the impact of an intervention can be defined as its effect on the prevalence of a particular problem within a given population (Society for Prevention Research, 2004). Specifically with reference to couple relationships, we base this chapter on the assumption that the collective aim of couple relationship education (CRE) providers is to increase the rates of couples with high relationship satisfaction and to reduce the prevalence of couple relationship problems, violence, and separations. These outcomes are valuable in their own right, as well as in their potential for improving individual well-being, reducing social costs of relationship problems, and enhancing economic productivity.

The impact of an intervention on prevalence is a function of the *effectiveness* and the *reach* of the intervention. *Effectiveness* is the change resulting from the intervention on key outcomes (e.g., relationship satisfaction, violence, and separation) or associated outcomes (e.g., health care utilization and child support costs after separation). *Reach* is the proportion of the population of interest that access that intervention.

In addition to reach, another contributor to the impact of an intervention is the potential gap between *efficacy* and *effectiveness* (Chambless & Ollendick, 2001). *Efficacy* refers to the impact of an intervention within randomized controlled trials of interventions. *Effectiveness* refers to the effects of intervention within more usual service delivery conditions. Typically efficacy assessments involve delivery of a clearly defined intervention, usually operationalized in a written manual, which is delivered by professionals highly trained in that approach. It is common practice to record sessions in efficacy studies to monitor adherence to the protocol and to use intensive supervision to enhance the quality of delivery (Waltz, Addis, Koerner, & Jacobson, 1993). Moreover, efficacy studies often have tight inclusion and exclusion criteria for participants to ensure the sample is adequately described. Collectively these procedures optimize the internal validity of efficacy trials and ensure the integrity and quality of the intervention being evaluated. However, the resources needed to implement these training, quality control, and supervision procedures typically are beyond that usually available in routine service delivery. Moreover, the criteria for selecting participants in efficacy trials often raise doubt about the generalizability of findings to routine service delivery.

In the vast majority of research evaluating CRE (Halford, in press) the focus has been on the efficacy of intervention. Relatively little attention has been given to the effectiveness of the intervention, and almost none to the impact of CRE. While testing efficacy is important, demonstrated efficacy of an intervention does *not* guarantee impact. Highly efficacious interventions can be difficult to deliver effectively (Society for Prevention Research, 2004). Highly efficacious interventions with compromised effectiveness can have minimal impact. In contrast, modestly efficacious interventions that are easier to deliver can achieve similar effectiveness as efficacy, which enhances the impact if adequate reach is also attained. Table 1 sets out a hypothetical (though we suggest quite realistic) example of efficacy, effectiveness, reach, and impact of an intensive 12-hour skill-based CRE program and a computerized assessment and report. We have assumed that delivering the 12-hour program is quite difficult and, even with training and supervision, effectiveness in routine service delivery is lower than efficacy. In contrast, assume that a computerized assessment and report is highly robust in delivery. The other assumption is that many more couples would access a web-based assessment and report than would attend a 12-hour program. It is noteworthy that the less efficacious program has 15 times the impact of the more intensive efficacious program.

Although Table 1 presents a partially hypothetical example, substantial gaps have been demonstrated between the efficacy and the impact of a range of psychological interventions. For example, Vos, Corry, Haby, Carter, and Andrews (2005) estimated the potential impact on the prevalence of depression (if all cases of depression were treated) of cognitive behavior therapy, a well-established efficacious treatment. They noted that, CBT is not only

Table 1. Efficacy, effectiveness, reach, and impact of CRE programs

	Programs	
Criterion	12-hour intensive skill training	Web-based assessment and report of relationship
Consumer satisfaction	High in those who complete	High in those who complete
Efficacy evaluated in randomized controlled trial	Reduces separations from 50 to 30% of couples	Reduces separations from 50 to 45% of couples
Effectiveness	Reduces separations from 50 to 40% of couples	Reduces separations from 50 to 45% of couples
Reach	1% of couples attend and complete program	50% of couples complete program
Impact	Reduces population separations by 0.1%	Reduces population separations by 2.5%

efficacious but also potentially cost-effective. The cost in dollars to deliver CBT for depression is offset many times over by the reduction in disability adjusted life years attributable to depression when it is treated with CBT. However, the actual impact of CBT on depression is quite low. The majority of depressed people do not receive any treatment at all, and those depressed people who are treated receive that treatment from their family doctor, who almost never has the expertise or time to deliver CBT (Issakidis & Andrews, 2006). As a consequence, CBT is provided to less than 1% of all depressed people, and the impact of CBT on depression is minimal despite its high efficacy and strong cost-effectiveness.

Exclusive reliance on efficacy to evaluate evidence-based interventions can distort research designs and generate findings that are misleading with respect to their implications for impact. For example, returning to our CRE example in Table 1, if a researcher compared the efficacy of the 12-hour program with the computerized assessment and report, then a sample of couples willing to be randomly assigned to either intervention would need to be recruited. In a typical efficacy trial recruiting 200 couples for intensive CRE would be a very big sample size. (Only one published study has ever been conducted with a similarly large sample, see Halford, in press). A study with these two conditions plus a control condition would have about 70 couples per condition. Given the power of $n = 70$ per condition to detect a dichotomous outcome of separation, the likely result would be a significant effect of the intensive program, which has a large effect size. In contrast, the study would likely produce a null finding for the efficacy of the computerized assessment and report, which has a small effect size. Such a finding could be used to justify the false conclusion that assessment and feedback was ineffective, and the intensive program should be disseminated. In seeking to produce a community-wide impact from CRE, the challenge is to develop programs that can be delivered with adequate effectiveness and reach.

The Efficacy of CRE

Existing evidence-based CRE is of two forms. The first is the use of structured inventory-based assessments with a 1–2-hour feedback session used to provide couples with information about their level of risk for future relationship problems (Larson, Newell, Topham, & Nichols, 2002). This approach is based on the assumption that such feedback can guide couples to take appropriate remedial action. The most widely used inventories provide scores on dimensions like shared realistic relationship expectations, effective communication, and effective personal stress management. These scores predict newlywed couple's future relationship satisfaction and stability (Larson et al., 2002), showing they do assess relevant aspects of couple relationships. However, it is unclear whether receiving feedback based on such assessments helps newlywed couples sustain high relationship satisfaction. There have been two randomized controlled trials of inventory assessment with feedback (with the Internet-based RELATE inventory). One study showed short-term increases in relationship satisfaction and relationship commitment in unmarried couples in committed relationships (long-term dating or engaged) (Larson, Vatter, Galbraith, Holman, & Stahmann, 2007). In a second study, Busby, Ivey, Harris, and Ates (2007) found RELATE assessment and computer-generated report produced sustained improvements in relationship satisfaction over a 6-month period. In both the Larson et al. and Busby et al. samples, participants were young and highly educated, and the generalizability to other groups was unclear. Moreover, the long-term effects of assessment and feedback are unknown. However, the two studies found consistent benefits of assessment and feedback.

The second approach to CRE teaches couples crucial relationship skills, typically in a face-to-face course of 12–15 contact hours with use of procedures like modeling, rehearsal, and feedback on skills. There is a well-established finding that skills-focused CRE teaches couples key relationship skills, such as positive communication and conflict management, and couples that initially have somewhat low relationship satisfaction show immediate increases in relationship satisfaction (Hawkins, Blanchard, Baldwin, & Fawcett, 2008). Moreover, these skills are maintained for at least a year or two after training (Halford, Markman, Stanley, & Kline, 2003). However, the long-term benefits of CRE are less well established (Hawkins et al., 2008).

There are benefits from skill-based CRE in helping couples sustain long-term relationship satisfaction, but these benefits seem to be primarily for couples at high risk for future relationship difficulties. Several quasi-experimental studies have shown long-term (3–4 years) universal benefits for couples from skill-based CRE (e.g., Bodenmann, Pihet, Shantinath, Cina, & Widmer, 2006; Markman, Renick, Floyd, Stanley, & Clements, 1993). These results are promising but, as Halford et al. (2003) and others have noted, these effects might be due to couples self-selecting into receiving CRE. Only randomized controlled trials with adequate followup can clearly establish an effect of CRE on maintaining relationship satisfaction and stability.

Halford (in press) summarized and reviewed 15 published randomized controlled trials of skill-based CRE. Couples who consistently show sustained benefits from CRE were couples in early stage relationships at high risk of future relationship problems; couples making the transition to parenthood (who also are at risk for future problems); and couples who already have some relationship distress. There is no evidence from long-term randomized controlled trials for a universal sustained benefit of skill-based CRE for couples in early stage relationships. Large ongoing trials being conducted in the US should clarify whether there are universal benefits of CRE. Whatever these additional data demonstrate, a key challenge to developing impact in CRE is achieving reach to couples at high risk of future relationship problems.

Selective Targeting of Relationship Education on High-Risk Couples

CRE provided to low-risk couples may make little difference to relationship satisfaction or stability, as many of these couples would have stable, mutually satisfying relationships without any education. In Australia more than 50% of couples who marry remain together for the rest of their lives, the vast majority of these couples report being satisfied in their relationship at least most of the time (Australian Bureau of Statistics, 2006), and most of these couples have not attended any form of CRE (Halford, O'Donnell, Lizzio, & Wilson, 2006).

It is possible to identify, albeit with limited accuracy, the couples who are at high risk for future relationship problems. For example, couples who have divergent or unrealistic expectations of their relationship; who have deficits in their expression of affection, sharing of positive activities, or supporting each other; or who have negative communication or ineffective conflict management, are at high risk of deteriorating relationship satisfaction and separation (Bradbury & Karney, 2004; Holman, 2001). Couples forming stepfamilies (Halford, Nicholson, & Sanders, 2007), who have low formal education, or come from socially disadvantaged groups (Cherlin, 2005; Thomas & Sawhill, 2005), are at high risk of future relationship problems. Unfortunately there is evidence that high-risk couples are under-represented in those who attend existing CRE (Halford et al., 2006; Stanley, Amato, Johnson, & Markman, 2006).

If the focus is on addressing the needs of high-risk couples, then CRE is likely to need some individual tailoring of content to address the particular risk factors which put a couple relationship at risk. However, in current practice, CRE with standardized curriculum typically is applied universally to all couples, with the implicit assumption that the information provided and skills trained will be of use to most, if not all, couples (Halford, in press). For example, all skill training CRE programs have a strong (though not exclusive) focus on communication. This goal of enhancing communication is based on the research showing that negative communication in newlyweds predicts poor couple outcomes (Heyman, 2001). However, this finding clearly depends on heterogeneity in the sample with at least some marrying couples exhibiting low levels of negative communication that are linked with high relationship satisfaction. It is unlikely that such couples with low negative communication will benefit from CRE focused on reducing their already low levels of negative communication. Consistent with this interpretation, Halford, Sanders, and Behrens (2001) found only couples with evidence of high rates of negative communication showed long-term (after 4 years) gains in relationship satisfaction from skill training CRE focused on communication.

Standardized skill training curriculum likely needs individual tailoring of content to address relationship risk factors that are: (a) usually not covered in universal skill training programs and (b) relevant to only some couples. For example, hazardous drinking early in relationships predicts aggression, deteriorating relationship satisfaction, and instability (Leonard & Mudar, 2003). Conversely, couple relationship problems predict increased risk of alcohol abuse (Whisman, Uebelacker, & Bruce, 2004). CRE can successfully incorporate a focus on reducing hazardous drinking (Bouma, Halford, & Young, 2004), but this content is likely to be useful to only a minority of couples. As a second example, stepfamilies are at high risk of relationship breakdown (Whitsett & Land, 1992). A predictor of distress and separation in stepfamilies is conflict over parenting and difficulties in forming a family identity (Phillips, Halford, Nicholson, & Bruce, 2009). These issues are important in work with stepfamilies, but specific to them (see Adler-Baeder and Higginbotham (2004) for a review of stepfamily CRE programs).

In addition to the challenges of reaching high-risk couples and providing them with education salient to their particular relationship risks, there is a further challenge of helping couples produce sustained changes in their relationships. No existing psychological interventions produce life-long protection against occurrence of psychological problems (Kendall, 1989), and it is probably unrealistic to expect that relationship education at the start of committed relationships could "inoculate" couples against relationship problems for the rest of their lives. In the longest term evaluations of skill-based CRE, effects did attenuate over a 3–4-year period in one study (Markman, Floyd, Stanley, & Storaasli, 1988), but were maintained in another over 5 years (Hahlweg, Markman, Thurmair, Engel, & Eckert, 1998). In work with couples married on average for 10 years, two booster sessions 1 and 3 months after the CRE weekend training program helped couples sustain relationship satisfaction (Braukhaus, Hahlweg, Kroeger, Groth, & Fehm-Wolfsdorf, 2003). Booster sessions might assist long-term maintenance of CRE effects in newlywed couples. However, this suggests our challenge is to design systems of delivery that continue to provide education and support to couples over sustained periods in an analogous manner to regular health checks.

Indicated Targeting of Relationship Education on Mildly Distressed Couples

As noted earlier, couples with early warning signs of distress show some immediate and longer-term benefits from skill-based CRE. Three recent studies, two quasi-experimental studies (Cordova, Warren, & Gee, 2001; Halford, Osgarby, & Kelly, 1996) and a randomized controlled trial (Cordova et al., 2005), showed a "relationship checkup" produced significant gains in relationship satisfaction maintained for up to 2 months. The checkup consisted of a systematic relationship assessment, feedback, and motivational interviewing to develop relationship goals. Cordova et al. (2001, 2005) worked with couples who had low relationship satisfaction, but were not clinically distressed, while Halford et al. (1996) worked with distressed couples. While none of the studies used any of the inventories widely used in CRE, the studies do suggest that CRE consisting of assessment with feedback can be helpful, at least for mildly distressed couples.

The CRE Currently Provided

CRE predominantly targets committed, married, premarital or remarrying couples, parents, and parents-to-be (Halford & Simons, 2005). In Australia and the US, most of the CRE provided is brief (one or two sessions) (Halford & Simons, 2005; Stanley et al., 2006). Often providers develop their own programs, usually in response to perceived local needs or in response to calls from funding providers to address the needs of identified target groups (Halford & Simons, 2005). Many of these programs are not documented in a way that permits evaluation (Halford & Simons, 2005). Where documentation is available, the programs often include stated goals of the acquisition of both knowledge and skills and address a variety of risk and protective factors identified in the literature. However, provider estimates of time spent on skill development (explaining the skill, demonstration, practice, and feedback) suggest there is limited skill training offered in most programs (Halford & Simons, 2005).

Influences on the Adoption of Evidence-Based Relationship Education

Standardized, evidence-based CRE programs have shown potential to be more widely adopted. Notably, assessment and feedback to couples using inventories has become widely used in a number of Western countries including Australia, the UK, and the US (Larson et al., 2002). The most widely used inventories of FOCCUS, PREPARE, and RELATE each predict the trajectory of relationship satisfaction in the early years of marriage (Fowers & Olsen, 1986; Holman, 2001; Larsen & Olson, 1989; Williams & Jurich, 1995). Thus, each inventory assesses factors relevant to relationship outcomes. There is structured training on the use of these inventories (e.g., Olsen, Dyer, & Dyer, 1997) which at least partially may explain the widespread adoption of inventory-based relationship education. However, the impact of inventory-based assessment and feedback on couple relationship problems is unproven. Given the skill deficits some couples bring to relationships, this approach alone seems unlikely to have large impact, though it might act as a channel through which couples can access other services.

Several efficacious, standardized skill-based programs, like Guerney and colleagues' Relationship Enhancement Program (Guerney, 1987) and Markman and colleagues' Premarital Relationship Enhancement Program (PREP) (Markman, Stanley, & Blumberg, 2001), have resource materials (e.g., audiovisual demonstration of key relationship skills, leader's manuals, and participant workbooks) available to assist in delivery, and training in program delivery is available. There have been several studies of PREP dissemination showing that with relatively brief training (a 3- or 4-day workshop) and the use of resource materials, a diverse range of people (e.g., rabbis, priests, welfare workers, prison officers, and other human service personnel) can successfully deliver the program (Markman, Stanley, Jenkins, Petrella, & Wadsworth, 2006). In fact, rabbis and ministers of religion who undertake 3 to 4 days of training in PREP achieve at least as good improvements in couple communication as university-based psychologists (Laurenceau, Stanley, Osmos-Gallo, Baucom, & Markman, 2004). In a nonreligious setting our research team trained midwives in a number of Australian maternity hospitals to deliver Couple CARE for Parents, a skill-based relationship education program that helps couples enhance their communication and relationship satisfaction when having their first child. Again the dissemination involved use of DVDs, structured workbooks, and other technology to train the midwives and support their delivery of the program.

All of these examples of adoption of evidence-based CRE use a relatively fixed curriculum. Yet the varying risk profiles of couples suggest that education might be more effective if it was individually tailored to each couple. The cost of increasing the variety of content in CRE programs is that the training and supervision of effective program delivery becomes more difficult. It also becomes questionable whether some of the current providers of standardized CRE, such as ministers of religion, can deliver programs that focus on complex issues like alcohol abuse. The challenge is to develop systems of delivery of CRE that can be widely adopted, and that provide content relevant to the needs of participants. In particular, programs need to address the needs of couples at high risk of future relationship problem and those who are experiencing the early stages of relationship distress.

Barriers to Couples Accessing Services

The barriers to couples attending CRE are many and varied. Couples often report they do not perceive a personal need for relationship education; see CRE as being for young people who lack experience in committed relationships; or that relationship education is for highly conservative or religious people (Simons, Harris, & Willis, 1994). These perceptions might inhibit older or less religious couples from attending. Some couples express concern that CRE might raise problems where none currently exist (Simons et al., 1994). Practical issues are also commonly cited reasons for nonattendance of CRE, like the difficulty of scheduling to attend a weekend or regular weekly sessions and a lack of child care for couples with children (Simons et al., 1994).

Expanding the range of formats in which CRE is offered could enhance the accessibility of such education. Most existing CRE programs are offered in face-to-face sessions

(Halford et al., 2003), but many adults prefer to access psychological education through self-directed programs that can be undertaken at times and places that suit participants, rather than through face-to-face programs (Christensen & Jacobson, 1994). Moreover, there are substantial numbers of people who prefer the web, DVDs, and the like to face-to-face contacts when seeking psychological information (Emmelkamp, 2005). Interestingly, there is increasing evidence that people might be more willing to disclose about sensitive issues like relationship functioning with web- or computer-based assessment than with face-to-face or written assessments (Kaltenthaler, Parry, & Beverly, 2004). At least some couples might prefer the flexibility and convenience of accessing CRE through web-based or other self-directed programs. Moreover, in geographically large countries like the US, Canada, and Australia, distance can make attendance of face-to-face programs difficult, and flexible-delivery programs might help overcome this barrier.

RELATE with Couple CARE

The RELATE with Couple CARE program developed from a collaboration between researchers at Griffith University and at Brigham Young University. Our aim has been to provide easily accessible CRE that provides tailored content of skill-based education to couples at high risk of future relationship problems. Couples complete RELATE over the web, or if they do not have Internet access, RELATE is provided in written form. The couples receive the computer-generated RELATE report that documents their relationship strengths and challenges. A 1-hour coaching session (usually by telephone, but can be face-to-face) is used to discuss this report of relationship strengths and challenges, and to assist couples to formulate specific relationship enhancement goals. Couples with many relationship strengths and few challenges (low-risk couples) are given brief advice to assist them fine-tune any areas of concern. Moderate to high-risk couples do the Couple CARE program (or selected units from Couple CARE) with the intent of achieving the stated relationship change goals. The Couple CARE program uses a DVD and self-instructional material to teach relationship skills, and can be completed by couples in their homes, though it also can be used as resource materials for more traditional face-to-face delivery.

The integrated RELATE with Couple CARE system provides a stepped approach to relationship education based on assessed risk, as depicted in Table 2. Couples at low risk need only complete the RELATE assessment. High-risk couples are encouraged to complete Couple CARE, with the focus of education being aligned with assessed needs.

RELATE Assessment and Feedback

RELATE is a 240-item comprehensive assessment of a couple's relationship. RELATE is completed by both partners and takes about an hour to complete (Busby, Holman, &

Table 2. RELATE with Couple CARE, a stepped individually tailored approach to CRE

Risk	Prevention			
	Low	Medium	High	Indicated
Intervention	RELATE			
		RELATE plus some Couple CARE		
			RELATE plus all of Couple CARE	
				Couple Therapy

Taniguchi, 2001). RELATE provides self- and partner reports of personal characteristics and values, self-reports of family-of-origin background and interaction processes, and self- and partner reports of current relationship satisfaction, communication, conflict management, and aggression. These factors predict marital satisfaction and stability in newlywed couples (Holman, 2001). Relationship risk is operationalized as the number of relationship challenges a couple has, as assessed by RELATE, which has been shown to predict newlywed's future relationship satisfaction and separation status (Holman, 2001).

Educators can have couples access the web site, complete the assessment, and access the report themselves. Alternatively, educators can register with the RELATE Institute and have the couple's report sent to them. The report is presented as a downloadable file, which can be printed either in color or in black and white. The home page of the web site is https://www.relate-institute.org.

The report generated from the RELATE assessment is quite detailed, but also easy to follow. As noted previously, couples can access the RELATE site, complete the assessments, and review the computer-generated report on their own. However, couples report that having a relationship educator guide them through the report is helpful (Larson et al., 2007). The RELATE report consists of a set of instructions to the couple on how to interpret the report, a report on each of the areas assessed, a summary relationship profile, and some suggested discussion questions for the couple to discuss their report. The RELATE web site also lists a range of resources and agencies that can provide further relationship education. This information is a useful resource for couples living in the US, but has limited utility for couples living elsewhere.

Couple CARE

Couple CARE is a 6-unit program in which couples are asked to complete each unit in about a week. Completing each unit consists of three steps. First, the couple watches a 12–15-minute segment of videotape that introduces key concepts and models relevant relationship skills. Second, they complete individual and conjoint tasks described in a

Table 3. Content of Couple CARE relationship education program

Unit	Content
1. Self-change	Introduction; relationship goal setting; relationship commitment and enhancement; self-change in relationships
2. Communication	Effective couple communication; self-evaluation of communication; self-change for communication enhancement
3. Intimacy and caring	Importance and review of expression of affection, social support and positive shared activities; self-change plan
4. Managing differences	The positive effects of differences; effective conflict management; self-evaluation of current conflict management; self-change plan
5. Sexuality	Sexuality myths; evaluating our sexual relationship; self-change
6. Adapting to change	Life events and relationships; managing likely couple life changes; maintaining a relationship focus in a busy life; self-change plan

guidebook given to each partner, which take ~ 50 minutes to complete. The tasks assist the couple to relate the concepts and skills shown in the videotape to their own relationship, to prompt relationship goal setting, and to self-direct change in their relationship behaviors. Third, the couple shares a telephone call of about 45 minutes with a psychologist who reviews the concepts covered in the unit and helps the couple implement individual self-change plans.

The content of each of the six units of Couple CARE is presented in Table 3. A distinguishing feature of Couple CARE is a focus on relationship self-regulation, which is the extent to which the partners each actively work on their relationship. Partners are assisted to self-evaluate their behavior across a range of domains of relationship interaction, to select goals for personal change, and to implement and evaluate their change efforts. For example, across Units 2 and 3 of Couple CARE, participants watch videotape segments illustrating positive couple communication. The guidebook describes communication tasks the partners do together, after which each partner self-evaluates his/her current communication skills using a form provided in the guidebook. Each identifies specific behavioral goals to improve one's own communication, again using a form provided in the guidebook. The self-evaluation and goals are discussed with the psychologist during the telephone call, and the partners are assisted to implement their self-change goals for communication enhancement.

The design of Couple CARE is intended to allow delivery of a relatively fixed curriculum, which enhances the ease of training of educators and widespread adoption of the program. At the same time, the self-change focus allows tailoring of the content to address the needs of the particular couple.

Distinctive Characteristics of RELATE with Couple CARE

The RELATE with Couple CARE approach to CRE differs from previous approaches in three important ways. First, it uses a flexible-delivery format, allowing couples to complete the program in their own time and in the privacy of their own home. This mode of delivery aims to facilitate couple recruitment and retention and to assist those who are more geographically isolated to access CRE. Second, there is an emphasis on self-change in which couples select areas to change that are most salient to them. Third, it uses a stepped approach in RELATE with Couple CARE which provides couples with only as much education as they need, and tailors the content to couples assessed risk factors. This stepped approach is aimed at maximizing cost-effectiveness by making less intensive and lower cost interventions (RELATE) broadly available and focusing more intensive and expensive interventions (Couple CARE) on people with the greatest need.

Adapting Content and Delivery Mode to Enhance Reach

The content and mode of delivery of RELATE with Couple CARE can be adapted to enhance the reach to a range of different couple target groups. For example, Couple CARE for Parents is a version of Couple CARE specifically adapted to address the needs of couples becoming parents for the first time. Couple CARE for Parents is provided to couples from the later stages of the woman's pregnancy through the first 4–5 months of the infant's life (Petch, Halford, & Creedy, 2009). The timing and content of each of the units is designed to reflect the challenges salient to most couples at particular points across the transition to parenthood. For example, the initial session delivered in the antenatal period focuses upon expectations of parenthood, with the intention that the couple can take actions that will allow them to realize their desired means of managing parenthood (e.g., arranging leave to allow them to share parenting in the early weeks of the baby's life). Unit 3, which is delivered about 4 weeks after the birth, includes a detailed review of how the couple handle challenges in infant care (breast feeding, sleep, and crying) that are commonly experienced around this time. Unit 4 focuses upon issues of sexuality, as it is often a couple of months after the birth that couples will begin having intercourse again, or at least be contemplating initiation.

The format of Couple CARE for Parents is intended to make the program easy to access. As our team usually delivers the program, 5 of the 6 units can be completed in the couple's home. Couples with a young baby are likely to find it difficult to attend regular sessions outside the home, and we use a mixture of home visits and flexible delivery (exercises done at home complemented by telephone-based coaching) to maximize ease of access. Only the first session (which is usually provided as a workshop to groups of couples in the late stages of pregnancy) involves the couple attending a face-to-face session. The couples who attend this antenatal workshop rate it as highly valuable (Petch et al., 2009) and often mention the value of meeting other expectant couples. However, this session also could be done as a home visit, if attending a group session is difficult.

While the transition to parenthood is a time of high risk for deteriorating relationship satisfaction, many couples experience only transient challenges in making the transition and manage these challenges successfully without relationship education. Currently we are developing a version of RELATE to assess level of risk for difficulty in making the transition to parenthood. Our long-term goal is to use this modified version of RELATE as a screening tool to assess the need for an intensive skill training program like Couple CARE for Parents.

We are seeking to expand the suite of CRE programs available in flexible-delivery mode to address the needs of different couples. Currently there are versions of Couple CARE being developed and evaluated for stepfamilies and for couples seeking to balance work and family. In each case RELATE is incorporating additional assessment items to identify particular challenges and strengths of these couples. Web-based delivery holds out the potential of cutting and pasting different learning resources into a uniquely structured program for each couple. For example, a module of developing shared expectations of the role of a stepparent could be added if the RELATE assessment shows that it is an issue of importance for a particular couple. Substantial research is still needed to test the efficacy, effectiveness, reach, and impact of this range of new CRE programs.

Does Technology Increase Reach or Impact?

One issue related to the use of technology and flexible delivery of relationship education is whether couples will complete programs. Table 4 summarizes the proportion of couples commencing flexible-delivery CRE that complete the program. There is variation across these studies in the target group. There also is variation in the extent of any face-to-face contact with educators ranging from zero to about half of the program being in face-to-face mode and half being flexible delivery. All programs involve the use of telephone contact with the educator, though the RELATE program could be offered without such contact. As can be seen, the completion rate through the programs is around 90%, with the exception of the RELATE with Couple CARE program evaluated by Halford, Busby et al. (2008).

There is some evidence that flexible-delivery CRE does extend reach of education. In a trial of the Couple CARE for Parents program, couples expecting their first child were offered the program while attending antenatal education services in five different maternity hospitals in South East Queensland, Australia. Forty-two percent of couples approached agreed to participate. Of couples who participated, 61% were married and 39% were cohabiting, 35% of women and 21% of women had previously sought help for psychological disorders, 39% of women and 34% of men had experienced parental separation, and only 15% had ever attended any previous relationship education. Thus, the take-up rate of couples who had not previously accessed relationship education was high and many of those couples who had participated were at high risk of future relationship problems.

In a trial of RELATE with Couple CARE we are undertaking at Griffith University (Halford, Busby et al., 2008), 60 couples who were recently married were recruited by mailing them information offering them access to the program. Of the couples who

Table 4. Retention of couples in flexible-delivery relationship education using web- or DVD-based technology

Study	Program	Participants	% completing
Halford, Moore, Wilson, Dyer, and Farrugia (2004)	Couple CARE: Face-to-face assessment, DVD, guidebook, and telephone calls	30 couples (cohabiting or married) in early stage relationships	90
Halford, Busby et al. (2008)	RELATE web-based assessment and telephone feedback	30 recently married couples	90
Halford, Busby et al. (2008)	RELATE web-based assessment and telephone feedback plus Couple CARE	30 recently married couples	60
Petch, Halford, and Creedy (2009)	Couple CARE for Parents: 1 antenatal group, 2 face-to-face home visits, 3 units of DVD, guidebook, and telephone calls	34 couples expecting first child	91

volunteered, 40% were forming stepfamilies, 60% reported that the parents of at least one partner had divorced, and 88% reported they had not previously accessed any form of relationship education. Again these data suggest flexible delivery is reaching high-risk couples who do not access existing relationship education programs.

Conclusion

Program designers need to begin with the end in mind if CRE. To impact on the prevalence of couple relationship problems, programs need to be structured such that they are easy to deliver and convenient for couples to access. We need to reach couples at high risk for future problems, which is more easily done if we can cost-effectively assess couple relationship strengths and challenges. However, the effectiveness of such tailoring is dependent upon the accuracy of assessment of couples' relationship strengths and risk profile, and more research is needed to evaluate that accuracy. CRE content needs to be salient to couples both in terms of the point of the developmental point in their relationship, and the risk profile of the couple relationship. There also is a need to identify windows of opportunity in which couples are receptive to education. RELATE, Couple CARE, and

Couple CARE for Parents are examples of our research team's current attempts to address these challenges. There are particular challenges in the design and effective delivery of relationship education using technology, and these are discussed in Chapter 14 in the current volume by Casey and Halford.

References

Adler-Baeder, F., & Higginbotham, B. (2004). The implications of remarriage and stepfamily formation for marriage education. *Family Relations, 53*, 448–458.

Australian Bureau of Statistics. (2006). *Australian social trends 2005*. Canberra, Australia: Australian Bureau of Statistics.

Bodenmann, G., Pihet, S., Shantinath, S. D., Cina, A., & Widmer, K. (2006). Improving dyadic coping in couples with a stress-oriented approach: A 2-year longitudinal study. *Behavior Modification, 30*, 571–597.

Bouma, R., Halford, W. K., & Young, R. McD. (2004). Evaluation of the controlling alcohol and relationship enhancement (CARE) program with hazardous drinkers. *Behaviour Change, 21*, 229–250.

Bradbury, T. N., & Karney, B. R. (2004). Understanding and altering the longitudinal course of intimate partnerships. *Journal of Marriage and Family, 61*, 451–463.

Braukhaus, C., Hahlweg, K., Kroeger, C., Groth, T., & Fehm-Wolfsdorf, G. (2003). The effects of adding booster sessions to a prevention training program for committed couples. *Behavioural and Cognitive Psychotherapy, 31*, 325–336.

Busby, D. M., Holman, T. B., & Taniguchi, N. (2001). RELATE: Relationship evaluation of the individual, family, cultural and couple contexts. *Family Relations, 50*, 308–317.

Busby, D. M., Ivey, D. C., Harris, S. M., & Ates, C. (2007). Self-directed, therapist-directed, and assessment based interventions for premarital couples. *Family Relations, 56*, 279–290.

Chambless, D. L., & Ollendick, T. H. (2001). Empirically supported psychological interventions: Controversies and evidence. *Annual Review of Psychology, 52*, 685–716.

Cherlin, A. J. (2005). American marriage in the 21st century. *The Future of Children, 15*, 33–56.

Christensen, A., & Jacobson, N. S. (1994). Who (or what) can do psychotherapy: The status and challenge of nonprofessional therapies. *Psychological Science, 5*, 8–14.

Cordova, J. V., Scott, R. L., Dorian, M., Mirgain, S., Yaeger, D., & Groot, A. (2005). The marriage checkup: An indicated preventive intervention for treatment-avoidant couples at risk for marital deterioration. *Behavior Therapy, 36*, 301–309.

Cordova, J. V., Warren, L. Z., & Gee, C. B. (2001). Motivational interviewing as an intervention for at-risk couples. *Journal of Marital and Family Therapy, 27*, 315–326.

Emmelkamp, P. M. G (2005). Technological innovation in clinical assessment and therapy. *Psychotherapy and Psychosomatics, 27*, 336–343.

Fowers, B. J., & Olsen, D. H. (1986). Predicting marital success with PREPARE: A predictive validity study. *Journal of Marital and Family Therapy, 12*, 403–413.

Guerney, B. G. (1987). *Relationship enhancement manual*. Bethseda, MD: Ideal.

Hahlweg, K., Markman, H. J., Thurmaier, F., Engl, J., & Eckert, V (1998). Prevention of marital distress: Results of a German prospective longitudinal study. *Journal of Family Psychology, 12*, 543–556.

Halford, W. K. (in press). *Marriage and relationship education: What works and how to provide it*. New York: Guilford.

Halford, W. K., Busby, D., Larson, J., Wilson, K. L., Holman, T., & Watson, B. (2008). The effects of couple relationship education: Does skill training enhance the effect of inventory based assessment and feedback? Manuscript in preparation.

Halford, W. K., Markman, H. J., Kline, G. H., & Stanley, S. M. (2003). Best practice in couple relationship education. *Journal of Marital & Family Therapy, 29*, 385–406.

Halford, W. K., Moore, E. M., Wilson, K. L., Dyer, C., & Farrugia, C. (2004). Benefits of a flexible delivery relationship education: An evaluation of the Couple CARE program. *Family Relations, 53*, 469–476.

Halford, W. K., Nicholson, J. M., & Sanders, M. R. (2007). Couple communication in step families. *Family Process, 46*, 471–483.

Halford, W. K., O'Donnell, C., Lizzio, A., & Wilson, K. L. (2006). Brief report: Do couples at high-risk of relationship problems attend pre-marriage education? *Journal of Family Psychology, 20*, 160–163.

Halford, W. K., Osgarby, S. M., & Kelly, A. B. (1996). Brief behavioural marital therapy: A preliminary quasi-experimental evaluation. *Behavioural and Cognitive Psychotherapy, 24*, 263–273.

Halford, W. K., Sanders, M. R., & Behrens, B. C. (2001). Can skills training prevent relationship problems in at-risk couples? Four-year effects of a behavioral relationship education program. *Journal of Family Psychology, 14*, 750–768.

Halford, W. K., & Simons, M. (2005). Couple relationship education in Australia. *Family Process, 44*, 147–259.

Hawkins, A. J., Blanchard, V. L., Baldwin, S. A., & Fawcett, E. B. (2008). Does marriage and relationship education work? A meta-analytic study. *Journal of Consulting and Clinical Psychology, 76*, 723–734.

Heyman, R. E. (2001). Observation of couple conflicts: Clinical assessment applications, stubborn truths, and shaky foundations. *Psychological Assessment, 13*, 5–35.

Holman, T. B. (2001). *Premarital prediction of marital quality or break up: Research, theory and practice*. New York: Kluwer.

Issakidis, C., & Andrews, G. (2006). Who treats whom? An application of the pathways to Care model in Australia. *Australian and New Zealand Journal of Psychiatry, 40*, 74–86.

Kaltenthaler, E., Parry, G., & Beverly, C. (2004). The use of the internet in delivering cognitive-behaviour therapy. *Behavioural and Cognitive Psychotherapy, 32*, 31–55.

Kendall, P. C. (1989). The generalization and maintenance of behaviour change: Comments, considerations, and the "no-cure" criticism. *Behavior Therapy, 20*, 357–364.

Larsen, A. S., & Olson, D. H. (1989). Predicting marital satisfaction using PREPARE: A replication study. *Journal of Marital and Family Therapy, 15*, 311–322.

Larson, J. H., Newell, K., Topham, G., & Nichols, S. (2002). A review of three comprehensive premarital assessment questionnaires. *Journal of Marital and Family Therapy, 28*, 233–239.

Larson, J. H., Vatter, R. S., Galbraith, R. C., Holman, T. B., & Stahmann, R. F. (2007). The relationship evaluation (RELATE) with therapist-assisted interpretation: Short-term effects on premarital relationships. *Journal of Marital & Family Therapy, 33*, 364–374.

Laurenceau, J. P., Stanley, S. M., Olmos-Gallo, A., Baucom, B., & Markman, H. J. (2004). Community-based prevention of marital dysfunction: Multi-level modeling of a randomized effectiveness study. *Journal of Consulting and Clinical Psychology, 72*, 933–943.

Leonard, K. E., & Mudar, P. (2003). Peer and partner drinking and the transition to marriage: Longitudinal examination of selection and influence processes. *Psychology of Addictive Behaviors, 17*, 115–125.

Markman, H. J., Floyd, F. J., Stanley, S. M., & Storaasli, R. D. (1988). Prevention of marital distress: A longitudinal investigation. *Journal of Consulting and Clinical Psychology, 56*, 210–217.

Markman, H. J., Renick, M. J., Floyd, F. J., Stanley, S. M., & Clements, M. (1993). Preventing marital distress through communication and conflict management training: A 4- and 5-year follow-up. Special section: Couples and couple therapy. *Journal of Consulting and Clinical Psychology, 61*, 70–77.

Markman, H. J., Stanley, S. M., & Blumberg, S. L. (2001). *Fighting for your marriage: Positive steps for preventing divorce and preserving a lasting love*. San Francisco, CA: Jossey-Bass.

Markman, H. J., Stanley, S. M., Jenkins, N. H., Petrella, J. N., & Wadsworth, M. E. (2006). Preventive education: Distinctive and directions. *Journal of Cognitive Psychotherapy, 20*, 411–433.

Olsen, D. H., Dyer, P., & Dyer, G. (1997). *Growing together: Leaders manual. A group program for couples*. Minneapolis: Life Innovations.

Petch, J., Halford, W. K., & Creedy, D. K. (2009). Promoting a positive transition to parenthood: A randomized controlled trial of couple relationship education. Manuscript under review.

Phillips, M., Halford, W. K., Nicholson, J. M., & Bruce, V. (2009). How couples describe their stepfamily life predicts their future. Manuscript under review.

Simons, M., Harris, R., & Willis, P. (1994). *Pathways to marriage: Learning for married life in Australia*. Adelaide, Australia: Centre for Research in Education and Work, University of South Australia.

Society for Prevention Research. (2004). *Standards of evidence: Criteria for efficacy, effectiveness and dissemination*. Fall Church, VA: Society for Prevention Research.

Stanley, S. M., Amato, P., Johnson, C. A., & Markman, H. J. (2006). Premarital education, marital quality, and marital stability: Findings from a large, random household survey. *Journal of Family Psychology, 20*, 117–126.

Thomas, A., & Sawhill, I. (2005). For love and money? The impact of family structure on family income. *Marriage and child well-being, 15*, 57–74.

Vos, T., Corry, J., Haby, M. M., Carter, R., & Andrews, A. (2005). Cost-effectiveness of cognitive-behavioural therapy and drug interventions for major depression. *Australian and New Zealand Journal of Psychiatry, 39*, 683–692.

Waltz, J., Addis, M. E., Koerner, K., & Jacobson, N. S. (1993). Testing the integrity of a psychotherapy protocol: Assessment of adherence and competence. *Journal of Consulting and Clinical Psychology, 61*, 620–630.

Whisman, M., Uebelacker, L. A., & Bruce, M. L. (2004). Longitudinal association between marital dissatisfaction and alcohol use disorders in a community sample. *Journal of Family Psychology, 20*, 164–167.

Whitsett, D., & Land, H. (1992). Role strain, coping, and marital satisfaction of step-parents. *Families in Society, 73*, 79–92.

Williams, L., & Jurich, J. (1995). Predicting marital success after five years: Assessing the predictive validity of FOCCUS. *Journal of Marital and Family Therapy, 21*, 141–153.

Kim Halford
School of Psychology
McElwain Building
University of Queensland
St. Lucia, Qld 4072
Australia
E-mail: k.halford@psy.uq.edu.au

Extending the Reach of Research-Based Couples Interventions

The Role of Relationship Education

Howard J. Markman,[1] Galena K. Rhoades,[1] Richard Delaney,[2] Lee White,[2] and Caesar Pacifici[2]

[1]University of Denver, CO, USA
[2]NorthWest Media, Inc., Eugene, OR, USA

Abstract

In this chapter we explore ways of extending the reach of research-based approaches to couples intervention to partners, service providers, and policy makers. We focus specifically on prevention and relationship education efforts over the past 30 years and summarize lessons learned from these efforts that can influence practice and social policy. We show how today these services are becoming the main way that empirically based couples interventions are reaching couples in general and underserved, high risk partners and individuals in particular. We conclude with a discussion of two new studies that illustrate some of the lessons learned and that highlight some of the key issues that our field faces as we move forward.

Prolog

Washington, DC, October 1963

The man dressed in a dark suit, who is destined to die less than a month later, reaches for the quill pen and signs his name for the last time to a piece of legislation. He smiles and may be thinking of his family background and the role that mental health problems had in shaping his future. He is determined to change forever how his country deals with community mental health and unbeknownst to him at the time, he has opened the door to increasing Federal involvement in the personal lives of children, adults, couples and families in the U.S. He leaves the room, perhaps thinking that a nightmare is brewing as he is sending U.S. advisors into a war zone in South East Asia or more optimistically of his dream and his promise to his nation to put a man on the moon by the end of the decade.

Zuoz, Switzerland, September 2007

The small group of scholars was walking in the beautiful valley under the light of the gibbous moon, the sound of the cow bells echoing in the distance. The distinguished man with the German accent was talking with two of his friends from the States about how the just completed meeting reminded him of a similar meeting in a castle 27 years earlier, where the beginnings of lifelong friendships and collaborations shaped the field they were all in. The field they were actually walking in ended suddenly at the shore of a lake and the group rested and each remembered in his or her own way the highlights of the meeting where they all had talked, shared, listened and learned.

One of the main goals of this chapter is to explore ways of extending the reach of research-based approaches to couples intervention to couples, service providers, and policy makers. One of the key issues in the family psychology field is that most divorcing couples do not receive any intervention and those who do receive services that are not research based. In this chapter we attempt to show how in the US, Relationship Education is becoming the main way that empirically based couples interventions are reaching couples in general and underserved, high risk couples and individuals in particular.

Prevention and Relationship Enhancement Program

When the first author started in this field over 30 years ago, he had a simple dream – understand relationship problems and, based on resulting theory and research, develop programs to help couples prevent problems and divorce and have successful marriages, and then get programs into the hands of couples at key transitions and institutions, starting with planning marriage. Since then, we have been involved in the development, testing, and refinement of a marriage education program (PREP; Markman, Stanley, & Blumberg, 2001). PREP stands for the Prevention and Relationship Enhancement Program. It is a program built around a best practices model of marriage education (Halford, Markman, Kline, & Stanley, 2003) and was designed as a program to prevent marital distress and divorce, based on an analysis of empirically determined risk factors. The goal of PREP is to help couples lessen known risks and increase protective factors. Along with the use of cognitive-behavioral techniques for helping couples better manage negative emotions and conflict, PREP targets key protective factors such as friendship, commitment, teamwork, fun, spiritual connection, and sensuality, mirroring advances in the field targeted at helping couples build and deepen the positive side of their relationships. PREP and variations of PREP have been studied by various research teams with a preponderance of evidence that shows a range of preventive effects of PREP (see Halford et al., 2003, for a review), resulting in PREP being classified as an efficacious marriage enrichment program (Jakubowski, Milne, Brunner, & Miller, 2004). As of 2007, PREP is now listed as the only (to our knowledge) empirically based marriage education program by Substance Abuse and Mental Health Services Administration on their national registry of empirically based interventions.

Throughout the first author's career, he has been strongly influenced by the field of community psychology, which when he was in graduate school was a new perspective or movement spurred in part by Community Mental Health Centers Act – the last piece of legislation signed by President John F. Kennedy (the man in Black from the prolog) before he was assassinated on November 22, 1963. The dream expressed in this act was to provide research-based services, including prevention and education to community members who needed the services the most in settings close to their home at low or no cost. Unfortunately, Kennedy's vision was not realized (Snow & Newton, 1976) due in part to one major mistake that we will cover later as one of the lessons learned. However, now in the US (under the Federal Governments Administration for Children and Families a team led at the time by Dr. Wade Horn, a psychologist) and in Europe (as seen by the Klaus-Grawe Think-Tank Meeting that spawned this book), we have a chance to provide research-based relationship education services to community members close to home, at no or low charge, and delivered by service providers who understand their audience (see Horn, 2003, for an overview of the US Healthy Marriage Initiative) to achieve the goal of making the dreams of a happy, healthy lifelong marriage come true for these couples and their children.

As discussed in more detail elsewhere (Halford, Markman, & Stanley, 2008; Markman, Stanley, Jenkins, Petrella, & Wadsworth, 2006; Stanley, 2001), we believe there is enough empirical support for widespread, population-wide dissemination efforts of research-based marriage education (RBME). There is more support for research-based marital education than other education interventions, although Stanley, Amato, Johnson, and Markman (2006) suggest that any form of premarital education may be somewhat effective. The time is right for both engaging in these efforts and for evaluating their impact. However, we realize that there are colleagues who believe we should be moving more slowly. Our field is in very good health for a young field, but we are feeling growing pains and have many options and challenges in front of us.

Lessons Learned from Research: Implications for Service Providers, Researchers, and Policy Makers

In the years that we have conducted couples' research, translated the results into programs for couples, trained trainers, and worked directly with couples, we have learned some major lessons that we want to share in this chapter.

Lesson 1: Remain Faithful to Prevention and Education Goals and Implementation; Do Not Slide into Therapy and Invest Efforts to Change Current Institutions that Train Service Providers

The first lesson is learned in part from one of the mistakes (alluded to earlier) of the community mental health center movement. During that movement, no research-based services were introduced into the field, nor were prevention and education services widely used (Snow & Newton, 1976). The reason for this outcome, according to the experts, was that no efforts were mounted to train the current or new generation of service providers in research-based interventions nor in prevention and education services. Instead, service providers did what they were trained to do in the first place – therapy.

A major emphasis for our field therefore is to devote careful consideration to how we will train the next generation of service providers who are trained in the field of marriage education (and its brother field of what is often called responsible fatherhood). We would suggest a training model that links research, practice, dissemination, and social policy regarding marital distress and divorce, in a synergistic loop.

Lesson 2: We Are Learning How to Extend Standard Programs to New Populations and Settings

The second lesson is about how to extend or disseminate RBME with new populations of couples and individuals in new settings. One of the grand achievements, and most surprising and meaningful to us, has been that RBME has been used in remarkably diverse institutions and with diverse couples and individuals. These settings and populations include: adoptive and foster parent couples, high schools, first offender youths and parents, transition to parenthood (Thuen & Loerum, 2005), work settings (Markman, Myrick, & Pregulman, 2006), prisons (Einhorn et al., 2008), the military (Stanley et al., 2005), individuals with low income levels (*Within My Reach*, Pearson, Stanley, & Kline, 2005), and couples with low income levels (*Within Our Reach*, Stanley, Markman et al., 2006). Next, we briefly list some of the reasons why we think this explosion of interest has happened:

(1) Numerous surveys have shown high levels of interest in marriage, people with low income levels showing even higher levels of interest than other community members (Johnson et al., 2002).
(2) Research has shown that both participants and service providers are typically satisfied with the curricula and programs (Markman, Stanley et al., 2006).
(3) Our interpretation of research and theory to date (e.g., Huang, 2005; Thuen & Loerum, 2005) suggests that there is a basic universality in what constitutes a healthy relationship and thus standard research-based programs can be used as a springboard for thoughtful adoptions.

(4) Many of these adaptations have sprung from our work with the Oklahoma Marriage Initiative (see www.OKmarriage.org) where we have followed our dissemination model (Markman, Williams, Einhorn, & Stanley, 2008) that involves training trainers who know their audiences (the messenger matters) and working with institutions that serve couples. We have also followed a model of prevention science applied to couples that suggests it is important to modify risk and protective factors for future distress or success at key developmental transitions (Coie et al., 1993). These include those developmental events that are planned (deciding to live together, planning marriage, transition to parenthood, kids entering school, empty nest, and retirement) and those that are unplanned (diagnosis with medical problem, other crises). Our dissemination model also recommends that when developing relationships with institutions, it is very important to get support from the top for the use of the intervention. For example, in our work with the military we call this command support.

(5) These adaptations have also followed some general principles including more activities, relevant examples and videos, modified and additional content based on emerging research (e.g., support and stress management), and flexibility in intensity and service delivery as seen in the work of Halford and associates (see Markman, Stanley et al., 2006, for a review).

Lesson 3: Researchers Can Increase Fidelity and Strength of Effects

A third set of lessons involves some simple truths from studies evaluating marital education programs:

(1) Fidelity in service delivery tends to drift. We have found that a checklist at the end of each module a leader presents helps keep them on track.

(2) There is an attenuation of findings over time (Hahlweg & Markman, 1988; Markman, Renick, Floyd, Stanley, & Clements, 1993). Booster sessions have been suggested as one way to bolster effects (Markman et al., 1993), but several studies to date have found it difficult to get couples to come in as part of a research trial – on our schedule versus theirs. New models of offering ongoing services to couples are using what we are calling community service providers to meet on an ongoing basis with couples, offering booster opportunities on a regular schedule, and also when couples feel they need some extra input. Also, community events for intervention participants are being offered to increase a sense of community connection in order to maintain and enhance initial intervention effects (Markman, Williams et al., 2008).

(3) Evidence suggests that as risk increases, so does our impact, and this reinforces calls for focusing our efforts on higher-risk couples (Halford et al., 2003). Interestingly, most of the new settings and populations that are using RBME are serving higher-risk couples.

Lesson 4: We Can Assess Key Dimensions Associated with a Healthy Relationship

A fourth lesson involves advancement in assessment. Specifically, we have developed a set of strong measures that enables us to assess components of a healthy marriage from an insider's perspective. These measures assess: (1) handling conflict and regulating negative affect, (2) positive connections, (3) confidence and commitment, (4) relationship happiness/satisfaction, and (5) stability (see www.prepinc.com, for copies of these measures). We recommend to service providers that all programs imbed a preassessment before the first intervention session and the post after the last.

Lesson 5: Marriage Education Programs Should Include Skills for Talking Without Fighting and an Understanding of Gender Differences in Relationships

A fifth lesson involves some key points about what should be included in all RBME programs. Thirty years ago, when we started, we discovered that it is not the differences as much as how they are handled – we focused on the negatives. Along with stability over time, being able to handle differences has come to define "a good enough" marriage (for kids, and maybe some husbands). But a stable, conflict-free marriage is not enough for a happy, healthy marriage in today's world. A healthy marriage also needs positive connections, fun, friendship, sensuality, and emotional support as well as high levels of sacrifice and forgiveness. Today's couples, especially those who are higher risk have more need for the negotiation skills offered in RBME. Today's couples have more challenges and differences, including: no clear roles, working women, parents living longer, more mobility, and less family support. We still believe that: "It's not the differences, but how they are handled."

The complex interplay between the waxing and waning of positives and negatives over time leads to a number of very important burning questions for the field including: (1) Why do positives diminish over time for most couples? (2) Are women more sensitive than men to emotional distance brewing (i.e., a decrease in positive connections), and are men more sensitive to an increase in negatives? (Stanley, Rhoades, & Markman, 2006) (3) Does this pattern lead to a cycle where women are raising concerns fueled by a perception of decreasing positives (he does not want to spend time with me) and then men perceiving these as negatives wherein they tend to avoid and withdraw, leading to the classic pursuit/withdrawal pattern (Christensen & Heavey, 1990; Markman & Kraft, 1989). (4) Why are most divorces low conflict (Amato, 2001; Amato & Booth, 1997) and filed for by women?

Lesson 6: In Future Longitudinal Outcome Studies Include Measures of Parenting, Child Outcomes, and the Use of Behavioral Observations

The sixth and final lesson is what we can do in terms of our research agenda for the next wave of outcome studies. I have chosen to focus on three major points. First there is a need to replicate and extend the findings from studies to date with the vast array of new populations mentioned earlier, using longitudinal studies in which the goals of prevention by definition are long term. Already three major multi-site studies are underway in the US evaluating RBME with unmarried couples who are having a child together (Building Strong Families – BSF), married couples with low income levels (Strong and Healthy Marriages – SHM), and in the prisons (go to www.acf.gov for details on these projects). In the rest of this section we focus on the need for including behavior observations evaluating parenting and child outcomes, health and work outcomes.

Behavioral Observation

The backbone of the couple's research field has been careful and systematic behavioral observation (see Markman & Notarius, 1987, for a history) of couples' interaction research. Discoveries from these studies have been a large part of the empirical basis of the RBME. As seen in part from the results of the meta-analyses reviewed earlier, the strongest and most consistent effects of RBME have been using observational data (both micro- and global systems, see Julien, Notarius, & Markman, 1989, for a review of issues with these two types of coding strategies). However, to our knowledge none of the large-scale federally funded evaluations of marriage education are using observational measures. The reason is often pragmatic and economical, but all of us should increase efforts to include observational measures in evaluation efforts. Another reason why it is important to do so is to evaluate mechanism of effects of interventions, an area that is very important to discuss, but is beyond the scope of this chapter (see Stanley, Rhoades, Olmos-Gallo, & Markman, 2007, for a discussion of this important issue).

Children and Parenting

The marriage education field has been powered by a concern for the best interests of children. The mantra of the movement has been that children who grow up in a stable marriage do better in life in general and in terms of school, work, mental health, and their own relationships (e.g., Amato, 2001; Nock, 1998; Waite & Gallagher, 2000). However, marriage education programs and research evaluating marriage education have widely ignored children and parenting in programs and evaluations. For example, the two major evaluations of relationship and marriage education programs in the US (Building Strong Families, Supporting Healthy Marriages) (described earlier) to my knowledge do not evaluate parenting or child outcomes. So how will we know if the large-scale national efforts (e.g., $150 million awarded in service grants in 2006 for marriage education efforts across the nation) ultimately will result in children doing better as a result of their parents participating in marriage education programs?

Applying the Lessons Learned in Our Newest Work

In the last section of this chapter, we will briefly describe two of our newest studies that both reflect and build on some (but alas not all) of the lessons learned discussed above and involve random clinical trials. The first study describes an Internet version of PREP for foster and adoptive parents, and the second a program tests the new version of PREP for couples with low income levels that address a key burning question in the field: Can we do marriage education with one person?

Marriage College: PREP Over the Internet

In one new project, we have been working with a team of innovative Internet-based service providers from Eugene, Oregon who had already developed a set of programs called Foster Parent College (see www.FosterParentCollege.com). We have also built on the innovative work of Braithwaite and Fincham (2007) who were the first to offer a computer-based version of the PREP.

We obtained funding (from the NIMH SBIR program) to develop a pilot of the first part of the PREP that included: (1) an overview of marriage today and why marriage education is important, (2) danger signs in relationships (including a quiz), (3) safety theory and taking a break (time out/stop action), and (4) speaker-listener skills. The innovations in the service delivery model included interactional questions and answers with animated foster parents and adoptive couples, showing these same couples learn and practice the skills while being coached by animated versions of Howard Markman and Scott Stanley, and mini-lectures of the PREP material taught by Scott Stanley and Howard Markman. We estimated that it would take 2–3 hours to complete the program.

We conducted a pilot study of the Internet intervention. We recruited foster, adoptive, and kinship couples for our sample by sending an email announcement about the study to about 13,000 parents who had previously taken a course through www.FosterParentCollege.com and also posted the announcement on the home page of the www.FosterParentCollege.com site. To be included in the study, both spouses had to participate and have access to a computer with high-speed Internet access. Interested parents were asked to respond by email. We received over 200 emails from interested couples in the first 24 hours after the email announcements were sent. We selected the first 100 qualified respondents (i.e., 50 couples) to participate in the study.

We randomly assigned those who agreed to participate to either an intervention condition or a comparison condition. Couples in the intervention group viewed the PREP course, while couples in the comparison group viewed another course offered on FosterParentCollege.com about visitation. Participants in both groups completed a set of pretest questionnaires and then had 1 week to view their respective training course (the *Marriage Relationships* course for the intervention group or the *Visitation* course for the comparison group) and to complete a set of posttest questionnaires after they finished viewing the course. The posttest questionnaires were the same as those given at pretest, without the background information questionnaire, but including user satisfaction questionnaire regarding their respective training course. At the beginning of the second week, all participants had the option of viewing the other course.

Results indicated that couples who participated in the *Marriage Relationships* course as compared to those who participated in the *Visitation* course had higher scores pre-to-post on the measure of knowledge of basic concepts and skills covered by the curriculum (e.g., ratings on use of communication skills and increased confidence in handling problems). There were no differences in ratings problems in their marriage. Participants in the *Marriage Relationships* program expressed great satisfaction with the training program, not only in their quantitative ratings on the satisfaction questionnaire items and in their responses to the questionnaire's open-ended items, but also in many emails at the end of the study.

The results suggest that we successfully modified both the content and service delivery for foster, adoptive, and kinship parents. Parents in the treatment group made significant gains in their knowledge of the PREP content and showed significant gains in their own perceptions of the communication skills they learned, a critical antecedent for and component of behavioral change. Intervention couples also reported very high levels of confidence in handling future problems. We expected to see decreases in negative communication for the intervention group, but they were not evident. It may be that there was not enough time between the intervention and our postassessment for couples to realize differences in the frequency of their negative communication patterns. Longer-term follow-ups are necessary to test this idea. In addition, the lack of differences in the negative communication measure may be at least in part due to very low negativity scores for both groups at pretest.

We have plans to expand the Internet program to make it relevant for all couples and then use the revised program for a variety of intervention purposes including having couples who miss sessions view the program and for booster sessions. At the same time, we are working on an Internet version of these same modules for all couples and then, if successful, a full Internet version of the PREP that can be tailored for a diverse set of populations and settings by having participants click on relevant examples for their situation. We already have this sort of flexibility built into our PREP leader training materials. Finally, the success of the strategy to recruit parents via email from the list of subscribers to www.FosterParentCollege.com far surpassed our highest expectations. Within hours of the announcement, we fulfilled our recruitment goals. Thus, the Internet as a tool for both service delivery and research has great potential.

New Fatherhood, Relationship, and Marriage Education Study

It has historically been difficult to enroll men in therapy and preventive interventions. Culprits include a combination of pragmatic challenges and philosophical assumptions of programs and enrollees (e.g., Costigan & Cox, 2001; Turbiville & Marquis, 2001). Pragmatic challenges include the difficulty of coordinating services for two parents with children at home, work schedules, child care issues, lack of interest, and military deployment. Philosophical problems include the assumptions that fathers will not enroll in an intervention and therefore explicitly targeting interventions to mothers (e.g., Turbiville & Marquis, 2001). Additionally, fathers and mothers report needing and/or wanting different information from interventions (Lengua et al., 1992). One way to address all of these obstacles is to offer relationship education services in groups for individuals as well as couples.

With the notable exception of the pioneering work by Bennum (1997), there are virtually no studies of the effects of couples interventions delivered to individuals. This is at least in part due to the findings that when there were marital issues, individual therapy had negative effects on the relationship (see review in Gurman & Fraenkel, 2002). Nevertheless, many models of psychotherapy and service provision depend on the ability of individuals to learn and apply skills on behalf of others, such as children and persons with disabilities. Applications of such models, such as parent training interventions, lend support to the idea that one member of a couple should be able to learn skills typically taught in couples interventions and apply them with their partner outside of the intervention (e.g., Boise, Congleton, & Shannon, 2005). The new study compares the efficacy of marriage education delivered to couples versus individuals to assess if couples and fathers benefit differentially when one only partner receives the intervention. *To our knowledge this is the first study in the entire couple's field to systematically address this very important question. The answers will not only have implications for the marriage education field but to the entire field of couples intervention.*

Specifically we are testing a new PREP for couples with low income levels, *Within Our Reach*, that has been adapted for use by both couples and individuals (see Markman, Stanley et al., 2006, for a discussion why marriage education is particularly important for low income couples and individuals). In addition to the core PREP skills, the adapted version of *Within Our Reach* (Stanley, Markman et al., 2006) incorporates several new emphases such as helping couples to identify and plan for overcoming barriers to meeting their goals, discovering new ways to cope with the specific stressors of economic strain, and units designed to foster parenting skills, community connection and involvement, and thinking about the future.

Our target population is individuals with low income levels in an ongoing committed relationship with at least one child together. All participants' income levels must be defined as "low income" based on 200% of the federal poverty line. Participants are clearly informed that 75% will be randomly chosen to participate in a marriage education program, and that all participants are asked to participate over a 5-year period in repeated assessments which will gather information on personal and relationship issues. Participants need to agree to these procedures and to serve in any of the four conditions before being signed up for the study. Interested couples who agree to be randomly assigned will be screened for the following criteria: involved in an ongoing committed relationship, have at least one child together, and be defined as low income based on 200% of the federal poverty level.

After completing preassessment, couples are randomly assigned to one of four conditions, control (N = 100), couples intervention (N = 100 couples), father intervention (N = 100), or the mother intervention (N = 100). After the intervention, couples complete a postassessment and then will be invited to complete regular follow-up assessments. Constructs assessed include individual adult and relationship functioning, parenting, and child outcomes.

The most interesting preliminary finding thus far is that, quite unexpectedly, the partners of the men in the male only group seem to be doing the best at posttest as compared to the other subgroups in the study. It is possible that the men are following instructions and teaching the skills they learn in the program to their partners and that their partners may be liking the idea that the men are interested enough in the relationship to do so. Many women we have interviewed over the years would certainly be happily surprised if their partner suggested the idea of having a couples meeting and talking about their relationship.

In sum, these new studies deal with one of the major challenges facing service providers working with delivering marriage education to general community populations: getting people in the room. Despite the success of reaching out to diverse groups of couples through institutions that serve them (a lesson learned concerning how to get RBME out to high risk couples), the biggest issue we hear from service providers is getting couples in the room. This does not seem to be due to a lack of interest in marriage education, as discussed earlier, it is very high, but due to dealing with barriers such as time constraints, child care, and coordinating schedules for both partners. Using the Internet and having just one partner in the room provide innovative ways to deliver marriage education services as we move forward.

Epilog

August 1969

The man in the white suit was trying to think about the lines he had rehearsed many times before, but was distracted by the by light show in the sky above and the darkness below, as he descended toward the realization of his dream and countless others who watched and listened from over 380,000 miles away. His personal success was truly built on the shoulders of giants who came before him, from the older generation of pioneers and friends Alan, Wally, John, and Scott to his own generation of explorers and colleagues and especially his shipmates Michael and Edwin. But perhaps most of all, he was making this one small step because of one man (John F. Kennedy) who had challenged our nation to put a man, who turned out to be this man (Neil Armstrong), on the moon by the end of the decade of the '60s.

September 2007

The small group looked up at the moon one more time and slowly walked away from the lake each thinking in his or own way that this was a very exciting time in their professional lives. In a previous article, we suggested that the time was right for a "marital moon shot" given unprecedented Federal support both in the U.S. and elsewhere for strengthening relationships and marriage. As in the early 60's, when we lacked a complete knowledge base and technology for achieving the monumental goal of a person walking on the moon, we know we have a lot more to know about marriage and couples interventions, but as Stanley (2001) notes, we know enough to act now and if we don't, we will lose an opportunity that may not come again any time soon. The marital equivalent of the Mercury astronauts (i.e., the Seniors in the field) have had the privilege to work together in a variety of ways and share incredible friendships and synergistic collaborations. As we share with the marital equivalent of the Gemini astronauts (i.e., the Juniors in the field), we hope we will go a long way to the Apollo generation who will take us to the marital moon and beyond into new frontiers of knowledge, discovery and achievements.

Acknowledgments

Preparation of this manuscript was supported in part by the grants from the National Institute of Child Health and Human Development (R01 HD053314 & R01HD48780) awarded to Howard Markman and Scott Stanley and from the Administration for Children, Youth and Family (36302) awarded to Howard Markman and Martha Wadsworth.

References

Amato, P. R. (2001). Children of divorce in the 1990s: An update of the Amato and Keith (1991) meta-analysis. *Journal of Family Psychology, 15*(3), 355–370.

Amato, P. R., & Booth, A. (1997). *A generation at risk: Growing up in an era of family upheaval.* Cambridge, MA: Harvard University.

Bennum, I. (1997). Couples interventions with one partner. In K. W. Halford & H. J. Markman (Eds.), *Clinical handbook of marriage and couples interventions*. Chichester, England: John Wiley & Sons.

Biose, L., Congleton, L., & Shannon, K. (2005). Empowering family caregivers: The powerful tools for caregiving program. *Educational Gerontology, 31*, 573–586.

Braithwaite, S. R., & Fincham, F. D. (2007). ePREP: Computer based prevention of relationship dysfunction, depression, and anxiety. *Journal of Social and Clinical Psychology, 26*(5), 609–622.

Christensen, A., & Heavey, C. L. (1990). Gender and social structure in the demand/withdraw pattern of marital conflict. *Journal of Personality and Social Psychology, 59*, 73–81.

Coie, J. C., Watt, N. F., West, S. G., Hawkins, J. D., Asarnow, J. R., Markman, H. J., et al. (1993). The science of prevention: A conceptual framework and some directions for a national research program. *American Psychologist, 48*, 1013–1022.

Costigan, C., & Cox, M. (2001). Fathers' participation in family research: Is there a self-selection bias? *Journal of Family Psychology, 15*(4), 706–720.

Einhorn, L., Williams, T., Stanley, S. M., Markman, H. J., & Eason, J. (2008). PREP inside and out: Marriage education for inmates. *Family Process, 47*, 341–356.

Gurman, A., & Fraenkel, P. (2002). The history of couple therapy. *Family Process, 41*, 199–260.

Hahlweg, K., & Markman, H. J. (1988). The effectiveness of behavioral marital therapy: Empirical status of behavioral techniques in preventing and alleviating marital distress. *Journal of Consulting and Clinical Psychology, 56*, 440–447.

Halford, K. W., Markman, H. J., Kline, G., & Stanley, S. M. (2003). Best practice in couple relationship education. *Journal of Marital and Family Therapy, 29*, 385–406.

Halford, K. W., Markman, H. J., & Stanley. (2008). Strengthening couples relationships with education: Social policy and public health perspectives. *Journal of Family Psychology, 22*, 497–505.

Horn, W. (2003). *Going to the chapel: The President's* healthy *marriage initiative*. Keynote address to the 7th annual meeting of Smart Marriages. NV: Reno.

Huang, W. (2005). An Asian perspective on relationship and marriage education. *Family Process, 44*, 161–173.

Jakubowski, S. F., Milne, E. P., Brunner, H., & Miller, R. B. (2004). A review of empirically supported marital enrichment programs. *Family Relations, 53*, 528–536.

Johnson, C. A., Stanley, S. M., Glenn, N. D., Amato, P. A., Nock, S. L., Markman, H. J., et al. (2002). *Marriage in Oklahoma: 2001 baseline statewide survey on marriage and divorce (S02096 OKDHS)*. Oklahoma City, OK: Oklahoma Department of Human Services.

Julien, D., Markman, H. J., & Lindahl, K. (1989). A comparison of a global and microanalytic coding system: Implications for future trends in studying interaction. *Behavioral Assessment, 11*, 81–100.

Lengua, L., Roosa, M., Schupak-Neuberg, E., Michaels, M., Berg, C., & Weschler, L. (1992). Using focus groups to guide the development of a parenting for difficult-to-reach, high-risk families. *Family Relations: Journal of Applied Family & Child Studies, 41*, 163–168.

Markman, H. J., & Kraft, S. (1989). Men and women in marriage: Dealing with gender differences in marital therapy. *The Behavior Therapist, 12*, 51–56.

Markman, H. J., Myrick, J., & Pregulman, M. (2006). Marriage education in the workplace. *Journal of Employee Assistance*, 3rd Quarter, 12–15.

Markman, H. J., & Notarius, C. (1987). Coding marital family interaction: Current status. In T. Jacob (Ed.), *Family interaction and psychopathology: Theories, methods, and findings* (pp. 329–390). New York, NY: Plenum Publishing.

Markman, H. J., Renick, M. J., Floyd, F., & Stanley, S. M. (1993). Preventing marital distress through effective communication and conflict management: A four- and five-year follow-up. *Journal of Consulting and Clinical Psychology, 61*, 70–77.

Markman, H. J., Stanley, S. M., & Blumberg, S. L. (2001). *Fighting for your marriage*. San Francisco: Jossey-Bass.

Markman, H. J., Stanley, S. M., Jenkins, N. H., Petrella, J. N., & Wadsworth, M. E. (2006). Preventive education: Distinctives and directions. *Journal of Cognitive Psychotherapy, 20*, 411–433.

Markman, H. J., Williams, T., Einhorn, L., & Stanley, S. M. (2008). The new frontier in relationship education: Innovations and challenges in dissemination. *The Behavior Therapist, 31*, 14–17.

Nock, S. L. (1998). *Marriage in men's lives*. New York: Oxford University Press.

Pearson, M., Stanley, S. M., & Kline, G. H. (2005). *Within my reach leader manual*. Denver, CO: PREP.

Snow, D., & Newton, P. (1976). Task, social structure and social process in the community mental health center movement. *American Psychologist, 31*, 582–594.

Stanley, S. M. (2001). Making the case for premarital education. *Family Relations, 50*, 272–280.

Stanley, S. M., Allen, E. S., Markman, H. J., Saiz, C. C., Bloomstrom, G., Thomas, R., et al. (2005). Dissemination and evaluation of marriage education in the Army. *Family Process, 44*, 187–201.

Stanley, S. M., Amato, P. R., Johnson, C. A., & Markman, H. J. (2006). Premarital education, marital quality, and marital stability: Findings from a large random household survey. *Journal of Family Psychology, 20*(1), 117–126.

Stanley, S. M., Rhoades, G. K., & Markman, H. J. (2006). Sliding vs. deciding: Inertia and the premarital cohabitation effect. *Family Relations, 55*, 499–509.

Stanley, S. M., Markman, H. J., Jenkins, N. H., Rhoades, G. K., Noll, L., & Ramos, L. D. (2006). *Within our reach leader manual*. Denver: PREP Educational Products.

Stanley, S. M., Rhoades, G. K., Olmos-Gallo, P. A., & Markman, H. J. (2007). Mechanisms of change in a cognitive behavioral couples prevention program: Does being naughty or nice matter? *Prevention Science, 8*, 227–239.

Thuen, F., & Loerum, K. T. (2005). A public/private partnership in offering relationship education to the Norwegian population. *Family Process, 44*, 175–186.

Turbiville, V., & Marquis, J. (2001). Father participation in early education programs. *Topics in Early Childhood Special Education, 21*(4), 223–231.

Waite, L. J., & Gallagher, M. (2000). *The case for marriage*. New York: Doubleday.

Howard J. Markman
Center for Marital and Family Studies
Frontier Hall
University of Denver
Denver, CO 80208
USA
E-mail: hmarkman@du.edu

New Themes in Couple Therapy

The Role of Stress, Coping, and Social Support

Guy Bodenmann

University of Zurich, Switzerland

Abstract

Stress and coping in couples are themes that have received increased attention in theory building and research in the last decades. Many findings show that everyday stress has a negative impact on relationship satisfaction and the likelihood of divorce. On the other hand, studies reveal that individual and, even more specifically, dyadic coping (the way couples deal with stress together) are powerful predictors of relationship functioning and the developmental course of close relationships. These findings suggest that it might be worthy to address stress issues in couple therapy and to focus on the improvement of dyadic coping (in addition to communication training and problem-solving training). One key target of coping-oriented couple therapy is improvement of dyadic coping.

Theoretical Background

Presently, different approaches and techniques are offered for the treatment of couples' problems and marital distress. These different methods are regularly presented and summarized in handbooks of couple therapy (e.g., Halford & Markman, 1997; Harway, 2005; Jacobson & Gurman, 2002; Wetchler, 2007) or in the context of prevention (Berger & Hannah, 1999). In the last few years, there have been several publications about the use of couple therapy as a promising psychological intervention for the improvement of marital distress among couples (Christensen & Heavey, 1999). According to these overviews, there are currently six different empirically supported treatments for couples in distress:

traditional behavioral couple therapy (TBCT; Jacobson & Margolin, 1979), cognitive-behavioral couple therapy (CBCT; Baucom, Epstein, LaTaillade, & Kirby, 2008), integrative behavioral couple therapy (IBCT; Jacobson & Christensen, 1996), emotionally focused couple therapy (EFCT; Johnson, 2004), integrated systematic couple therapy (ISCT; Greenberg & Goldman, 1985), and insight-oriented marital therapy (IOMT; Snyder, Wills, & Grady-Fletcher, 1991).

Among these different evidence-based approaches, behavioral and cognitive-behavioral couple therapies are the only approaches that are widely used in Europe (but still much less than systemic or psychoanalytic marital therapy). Initially inspired by empirical research drawn from social learning theories from the 1970s, behavioral couple therapy offers a large set of evidence-based intervention tools (e.g., Garfield & Bergin, 1986; Halford & Markman, 1997) that are well evaluated.

These interventions exhibit excellent efficacy with internationally established high effect sizes (mean effect size of $d = 0.95$; e.g., Dunn & Schwebel, 1995; Grawe, Donati, & Bernauer, 1994; Hahlweg & Markman, 1988; Shadish & Baldwin, 2003; Shadish, Montgomery, Wilson, Bright, & Okwumabua, 1993). Although these approaches are promising and show treatment efficacy, there is a constant need for further consideration of new insights of basic research. This link between basic research and clinical practice results in a general interest in further improving the efficacy of couple therapy by integrating new developments and techniques. This is the main purpose of the current chapter, namely to summarize findings from one line of basic research (stress and coping research in couples) and to try to build a bridge from this body of research to clinical practice. We refer to stress and coping (or social support) research because these issues have received increased attention in the last decade and have contributed significantly to new developments in couple therapy. In current couple therapies, we find certain theoretical concepts underrepresented that are significant for the understanding of marital functioning in basic research such as the concepts of stress, coping, and social support. Thus far, many couple therapy approaches only marginally deal (or not at all) with these factors that have proven to be highly important in the development of close relationships and their likelihood of success or divorce.

The de-emphasis of these factors is documented in multiple ways. First, we find few publications dealing with the question of how stress, coping, and social support issues might beneficially be used in couple therapy. Second, scholars in the field de-emphasize these factors in their practice and empirical research. An evaluation of the subject index of the currently available handbooks of couple therapy revealed that in most of these handbooks no reference is made either to stress, coping or social support. To our knowledge, exceptions are Bodenmann (2004) and Epstein and Baucom (2006), who address these issues. But what is the benefit of including these concepts in modern couple therapy, and what does basic research tell us about the importance of these concepts for the functioning of couples? We will try to briefly summarize these findings and to establish their significance for clinical practice. In this analysis we focus only on stress and social support (or dyadic coping). This is reasonable as social support (or dyadic coping), a chief concept that needs to be further integrated into couple therapy, is closely related to stress experience.

People need support mainly in times of stress, and we believe that couples facing high levels of stress in their individual and shared lives create multiple opportunities for the partners to support one another. As Lyons, Mickelson, Sullivan, and Coyne (1998, p. 580) wrote, "Solo performances are rare and each event draws a cast of characters who confront the issue individually and together." Thus, stress, coping, and social support are closely linked to each other and need to be addressed together in couple therapy.

> "Furthermore, when people are embedded in an intimate relationship, solution of the immediate problem is not the only goal of coping. Protecting the relationship is as important as preventing harm to each individual" (Cutrona & Gardner, 2006, p. 501).

Empirical Findings on Stress in Close Relationships and Their Significance for Couple Therapy

For the past 10 years, scholars in stress research have begun to investigate how *external stress* (stress originating from outside the close relationship, such as stress at the workplace or stress with neighbors, family of origin, or children) affects marital quality, the development of close relationships, and the risk of divorce. This line of research has yielded evidence for harmful spillover effects of external stress on close relationships by: (a) decreasing the quality of dyadic communication, (b) undermining relationship quality and satisfaction, and (c) by increasing the likelihood of divorce.

The Association Between External Stress and Dyadic Communication

A number of recent studies have shown that external stress is significantly associated with lower quality of marital communication by decreasing positivity (such as tenderness, compliments, agreement, affirmation, and care) and increasing verbal and nonverbal negativity (such as criticism, contempt, belligerence, and withdrawal) or verbal aggression (e.g., Bodenmann, 2005; Crouter, Perry-Jenkins, Huston, & Crawford, 1989; Frye & Karney, 2006; Halford, Gravestock, Lowe, & Scheldt, 1992; Repetti, 1989; Schulz, Cowan, Cowan, & Brennan, 2004). Furthermore, the work by Crouter et al. (1989) and Repetti (1989) highlighted the *spillover effect* of work stress on marital communication. Based on objective indicators of work stress (e.g., for the air-traffic controllers studied by Repetti, this involved daily weather conditions and number of airplanes landing each day) and systematic behavioral observations at home, these authors report that daily workload led to more negative interaction between partners in the evening when they were together. Stressed individuals were either more withdrawn from their partners at home or they showed more anger and hostile behavior. These findings were further supported by an investigation conducted by Schulz et al. (2004). These authors confirmed that workday stress predicted negative changes in women's and men's marital behavior. All in all, their study replicated previous findings showing that, when under stress, women become angrier and men become more withdrawn. Similar findings were reported by Halford et al. (1992) using a diary approach. Partners reported more negative interactions during the week and more positive interactions during the weekend because their daily stress level was lower during the weekend. Along similar lines, Bolger, DeLongis, Kessler, and Wethington (1989) revealed not only that conflicts at work were significantly correlated with a higher degree of marital conflicts, but also that marital stress resulted in a higher amount of stress at work. Frye and Karney (2006) found corresponding results in their longitudinal study conducted with 82 couples within their first 3 years of marriage. Husbands reporting higher scores of chronic stress showed a higher tendency toward the use of physical aggression and "were more likely to engage in physical aggression when they were experiencing higher than average levels of acute stress" (Frye & Karney, 2006, p. 12).

In two laboratory experiments (EISI-experiment), Bodenmann (2005) found that stress exerted a direct negative influence on marital interaction. Systematic observational analysis revealed that the quality of marital communication decreased by 40% after stress induction. Under stress, couples' positive interactions (e.g., active listening, interest, and empathy) were reduced, and their negative behavior (e.g., criticism, contempt, belligerence, and withdrawal) increased significantly. Similarly, marital conflicts have been found to be associated with heightened blood pressure and accelerated heart rate, which are commonly interpreted as signs of stress arousal (e.g., Broadwell & Light, 1999; Ewart, Taylor, Kraemer, & Agras, 1991; Flor, Breitenstein, Birbaumer, & Furst, 1995). Furthermore, studies on endocrine functioning report elevated levels of catecholamines and hypothalamic-pituitary-adrenal axis hormones in those subjects showing negative and hostile behavior during marital conflict discussions (Malarkey, Kiecolt-Glaser, Pearl, & Glaser, 1994). Thus, Cutrona and Gardner (2006) summarize that there is a sufficient body of research showing that couples are more likely to have fights at home when the husband or wife has had a difficult day at work. These negative communication behaviors are well known for their predictive power for negative marital outcome (e.g., Gottman, 1994). However, very often stress may be a causal factor for poor communication and subsequently for low relationship satisfaction. Thus, not all partners have *a priori* deficits in communication skills, but they do lose their communication skills during stressful times. The real problem is, therefore, not poor communication itself but inadequate individual and dyadic coping competencies that do not sufficiently buffer the harmful influence of stress on dyadic communication. Consequently, one additional target of couple therapy might be the improvement of coping skills in order to maintain adequate communication levels within the relationship (Bodenmann & Shantinath, 2004).

The Association Between External Stress and Marital Quality

Another line of research examined the relationship between external stress and marital quality and satisfaction. These studies revealed that daily hassles are significantly negatively associated with relationship quality and satisfaction. The higher the level of everyday chronic stress was, the lower was the self-reported marital quality in both partners (e.g., Bodenmann, 2005; Neff & Karney, 2004). In the framework of their mediator analyses, Bodenmann, Ledermann, and Bradbury (2007) reported that external stress triggers internal stress (tensions and conflicts in the dyad) that in turn is negatively associated with relationship quality, sexual activity, and sexual satisfaction. It is noteworthy that only daily hassles but not major critical life events were significant predictors of internal stress and poor marital outcome (also see Williams, 1995). Different mediational models describe the paths between external stress and marital quality. Similarly, Conger, Ge, and Lorenz (1994) found that the relationship between economic stress and marital quality was significantly explained through both warm/supportive as well as hostile behavior which acts as a parallel mediator. Results reported by Matthews, Conger, and Wickrama (1996) indicate that the association between work-family conflict and marital quality is mediated through psychological distress and, on the dyadic level, through marital interaction, which were serially linked. In sum, empirical evidence exists that chronic, everyday stress erodes relationship quality by means of mutual alienation, emotional distance, and poor dyadic communication (Randall & Bodenmann, 2009).

The Association Between External Stress and the Likelihood of Divorce

Another series of studies support the notion that external stress is not only correlated with poor marital functioning and low marital satisfaction but is also causally responsible for a higher likelihood of divorce (e.g., Bodenmann & Cina, 2006; Rogge, Leonard, & Bradbury, 2007). In their longitudinal study with 488 married couples, Rogge et al. (2007) demonstrated that couples were more likely to be divorced 3 years later to the extent that wives, as newlyweds, perceived more stress in their lives. Similarly, Bodenmann and Cina (2006) found that stress was a significant predictor for relationship status 5 years later (i.e., stable satisfied; stable distressed; separated/divorced). At the time of the first measurement, all three groups differed significantly in their stress level. On average, the stable-satisfied couples were characterized by a significantly lower level of external everyday stress. At the end of the 5-year period, it was possible to classify couples with 62% accuracy into stable-satisfied, stable-distressed, or separated/divorced couples. The relevance of stress was also supported in a retrospective study in which divorced subjects were asked what reasons, facilitating conditions, inhibiting conditions (barriers), or triggers they thought had led to the divorce (Bodenmann, Charvoz, et al., 2007). This study revealed that low commitment and deficits in interpersonal competencies (communication, problem solving, and coping) were more likely to be perceived as reasons for divorce than stress. However, divorced subjects considered stress (accumulation of everyday stress) to be an important trigger in their decision to divorce. They assumed that a high stress level in everyday life might increase the risk of alienation and would trigger the decision to divorce in unhappy relationships (Bodenmann, Charvoz, et al., 2007). In sum, previous findings suggest that the variables most harmful to close relationships are external, chronic micro-stressors that spill over into the couple's relationship. These stressors cause tension and conflicts within the dyad and alienation between the partners, which increases the likelihood of divorce.

The Role of Dyadic Coping or Social Support in Alleviating Negative Effects of Stress on Close Relationships

Social support or dyadic coping are concepts that are increasingly discussed in the context of stress and close relationships and marriage (e.g., Acitelli & Antonucci, 1994; Bodenmann, 2005; Cutrona, 1996). Consequently, the body of research conducted in this field is growing, especially in the context of close relationships (Cutrona & Gardner, 2006). Many of these studies suggest that social support provided by the partner or dyadic coping differ significantly from social support from kin, friends, or other members of the social network (e.g., Bodenmann, 2005; Cutrona, 1996; Denoff, 1982; Williamson & Clark, 1992; Veiel, Crisand, Stroszeck-Somschor, & Herrle, 1991). Social support by the partner or dyadic coping reveal to be important powerful buffer variables that alleviate the negative impact of stress on close relationships (e.g., Badr, 2004; Bodenmann, 2005; Dehle, Larsen, & Landers, 2001; Pasch & Bradbury, 1998; Walen & Lachman, 2000). The effects of external chronic minor stress on close relationships can be moderated by means of appropriate and effective dyadic coping (Bodenmann, 2005). Assuming that in many cases, external stress (e.g., stress experienced at the workplace) spills over into the dyad and therefore increases the risk for marital conflicts and escalation, this negative spillover may be reduced if both partners cope efficiently with their own stress (individual stress) or if they are able to handle stress on a dyadic level (dyadic coping). A number of studies have shown that couples in which the partners are able to deal with daily stress in a more efficient way show better relationship functioning and, therefore, exhibit a reduced risk of destructive dyadic interaction (e.g., Bodenmann, 2005). Thus, we are convinced that the improvement of dyadic coping may be an important target of interventions in the context of couple therapy.

What Do These Findings Mean for Couple Therapy?

The fact that dyadic coping and social support by the partner are meaningful buffer variables between external stress and relationship outcome is important for couple therapy, as this means that one goal of couple therapy might be to enhance and foster dyadic coping. The better both partners are able to support each other or the better the couple is able to cope together with common stress, the better is the prognosis of the relationship. This suggests that couple therapy should not only address general issues of dyadic communication by introducing speaker and listener rules, but should also teach couples how to engage in mutual dyadic coping. Couples should learn: (a) that if the partner comes home in a bad mood (withdrawn or hostile), it is often because he/she has experienced a hard and stressful day and that this bad mood is not related to the partner but to these negative circumstances (no attribution to oneself but to external conditions), (b) that he/she should ask the partner what happened, why he/she is in this bad mood (inviting the partner to communicate about his/her stress experience), (c) to display active listening and to try to understand the partner and his/her experience, and (d) to engage in supportive dyadic coping. All these competencies can be taught in couple therapy with the aim of helping the couple to enlarge their repertoire of dyadic coping competencies. This suggests that couple therapy should to a greater extent consider the enhancement of dyadic coping or social support provided by the partner to increase efficacy of the treatment, namely by: (a) improving the appraisal of stress in partners (enhancement of mutual stress perception), (b) improving the way partners communicate with one another about the stress that they experienced (enhancement of stress communication), and (c) improving the dyadic coping repertoire of a couple (enhancement of dyadic coping).

Couple Interventions That Address Stress and Coping Issues

Although many of the classical couple therapies cited above do not explicitly address stress or coping issues and do not propose specific intervention tools for helping couples to deal with stress and to enhance their dyadic coping, we find a number of approaches in the literature that try to help couples with major critical life events as their meaning for couples is largely acknowledged (Revenson & Majerovitz, 1991). However, most of these approaches do not consider the handling of daily stress but more so the management of severe life events that have a big impact on couples' lives. These interventions mostly focus on *important transitions in a couple's biography* such as the transition to parenthood (e.g., Cowan & Cowan, 1997) or the loss of a child (e.g., Murray, Terry, Vance, Battistutta, & Connolly, 2000), or *severe chronic illness.* Among couple approaches that help partners deal better with health-related demands or that integrate the notion of social support, illnesses such as cancer, AIDS, dementia, or chronic arthritis are addressed (Baucom et al., 2009; Blanchard, Toseland, & McCallion, 1996; Bultz, Speca, Brasher, Geggie, & Page, 2000; Cano & Leonard, 2006; Christensen, 1983; Goldberg & Wool, 1985; Halford, Scott, & Smythe, 2000; Heinrich & Schag, 1985; Kayser, 2005; Quayhagen et al., 2000; Pakenham, Dadds, & Lennon, 2002; Sabo, Brown, & Smith, 1986; Samarel & Fawcett, 1992; Serovich, 2000; Weber et al., 2004). Another field in which couple therapy refers to social support issues relates to *psychological disorders* (e.g., alcoholism, drug abuse, and depression) (e.g., Epstein & McCrady, 1998).

Among these disorders, depression plays an eminent role. Many therapists are aware of the important role that the partner plays in the etiology and maintenance of depression and the risk of relapse (Beach, Jones, & Franklin, 2008). Thus, several clinicians point out that social support should be strengthened in these couples and should be a part of the intervention (e.g., Misri, Kostaras, Fox, & Kostaras, 2000). Most of these interventions include psycho-education about the specific stressor (i.e., illness, parenthood, and psychological disorder) and the role of the partner in the stress process. Other components that are found in nearly all of these interventions are classical ingredients of behavior couple therapy such as problem-solving training (structured procedure to find suitable solutions to a problem) and communication training. Typically, problem solving addresses stressor-specific solutions (e.g., dealing with medical issues, medication compliance, and how the stressor impinges on daily task resolution) as well as relationship-related topics that are related to the stressor (e.g., speaking about the partners' worries concerning the impact of the illness on the close relationship). Additionally, several approaches also integrate discussions about the role of social support or dyadic coping. In some approaches, work on empathy (e.g., with the integrative therapy approach) is reported (e.g., Cano & Leonard, 2006). Stress and coping issues are, however, even more specifically addressed in cognitive-behavioral approaches such as the Couples' Coping Enhancement Training (CCET;

Bodenmann & Shantinath, 2004), The Partners in Coping Program (Kayser, 2005; Kayser & Scott, 2008), CanCope (Scott, Halford, & Ward, 2004), CanThrive (Baucom, 2003), Couple-focused Group Intervention for Women with breast cancer (Manne et al., 2005), or Side to Side (Seite an Seite; Heinrichs & Zimmermann, 2008). While the CCET is designed for all couples (universal, indicated, or selective prevention) and aims to help couples deal with everyday stress, the other intervention programs address couples in which one partner suffers from cancer (in most of the cases breast or prostate cancer). All the cancer intervention programs address psycho-education (teaching couples about the illness and the implication for the couples' lives), problem-solving training, communication training, and support issues. Some also address psycho-education about sexuality and cancer. The programs have a mean duration of 4–6 sessions (often followed by telephone contacts) and last on average 10 hours. All these programs have been evaluated in randomized controlled trials and have shown their efficacy.

The 3-Phase-Method

The key element of the CCET or the coping-oriented couple therapy (COCT) is the improvement of dyadic coping by means of the 3-phase-method (Bodenmann, 2007). This method is well grounded in Bodenmann's stress and coping theory in couples (Bodenmann, 2005) as well as in cognitive therapy (Beck, Rush, Shaw, & Emery, 1979). The aim of the 3-phase-method is to help the stressed partner to better understand his/her own psychological functioning while simultaneously helping the other partner enhance his/her understanding of his/her partner. Because external stress experienced by one partner can often affect the relationship between both partners (mostly by triggering problematic personality traits that irritate the other partner and easily lead to arguments and escalation), it is very important that both individuals understand that a negative mood expressed within the context of the couple's relationship may in fact have nothing to do with the relationship itself. Instead, the mood might result from the "spillover" of stress from outside of the marriage into the marriage, and this stress may trigger personal vulnerabilities of the partner. Sharing the insight that each partner brings strengths and weaknesses into the relationship helps promote a sense of "we-ness" and encourages both partners to cease "wearing masks" in attempts to cover personal imperfections.

To enhance dyadic coping, COCT and CCET focus on strengthening the couple's ability to effectively communicate stress, the ability to perceive and understand the partner's stress, and in turn to engage in effective dyadic coping. These skills are learned through the 3-phase-method which aims at: (a) enhancing the ability to clearly communicate stress to the partner (phase 1), (b) adapting support to the specific needs of the other (phase 2); and (c) refining the ability to offer dyadic coping based on the partner's feedback (phase 3) (Bodenmann, 2007).

Lasting approximately 30 minutes, phase 1 consists of exploring the emotional stress by means of the funnel method. In this method, one partner (partner A) begins with the broader aspects of his/her stress (top of the funnel, metaphorically speaking) and begins to further explore the deeper aspects of the stressful event (bottom of the funnel). First, partner A gives a short description of the stressful event and explores his/her emotions, thoughts, and perceptions linked to that specific event. The role of the therapist is to ask open-ended questions (such as "How did you feel?", "What did this mean to you?", and "Why was this so stressful?") in order to promote emotional self-disclosure of the stressed partner. Concurrently, partner B is encouraged to listen and summarize the important aspects of what partner A is saying. The central goal of phase 1 is for partner B to understand the meaning of what partner A experienced in order to be able to provide adequate emotion-focused dyadic coping (Bodenmann, 2007).

The second phase in which partner B is asked to provide positive support during dyadic coping (at the level of emotional self-disclosure) lasts approximately 10 minutes. Through expression of empathy and interest, partner B shows that he/she is aware of the underlying meaning of partner A's stressful event. The therapist invites partner B to provide, firstly, emotion-focused coping and secondly, also problem-focused forms of dyadic coping such as

> "helping to positively reframe the situation, promoting a sense of solidarity with the partner, telling the partner how he or she is appreciated, pointing out the partner's quality and strengths, helping the partner to slow down and relax, or helping the partner to actively find solutions for the problem" (Bodenmann, 2004, p. 481).

Lasting approximately 5 minutes, in phase 3, partner A is now encouraged to give feedback to partner B regarding how satisfied he/she was with the dyadic coping of the partner, how helpful he/she experienced the partner's support to be, and what else he/she would have liked to receive from partner B in order to feel better. Prior to completing the exercise, the partners switch roles so that both partners can benefit from this specific experience (Bodenmann, 2007).

The purposes of this deep personal self-disclosure when talking about one's stress experience are that: (a) the partners learn to provide supportive dyadic coping in a way that truly meets the needs of the other and is neither superficial ("this is not so bad, do not worry") nor inappropriate (providing support that the partner does not need or does not want), and (b) this experience strengthens the feeling of "we-ness" (i.e., cohesion, intimacy, solidarity, and mutual trust; see also Bodenmann, 2005; Cutrona, 1996). The 3-phase-method and the coping-oriented couple therapy have shown that the experience of being understood and supported by the partner is a very profound and essential one for relationship well-being. The efficacy of the 3-phase-method has been evaluated in several studies, showing that this method is a powerful therapeutic intervention (e.g., Bodenmann & Shantinath, 2004; Bodenmann, Pihet, Cina, Widmer, & Shantinath, 2006; Ledermann, Bodenmann, & Cina, 2007).

Discussion

As this overview has shown, stress and coping (mainly dyadic coping) play an important role in understanding relationship functioning and outcomes. It has been shown that external (chronic) stress often spills over into the close relationship, increases the likelihood of dyadic conflicts, arguments, and divorce, and simultaneously decreases relationship quality. On the other hand, individual and dyadic coping (or social support by the partner and others) are relevant buffer variables that alleviate the harmful effects of stress on close relationships. Based on these findings, we believe that modern couple interventions should, in addition to current evidence-based methods and techniques (such as behavior exchange techniques, communication training, problem-solving training, acceptance work, or emotion-focused interventions), also integrate methods that allow partners to improve their individual and dyadic coping competencies. A main focus of this approach should be the strengthening of dyadic coping which has been shown to be an important predictor of relationship quality and divorce (e.g., Bodenmann, 2005; Bodenmann & Cina, 2006). However, our analysis of current practice in couple therapy reveals that there is nearly no or only minor consideration of these issues in the treatment of distressed couples, yet we find an integration of stress and coping issues in couple therapies dealing with major life events (i.e., transition to parenthood, severe illness, and psychological disorders). In fact, nearly no couple therapy approach for distressed couples currently addresses the role of external stress that spills over into the close relationship and negatively affects relationship functioning, and only a few of these approaches explicitly address mutual support. Psychoeducation addressing these issues is found in only some current evidence-based treatments for distressed couples (e.g., Bodenmann, 2007). Ironically, as soon as major life events are involved, couple therapy approaches propose such tools for the enhancement of mutual understanding and support. This demonstrates that modern couple therapy could benefit from increasing the focus on these concepts for all couples. As everyday stress is a relevant factor for relationship deterioration, all couples (and not only those dealing with major life events) can benefit from daily experiences of mutual support, and all couples may benefit from the knowledge that they should protect their relationship from external stress. Although several approaches (cognitive couple therapy, integrative couple therapy, insight-oriented couple therapy, and emotion-focused couple therapy) touch some facets of social support to some degree (e.g., empathy), techniques to enhance social support or dyadic coping in couples should be more explicitly proposed and should become integral components of modern couple therapies. Empirical evidence of the benefit of coping-oriented couple therapy is demonstrated by studies conducted with the CCET or the coping-oriented couple therapy by Bodenmann (2007). Thus, the enhancement of dyadic coping through the improvement of one's own stress communication, the enhancement of one's ability to understand the partner's stress, and the enhancement of mutual dyadic coping can be viewed as an influential approach in an attempt to improve close relationships and furthermore reduce the risk of divorce. As Cutrona and Gardner (2006) noted, interventions on social support do not only help couples reduce stress and find their personal homeostasis, but they also help improve and strengthen the relationship quality in a way that goes beyond classical intervention methods as in communication training or problem-solving trainings. In an attempt to improve efficacy and widen the range of intervention tools for assisting distressed couples, we are convinced that couple therapy should integrate methods focusing on the enhancement of couples' coping.

References

Acitelli, L. K., & Antonucci, T. C. (1994). Gender differences in the link between marital support and satisfaction in older couples. *Journal of Personality and Social Psychology, 76*, 688–698.

Badr, H. (2004). Coping in marital dyads: A contextual perspective on the role of gender and health. *Personal Relationships, 11*, 197–211.

Baucom, D. (2003). *Canthrive: Helping couples respond to breast cancer: Treatment manual*. Chapel Hill: University of North Carolina.

Baucom, D. H., Epstein, N., LaTaillade, J. J, & Kirby, J. S. (2008). Cognitive behavioral couple therapy. In A. S. Gurman & N. S. Jacobson (Eds.), *Clinical handbook of couple therapy* (4th ed., pp. 31–72). New York: Guilford.

Baucom, D. H., Porter, L. S., Kirby, J. S., Gremore, T. M., Wiesenthal, N., Aldridge, W., et al. (2009). A couple-based intervention for female breast cancer. *Psychooncology, 18*, 276–283.

Beach, S. R. H., Jones, D. J., & Franklin, D. (2008). Marital, family, and interpersonal therapies for depression in adults. In H. Gotlib & C. L. Hammen (Eds.), *Handbook of depression* (2nd ed., pp. 624–641). New York: Guilford.

Beck, A. T., Rush, A. J., Shaw, B. F., & Emery, G. (1979). *Cognitive therapy of depression*. New York: Guildford Press.

Berger, R., & Hannah, M. T. (1999). *Preventive approaches in couples therapy*. New York: Brunner/Mazel.

Blanchard, C., Toseland, R., & McCallion, P. (1996). The effects of a problem-solving intervention with spouses of cancer patients. *Journal of Psychosocial Oncology, 14*(2), 1–21.

Bodenmann, G. (2004). *Verhaltenstherapie mit Paaren* [Cognitive behavioral therapy with couples: coping-oriented approach]. Bern: Huber.

Bodenmann, G. (2005). Dyadic coping and its significance for marital functioning. In T. Revenson, K. Kayser & G. Bodenmann (Eds.), *Couples coping with stress: Emerging perspectives on dyadic coping* (pp. 33–50). Washington, DC: American Psychological Association.

Bodenmann, G. (2007). Dyadic coping and the 3-phase-method in working with couples. In L. VandeCreek (Ed.), *Innovations in clinical practice: Focus on group and family therapy* (pp. 235–252). Sarasota: Professional Resources Press.

Bodenmann, G., Charvoz, L., Bradbury, T. N., Bertoni, A., Iafrate, R., Giuliani, G., et al. (2007). The role of stress in divorce: A retrospective study in three nations. *Journal of Social and Personal Relationships, 24*, 707–728.

Bodenmann, G., & Cina, A. (2006). Stress and coping among stable-satisfied, stable-distressed, and separated/divorced Swiss couples: A 5-year prospective longitudinal study. *Journal of Divorce and Remarriage, 44*, 71–89.

Bodenmann, G., Ledermann, T., & Bradbury, T. N. (2007). Stress, sex, and satisfaction in marriage. *Personal Relationships, 14*, 407–425.

Bodenmann, G., Pihet, S., Cina, A., Widmer, K., & Shantinath, S. (2006). Improving dyadic coping in couples with a stress-oriented approach: A 2-year longitudinal study. *Behavior Modification, 30*, 571–597.

Bodenmann, G., & Shantinath, S. D. (2004). The couples coping enhancement training (CCET): A new approach to prevention of marital distress based upon stress and coping. *Family Relations, 53*, 477–484.

Bolger, N., DeLongis, A., Kessler, R. C., & Wethington, E. (1989). The contagion of stress across multiple roles. *Journal of Marriage and the Family, 51*, 175–183.

Broadwell, S. D., & Light, K. C. (1999). Family support and cardiovascular responses in married couples during conflict and other interactions. *International Journal of Behavioral Medicine, 6*, 40–63.

Bultz, B. D., Speca, M., Brasher, P. M., Geggie, P. H. S., & Page, S. A. (2000). A randomized controlled trial of a brief psychoeducational support group for partners of early stage breast cancer patients. *Psycho-Oncology, 9*, 303–313.

Cano, A., & Leonard, M. (2006). Integrative behavioural couple therapy for chronic pain: Promoting behaviour change and emotional acceptance. *Journal of Clinical Psychology: In Session, 62*, 1409–1418.

Christensen, D. (1983). Postmastectomy couple counseling: An outcome study of a structured treatment protocol. *Journal of Sex and Marital Therapy, 9*, 266–275.

Christensen, A., & Heavey, C. L. (1999). Interventions in couples. *Annual Review of Psychology, 50*, 165–190.

Conger, R. D., Ge, X. J., & Lorenz, F. O. (1994). Economic stress and marital relationships. In R. D. Conger & G. H. Elder (Eds.), *Families in troubled times* (pp. 187–203). New York: Walter de Gruyter.

Cowan, C. P., & Cowan, P. A. (1997). Working with couples during stressful transitions. In S. Dreman (Ed.), *The family on the threshold of the 21st century: Trends and implications* (pp. 17–47). Mahwah, NJ: Lawrence Erlbaum Associates.

Crouter, A. C., Perry-Jerkins, M., Huston, T. L., & Crawford, D. W. (1989). The influence of work-induced psychological states on behavior at home. *Basic and Applied Social Psychology, 10*, 273–292.

Cutrona, C. E. (1996). *Social support in couples. Marriage as a resource in times of stress*. Thousand Oaks, CA: Sage.

Cutrona, C. E., & Gardner, K. A. (2006). Stress in couples: The process of dyadic coping. In A. L. Vangelisti & D. Perlman (Eds.), *The Cambridge handbook of personal relationships* (pp. 501–516). Cambridge: University Press.

Dehle, C., Larsen, D., & Landers, J. E. (2001). Social support in marriage. *The American Journal of Family Therapy, 29*, 307–324.

Denoff, M. S. (1982). The differentiation of supportive functions among network members: An empirical inquiry. *Journal of Social Service Research, 5*, 45–59.

Dunn, R. L., & Schwebel, A. I. (1995). Meta-analytic review of marital therapy outcome research. *Journal of Family Psychology, 9*, 58–68.

Epstein, E. E., & McCrady, B. S. (1998). Behavioral couples treatment of alcohol and drug use disorders: Current status and innovations. *Clinical Psychology Review, 18*, 689–711.

Epstein, N. B., & Baucom, D. H. (2006). *Enhanced cognitive-behavioral therapy for couples* (2nd ed.). Washington, DC: American Psychological Association.

Ewart, C. K., Taylor, C. B., Kraemer, H. C., & Agras, W. S. (1991). High blood pressure and marital discord: Not being nasty matters more than being nice. *Health Psychology, 10*, 155–163.

Flor, H., Breitenstein, C., Birbaumer, N., & Furst, M. (1995). Psychophysiological analysis of spouse solicitousness towards pain behaviors, spouse interaction, and pain perception. *Behavior-Therapy, 26*(2), 255–272.

Frye, N. E., & Karney, B. R. (2006). The context of aggressive behavior in marriage: A longitudinal study of newlyweds. *Journal of Family Psychology, 20*, 12–20.

Garfield, S. L. & Bergin, A. E. (Eds.). (1986). *Handbook of psychotherapy and behavior change*. New York: Wiley.

Goldberg, R. J., & Wool, M. S. (1985). Psychotherapy for the spouses of lung cancer patients: Assessment of an intervention. *Psychotherapy Psychosomatics, 43*, 141–150.

Gottman, J. M. (1994). *What predicts divorce?* Hillsdale, NJ: Erlbaum.

Grawe, K., Donati, R., & Bernauer, F. (1994). *Psychotherapie im Wandel. Von der Konfession zur Profession* [Psychotherapy in change]. Göttingen: Hogrefe.

Greenberg, L. S., & Goldman, A. (1985). *Integrated systemic couples' therapy: A treatment manual.* Unpublished manuscript. University of British Columbia, Vancouver, Canada.

Hahlweg, K., & Markman, H. J. (1988). Effectiveness of behavioral marital therapy: Empirical status of behavioral techniques in preventing and alleviating marital distress. *Journal of Consulting and Clinical Psychology, 56*, 440–447.

Halford, W. K., Gravestock, F. M., Lowe, R., & Scheldt, S. (1992). Toward a behavioral ecology of stressful marital interactions. *Behavioral Assessment, 14*, 199–217.

Halford, W. K. & Markman, H. J. (Eds). (1997). *Clinical handbook of marriage and couples intervention*. New York: Wiley.

Halford, W. K., Scott, J. L., & Smythe, J. (2000). Couples and coping with cancer: Helping each other through the night. In K. B. Schmaling & T. G. Sher (Eds.), *The psychology of couples and illness: Theory, research, and practice* (pp. 135–170). Washington, DC: American Psychological Association.

Harway, M. (Ed.). (2005). *Handbook of couple therapy.* New York: Wiley & Sons.

Heinrich, R. L., & Schag, C. C. (1985). Stress and activity management: Group treatment for cancer patients and spouses. *Journal of Consulting and Clinical Psychology, 53*, 439–446.

Heinrichs, N., & Zimmermann, T. (2008). *Bewältigung einer gynäkologischen Krebserkrankung in der Partnerschaft. Ein psychoonkologisches Behandlungsprogramm für Paare* [Mastery of a gynecological cancer disease in partnership. A psychooncological treatment program for couples]. Göttingen: Hogrefe.

Jacobson, A. S., & Gurman, N. S. (2002). *Clinical handbook of couple therapy.* New York: Guilford Press.

Jacobson, N. S., & Christensen, A. (1996). *Integrative behavioral couple therapy.* New York: Norton.

Jacobson, N. S., & Margolin, G. (1979). *Marital therapy: Strategies based on social learning and behavior exchange principles*. New York: Brunner/Mazel.

Johnson, S. M. (2004). *The practice of emotionally focused couple therapy* (2nd ed.). New York: Brunner-Routledge.

Kayser, K. (2005). Enhancing dyadic coping during a time of crisis: A theory-based intervention with breast cancer patients and their partners. In T. A. Revenson, K. Kaiser & G. Bodenmann (Eds.), *Couples coping with stress: Emerging perspectives on dyadic coping* (pp. 175–194). Washington, DC: American Psychological Association.

Kayser, K., & Scott, J. L. (2008). *Helping couples cope with women's cancer.* New York: Springer.

Ledermann, T., Bodenmann, G., & Cina, A. (2007). The efficacy of the couples coping enhancement training (CCET) in improving relationship quality. *Journal of Social and Clinical Psychology, 26*, 940–959.

Lyons, R. F., Mickelson, K. D., Sullivan, M. J., & Coyne, J. C. (1998). Coping as a communal process. *Journal of Social and Personal Relationships, 15*, 579–605.

Malarkey, W. B., Kiecolt-Glaser, J. K., Pearl, D., & Glaser, R. (1994). Hostile behavior during marital conflict alters pituitary and adrenal hormones. *Psychosomatic Medicine, 56*, 41–51.

Manne, S., Winkel, G., Grana, G., Ross, S., Ostroff, J. S., & Fox, K. (2005). Couple-focused group intervention for women with early stage breast cancer. *Journal of Consulting and Clinical Psychology, 73*, 634–646.

Matthews, L. S., Conger, R. D., & Wickrama, K. A. S. (1996). Work-family conflict and marital quality: Mediating processes. *Social Psychology Quarterly, 59*, 62–79.

Misri, S., Kostaras, X., Fox, D., & Kostaras, D. (2000). The impact of partner support in the treatment of postpartum depression. *The Canadian Journal of Psychiatry, 45*, 554–558.

Murray, J. A., Terry, D. J., Vance, J. C., Battistutta, D., & Connolly, Y. (2000). Effects of a program of intervention on parental distress following infant death. *Death Studies, 24*, 275–305.

Neff, L. A., & Karney, B. R. (2004). How does context affect intimate relationships? Linking external stress and cognitive processes within marriage. *Personality and Social Psychology Bulletin, 30*, 134–148.

Pakenham, K. I., Dadds, M. R., & Lennon, H. V. (2002). The efficacy of a psychosocial intervention for HIV/AIDS caregiving dyads and individual caregivers: A controlled treatment outcome study. *AIDS care, 14*, 731–750.

Pasch, L. A., & Bradbury, T. N. (1998). *Social support in marriages. Coding system*. Los Angeles: UCLA. Unpublished manual.

Quayhagen, M. P., Quayhagen, M., Corbeil, R. R., Hendrix, R. C., Jackson, J. E., & Snyder, L. (2000). Coping with dementia: Evaluation of four nonpharmacologic interventions. *International Psychogeriatrics, 12*, 249–265.

Randall, A. K., & Bodenmann, G. (2009). The role of stress on close relationships and marital satisfaction. *Clinical Psychology Review, 29*, 105–115.

Repetti, R. L. (1989). Effects of daily workload on subsequent behavior during marital interaction: The roles of social withdrawal and spouse support. *Journal of Personality and Social Psychology, 57*, 651–659.

Revenson, T. A., & Majerovitz, D. M. (1991). The effects of chronic illness on the spouse: Social resources as stress buffers. *Arthritis Care and Research, 4*, 63–72.

Rogge, R. D., Leonard, K., & Bradbury, T. N. (2007). Stress and the prediction of adverse marital outcomes. Manuscript in preparation.

Sabo, D., Brown, J., & Smith, C. (1986). The male role and mastectomy: Support groups and men's adjustment. *Journal of Psychosocial Oncology, 4*(1/2), 19–31.

Samarel, N., & Fawcett, J. (1992). Enhancing adaptation to breast cancer: The addition of coaching to support groups. *Oncology Nursing Forum, 19*, 591–596.

Schulz, M. S., Cowan, P. A., Cowan, C. P., & Brennan, R. T. (2004). Coming home upset: Gender, marital satisfaction, and the daily spillover of workday experience into couples interactions. *Journal of Family Psychology, 18*, 250–263.

Scott, J., Halford, K., & Ward, B. (2004). United we stand? The effects of a couple-coping intervention on adjustment to early stage breast or gynecological cancer. *Journal of Consulting and Clinical Psychology, 72*(6), 1122–1135.

Serovich, J. M. (2000). Helping HIV-positive persons to negotiate the disclosure process to partners, family members, and friends. *Journal of Marital and Family Therapy, 26*, 365–372.

Shadish, W. R., & Baldwin, S. A. (2003). Meta-analysis of MFT interventions. *Journal of Marriage and Family Therapy, 29*, 547–579.

Shadish, W. R., Montgomery, L. M., Wilson, P., Bright, I., & Okwumabua, T. (1993). The effects of family and marital psychotherapies: A meta-analysis. *Journal of Consulting and Clinical Psychology, 59*, 883–893.

Snyder, D. K., Wills, R. M., & Grady-Fletcher, A. (1991). Long-term effectiveness of behavioral versus insight-oriented marital therapy: A 4-year follow-up study. *Journal of Consulting and Clinical Psychology, 59*, 138–141.

Veiel, H. O., Crisand, M., Stroszeck-Somschor, H., & Herrle, J. (1991). Social support networks of chronically strained couples: Similarity and overlap. *Journal of Social and Personal Relationships, 8*, 279–292.

Walen, H. R., & Lachman, M. E. (2000). Social support and strain from partner, family, and friends: Costs and benefits for men and women in adulthood. *Journal of Social and Personal Relationships, 17*, 5–30.

Weber, B. A., Roberts, B. L., Renick, M., Deimling, G., Zauszniewski, J. A., Musil, C., et al. (2004). The effect of dyadic intervention on self-efficacy, social support, and depression for men with prostate cancer. *Psycho-Oncology, 13*, 47–60.

Wetchler, J. L. (Ed.). (2007). *Handbook of clinical issues in couple therapy.* New York: The Haworth Press.

Williams, L. M. (1995). Association of stressful life events and marital quality. *Psychological Reports, 76*, 1115–1122.

Williamson, G. M., & Clark, M. S. (1992). Impact of desired relationship type on affective reactions to choosing and being required to help. *Personality and Social Psychology Bulletin, 18*, 10–18.

Guy Bodenmann
Department of Psychology
Binzmühlestrasse 14/23
8050 Zurich
Switzerland
E-mail: guy.bodenmann@psychologie.uzh.ch

Translating Basic Science Research on Premarital Cohabitation into Clinical Practice

Galena K. Rhoades, Scott M. Stanley, and Howard J. Markman

University of Denver, CO, USA

Abstract

Cohabitation is increasingly common in the US, with the majority of couples now living together before marriage. This chapter briefly reviews research on cohabitation, its association with marital distress and divorce for those who marry (the cohabitation effect), gender differences, and theories underlying this association. Suggestions are made for future areas of exploration in this field and the implications of the existing research for relationship education efforts and clinical intervention with couples are discussed. The accumulating evidence favors discussing the cohabitation effect in relationship education settings and helping individuals explore their own expectations about cohabitation as well as how cohabitation may or may not change their relationships and influence future relationship goals. With regard to cohabiting couples presenting for therapy, it may be important for clinicians to help them consider their pathways into cohabitation, their commitment levels, plans for the future, and power dynamics. For married couples in therapy, it may be useful for some to look at the process by which they married and to recommit to decisions they made together.

In recent decades, living together before marriage has become increasingly common in the US. At least 50–70% of couples married during the 1990s cohabited premaritally (Bumpass & Lu, 2000; Stanley, Whitton, & Markman, 2004). Historically, cohabitation has been studied mainly by researchers in sociology and demography, professions typically not occupied with intervention. Perhaps because of this, little of the empirical knowledge about the risks of cohabitation for some couples has made it into the hands of practitioners of either couple therapy or couples' education. The purposes of this chapter are to briefly review what is known about premarital heterosexual cohabitation and to translate these major findings into tangible ideas for clinical practice. We limit our review to the US because, as Kiernan (2002) demonstrates, the rates of cohabitation as well as its meaning in society differ dramatically by country.

Basic Research Findings

What We Know

Why Do Couples Cohabit?

The rise of cohabitation rates is linked with other important shifts in family patterns. In particular, the increase in the age of first marriage is likely not a coincidence (Bumpass, Sweet, & Cherlin, 1991). In 2003, the average age for first marriage was 25.3 for women and 27.1 for men, according to the US Census Bureau (Fields, 2004). It is widely understood that couples have been delaying marriage but not living-together arrangements. Hence, it is not the case that young adults are extending singlehood as much as they are delaying marriage. In part, this means that people have replaced a more stable relationship union type (marriage) with a less stable union (cohabitation) in the early to mid-20s (Bumpass et al., 1991).

Although many have speculated that couples cohabit as a way to test their relationships, couples' own reports suggest that many do not give the transition from dating to cohabiting quite so much thought. Instead, they report that living together just sort of happened (Lindsay, 2000) or that they slid into it (Manning & Smock, 2005). In one of the first quantitative studies of reasons for cohabitation, Rhoades, Stanley, and Markman (2009) found that cohabiting couples most often report that they started living together so that they could spend more time together. In fact, only about 15% ranked testing the relationship as the top reason for their own cohabitations. Nevertheless, the majority of young adults in general believe that cohabitation provides a good test for compatibility (Glenn, 2005) and that it lowers the likelihood of marital distress and divorce, once married (Johnson et al., 2002).

The Cohabitation Effect

Premarital cohabitation has been shown to be associated with higher rates of divorce in several US samples (e.g., DeMaris & Rao, 1992; Kamp Dush, Cohan, & Amato, 2003). Many studies demonstrate links between premarital cohabitation and lower marital quality. After marriage, those who cohabited premaritally have lower satisfaction (Stanley et al., 2004), more negative observed communication (Cohan & Kleinbaum, 2002), more conflict (Thomson & Colella, 1992), more physical violence (Brownridge & Halli, 2000; Stanley et al., 2004), and higher rates of infidelity for wives (Forste & Tanfer, 1996) than those who did not cohabit premaritally. This association between premarital cohabitation and marital distress and divorce has been termed the cohabitation effect.

Selection Versus Experience

Although the linkages for risk are well documented across many studies, there exists a debate in the cohabitation literature as to whether it is the type of people who cohabit (i.e., the selectivity perspective) or the experience of cohabitation itself that accounts for the cohabitation effect (e.g., Brown & Booth, 1996). There is evidence for both positions. Selectivity can account for at least part of the association between premarital cohabitation and divorce. Woods and Emery (2002) found that the association between premarital cohabitation and divorce was negligible after controlling for variables that were connected to both premarital cohabitation and divorce (i.e., ethnicity, religiousness, and a history of delinquency). Such findings suggest that selection factors can account for the risks associated with premarital cohabitation. On the other hand, as it has been traditionally conceptualized, selectivity does not account for all of the cohabitation effect. For example, Cohan and Kleinbaum (2002) and Kamp Dush et al. (2003) carefully controlled for a number of possible selection variables and continued to find that those who had cohabited premaritally were at higher risk for distress and divorce (also see Amato & Rogers, 1999; Stanley, Amato, Johnson, & Markman, 2006). Thus, while there are known differences between couples who live together before marriage and those who do not (e.g., religiousness; Stanley et al., 2004), the differences do not fully explain the cohabitation effect. There is more to the story. Next, we describe a new perspective on how the experience of cohabitation may increase risk for divorce in some couples.

Inertia

Stanley, Rhoades, and Markman (2006) suggest that cohabitation may lead some couples to slide into marriages they otherwise would not have chosen. This "inertia theory" rests on both prior findings as well as commitment theories that distinguish between constraint forces and more intrinsic elements of commitment (see Johnson, Caughlin, & Huston, 1999; Stanley & Markman, 1992). Constraints reflect forces that can serve to raise the costs of leaving a relationship. They can come from many sources, such as financial limitations, the difficulty of dividing possessions and moving, legal considerations such as a lease or division of assets, fears of being alone, and moral dimensions. Theoretically, constraints can keep couples together, even when times are tough and when dedication may be low. Dedication, on the other hand, reflects the intrinsic desire to maintain the relationship into the future (Stanley & Markman, 1992).

There is likely great variability in terms of commitment levels during cohabitation, but on average, cohabitation is a relationship form that, at least in the US, is associated with lower dedication than marriage (Stanley et al., 2004), though many of the constraints associated with marriage also apply to cohabitation. The key issue identified by Stanley, Rhoades et al. (2006) is that the average couple would likely find it harder to break up if they were cohabiting than if they were dating and not cohabiting because cohabitation involves a higher level of constraints. For example, cohabitation may involve increased financial commitments (e.g., a lease), increased difficulty to move on (e.g., moving out and finding another place to live), and increased social pressure to stay together (e.g., friends and family beginning to expect more of the relationship, including, in many cases, marriage). Thus, cohabitation could increase the likelihood of marriage, even among couples who are at higher risk for divorce or marital distress. If this reasoning holds, the inertia (or accumulated weight of the relationship in its current state) could be part of the explanation for the cohabitation effect.

Relatively higher levels of inertia would favor relationship continuance when levels of dedication and satisfaction were otherwise equivalent (Stanley, Rhoades et al., 2006).

The Timing of the Decision to Marry

When considering the cohabitation effect, there is evidence that it is important to distinguish between couples who had made mutual decisions to marry before starting to cohabit and those who develop plans for marriage during cohabitation. Brown and Booth (1996) found that the relationship quality of cohabiting couples with plans for marriage was similar to married couples' relationship quality. More directly, Kline et al. (2004) found that married couples who lived together before engagement had more negative interactions, lower relationship quality, and lower relationship confidence than those who did not cohabit until after engagement or marriage. In the same study, there were no significant differences between couples who lived together only after engagement and those who did not cohabit premaritally. Though replication in a more representative sample is necessary, these findings suggest that living together may be a risky choice primarily for those who do not already have plans to marry. They are consistent with the idea of inertia because couples who cohabited before engagement would be the ones most at risk for sliding into marriage because of the increased constraints associated with cohabitation.

Gender Differences in Commitment

There is also evidence for important differences between married men and women in commitment based on cohabitation history. These differences have important implications for clinical work with couples and for preventive efforts. In an aforementioned national survey, married men who cohabited with their partners before marriage reported lower levels of dedication than men who did not cohabit premaritally (Stanley et al., 2004). There was no significant difference for women in that study. Other research with a smaller sample of couples showed that among married couples who had cohabited before engagement, husbands were significantly less dedicated than their wives (Rhoades, Stanley, & Markman, 2006). Surprisingly, little other research on cohabitation has considered either commitment or gender, though both seem important, given that they may relate to power dynamics in relationships.

What We Need to Know

Before considering practice implications, it is important to note limitations to the cohabitation literature and gaps in the existing knowledge base. First, many studies published on cohabitation have been based on a single data set, the National Survey of Families and Households. Although it comprises a random sample of the US population, it is now somewhat outdated, for the first wave occurred in the late 1980s. Given the quickly changing nature of cohabitation in terms of both its popularity and its meaning in the US (Smock, 2000), replication studies are very important to this field, but they are not widely published.

Second, it is difficult to isolate the relative contributions of variables to the cohabitation effect. For example, it impossible to know from the current literature how religiousness

(Stanley et al., 2004), previous number of cohabitation and sexual partners (Teachman, 2003), delinquent behavior history (Woods & Emery, 2002), and living together before engagement (Kline et al., 2004) may interact in explaining the cohabitation effect because not all of these constructs have been measured in a single study. Longitudinal studies that follow participants from very early in relationship development through cohabitation to break-up or marriage and that include comprehensive measurement of a multitude of variables are needed to fully understand the relative risks related to cohabitation.

Third, good estimates of the strength of the association between premarital cohabitation and divorce are not available. For example, studies have shown that those who cohabited premaritally experienced a divorce rate that was somewhere between 1.29 and 1.86 times greater than the rate for those who did not cohabit premaritally (DeMaris & Rao, 1992; Kamp Dush et al., 2003; Teachman, 2003). However, these estimates are based on couples who married as early as the 1960s and none of these studies included participants who married later than the 1990s. Updated samples will be necessary before steadfast conclusions can be drawn about the degree of risk for divorce.

Aside from these specific criticisms of the available data, there are several advances that would help researchers and clinicians better understand the cohabitation effect and better direct us toward effective interventions. As noted already, little research has incorporated existing theory about couples and relationship processes into research on cohabitation. Broadening this field to incorporate more literature on topics such as commitment, feminist theory, attachment theory, and power in relationships would likely aid our understanding of this dynamic new stage in American romantic relationships. International research comparing the meaning and institutionalization of cohabitation in different countries and cultures could also illuminate the circumstances under which cohabitation is most associated with risk (see Kiernan, 2002).

Practice Implications

It is clear that the literature does not contain all the answers regarding the association between premarital cohabitation and marital distress and divorce. As the field moves forward, research will further elucidate the circumstances under which cohabitation is a risk factor for distress and divorce and more precisely characterize the mechanisms that explain the cohabitation effect. In the meantime, enough knowledge exists to begin incorporating research on cohabitation and the cohabitation effect into couple therapy and relationship education efforts. Below we outline practice implications for psychoeducation and therapy for individuals as well as for couples.

Relationship Education with Individuals

Relationship education is typically aimed at couples who are already in fairly committed, viable relationships. However, the cohabitation literature demonstrates that early relationship development and the steps that come before marriage also influence a marriage's outcomes. Individuals can be educated about relationships before they make commitments to them and it seems clear that individuals should be made aware of research demonstrating links between cohabitation and subsequent marital distress and divorce. It is our impression that most young adults are unaware of the cohabitation effect, for the majority believes cohabiting will improve one's chances in marriage (e.g., Glenn, 2005). Providing basic information in relationship education programs on what is known about cohabitation from research may help some young adults think critically about what is right for them with regard to cohabitation. Further, it is a fact that no study shows advantages to premarital cohabitation as a strategy to reduce risk for marital problems or divorce.

Does the research on the cohabitation effect mean that those delivering relationship education programs should dissuade couples from cohabiting? In settings with a focus on religious values, this approach might be well received as it would fit with most traditional religious beliefs about the best way to enter marriage. More broadly, we believe that practitioners of all backgrounds will be most effective in psychoeducational contexts if they help individuals consider their expectations about cohabitation, their partners' expectations about the relationship, their beliefs and values, their own circumstances, and the available research evidence.

Stanley, Rhoades and colleagues (2006) suggested terminology to help individuals make healthy decisions about relationships: "sliding versus deciding." It is an easy-to-remember phrase reminding individuals to consider the constraints that can build with new relationship transitions (such as from dating to cohabiting) and that making decisions is generally better than sliding into new phases. Terminology like this could be useful in relationship education curricula aimed at helping individuals make positive relationship choices. Relationship education programs for teenagers and adults could review research on cohabitation and encourage individuals to think critically about their reasons for wanting to live together (e.g., becoming closer, doubts about the relationship, pressure from partner, finances, and convenience) and about the potential costs of cohabiting, such as giving up other options. Guidelines for talking with partners about the future, commitment levels, and the meaning of cohabitation could also be provided.

Given the commitment differences between men and women based on cohabitation history reviewed earlier, psychoeducational efforts about premarital cohabitation may be especially important to women. Most women likely would not want to find themselves more committed than their partners in marriage. As Rhoades et al. (2006) suggest, talking with both men and women about ways to judge a partner's commitment level and about the importance of communication about commitment and the future of the relationship could reduce the risk of winding up with asymmetrical commitment levels in marriage.

For an example of how these ideas have been applied in relationship education curricula for individuals, readers may be interested in *Within My Reach* (Pearson, Stanley, & Kline, 2005). This curriculum was developed specifically for individuals and is now used by welfare and Head Start programs across the US. The literature on gender differences in sacrificing for one's relationship may also be helpful to practitioners interested in helping individuals make healthy relationship choices (e.g., Stanley, Whitton, Low, Markman, & Clements, 2006; Whitton, Stanley, & Markman, 2002).

Relationship Education with Couples

The selection perspective (i.e., that selection factors account for the association between premarital cohabitation and lower marital satisfaction) suggests that individuals who tend to cohabit tend to also have characteristics that put them at increased risk for divorce. Thus, cohabiting couples may be good candidates for couple relationship education or premarital training programs. Calls have been made to begin identifying couples most at risk for marital distress and divorce as the best candidates for relationship education (Halford, Markman, Kline, & Stanley, 2003; Halford, Sanders, & Behrens, 2001) and cohabitation may be indicative of risk.

More specifically, given the different commitment dynamics in marriage versus cohabitation (e.g., Stanley et al., 2004), specific educational material regarding what commitment means and how it is beneficial in long-term relationships may be useful for cohabiting couples. Programs could also encourage and provide guidelines for conversations between partners about their perspectives on the future of their relationships and what their expectations are regarding marriage.

Additionally, we know that those who cohabit premaritally are more prone to negative marital communication (Cohan & Kleinbaum, 2002; Stanley et al., 2004), especially if they lived together before becoming engaged (Kline et al., 2004). Communication skills training is typically included in premarital training programs and could be particularly beneficial for those who are cohabiting. At the same time, their lower level of religiousness means that they are not likely to have easy access to such services (Stanley, Amato et al., 2006). Thus, better access to basic relationship education, especially programs with a focus on communication skills training and commitment, would be beneficial to cohabiting couples.

United States Census Bureau data show that at least 40% of cohabiting couples have children (Fields & Casper, 2001), adding an extra layer of complication that traditional relationship education typically has not been addressed. In many cases, the children are not the biological children of both partners, but rather children by previous partners. Especially in the context of unmarried relationships, having children by previous partners can cause feelings of jealousy and distrust if parents continue to have parenting relationships with their previous partners (see Hill, 2007; Monte, 2007). Relationship education curricula could target such issues directly and help couples discuss their expectations about contact with previous partners. More generally, having children (either together or by previous partners) also means that cohabiting partners must parent together. Parenting and co-parenting skills should therefore be incorporated into relationship education materials for cohabiting couples.

Couple Therapy with Cohabiting Couples

Therapeutic interventions could also benefit from greater consideration of cohabitation dynamics and patterns. Couple therapists are likely seeing more and more cohabiting couples in their practices. Cohabiting couples are different from married couples in a number of ways and the most significant difference may be in terms of the salience of commitment issues. In the US, cohabitation represents an ambiguous commitment between partners and to their communities (see Heuveline & Timberlake, 2004). Cohabiting partners may have unidentified or unspoken differences about the meaning of cohabitation and future goals for the relationship. Hence, couple therapists who are used to working with married couples need to realize that cohabiting couples may have special needs with regard to commitment. Few cohabiting couples who enter a therapy office will have decided what their futures will look like. Or, one partner may have decided while the other is ambivalent. In our experience, it is sometimes difficult for a couple to directly acknowledge this core relationship issue; the less dedicated partner may not wish to upset the *status quo* and the more dedicated partner may wish to retain some level of denial about the reality of the situation. Of course, the therapy issues will depend on the specific needs of the couple, but therapists seeing cohabiting couples may need to make space for conversations about commitment, differences in partners' commitment levels, and plans for the future of the relationship.

Marital Therapy

In terms of therapy with couples who are already married, the research and ideas presented here may have important implications, as well. A colleague recently asked us whether we would do anything differently in marital therapy based on a couple's premarital cohabitation history. On the surface, it seems as though what we know from research about cohabitation would be irrelevant to couples who are already married. Yet, couples who cohabited before making a decision to marry may have special needs around commitment dynamics and the ways in which they make decisions in their relationships, as well as higher levels of risk. Those who may have been strongly influenced by constraints in their transition to marriage could encounter problems related to commitment later on in their marriages. Attributions for why one is in a relationship that is based more on inertia (e.g., we got married because we were already living together) may translate into difficulty following through on commitments made later on (Stanley, Rhoades et al., 2006). Further, given that cohabitations that began before strong, mutually clear commitment to marriage had developed are more prone to asymmetries in marital dedication (Rhoades et al., 2006), such couples may experience ongoing power struggles, as it is generally believed that he or she who is least committed has the most power (Stanley, 2005). (This idea is a direct extension of Waller's (1937) principle of least interest.) Based on this reasoning, we have wondered whether a couple who experienced a significant number of constraints around the transition to marriage might benefit from making a recommitment to their decision to be married. Making a new, mutual commitment, even if it comes late in the relationship, may help a couple follow through on commitment to marriage when times are tough.

Conclusion

The rise in rates of cohabitation has widespread implications for practitioners who work with couples or with individuals about relationship issues. The meaning of marriage has historically been much clearer than the meaning of cohabitation is today. In the US, cohabitation is an ambiguous relationship stage in many ways. For some couples cohabitation means a long-term commitment to a future together, for others it may symbolize little more than being roommates. This ambiguity complicates clinical practice because practitioners cannot be sure that even partners share the same sense of what a cohabiting relationship means. This chapter has reviewed recent research on cohabitation (and specially the premarital cohabitation effect) and provides recommendations for using this research in relationship education programs and interventions for individuals and couples.

References

Amato, P. R., & Rogers, S. J. (1999). Do attitudes toward divorce affect marital quality? *Journal of Family Issues, 20*(1), 69–86.

Brown, S. L., & Booth, A. (1996). Cohabitation versus marriage: A comparison of relationship quality. *Journal of Marriage and Family, 58*(3), 668–678.

Brownridge, D. A., & Halli, S. S. (2000). "Living in sin" and sinful living: Toward filling a gap in the explanation of violence against women. *Aggression and Violent Behavior, 5*(6), 565–583.

Bumpass, L. L., & Lu, H.-H. (2000). Trends in cohabitation and implications for children's family contexts in the United States. *Population Studies, 54*(1), 29–41.

Bumpass, L. L., Sweet, J. A., & Cherlin, A. (1991). The role of cohabitation in declining rates of marriage. *Journal of Marriage and Family, 53*, 913–927.

Cohan, C. L., & Kleinbaum, S. (2002). Toward a greater understanding of the cohabitation effect: Premarital cohabitation and marital communication. *Journal of Marriage and Family, 64*(1), 180–192.

DeMaris, A., & Rao, V. (1992). Premarital cohabitation and subsequent marital stability in the United States: A reassessment. *Journal of Marriage and Family, 54*(1), 178–190.

Fields, J. (2004). *America's families and living arrangements: March 2003.* Current Population Report, P20-553. Washington, DC: US Census Bureau.

Fields, J., & Casper, L. (2001). *America's families and living arrangements: March 2000.* Current Population Report, P20-537. Washington, DC: US Census Bureau.

Forste, R., & Tanfer, K. (1996). Sexual exclusivity among dating, cohabiting, and married women. *Journal of Marriage and Family, 58*, 33–47.

Glenn, N. D. (2005). *With this ring: A national survey on marriage in America.* Gaithersburg, MD: National Fatherhood Organization.

Halford, W. K., Markman, H. J., Kline, G. H., & Stanley, S. M. (2003). Best practice in couple relationship education. *Journal of Marital and Family Therapy, 29*(3), 385–406.

Halford, W. K., Sanders, M. R., & Behrens, B. C. (2001). Can skills training prevent relationship problems in at-risk couples? Four-year effects of a behavioral relationship education program. *Journal of Family Psychology, 15*(4), 750–768.

Heuveline, P., & Timberlake, J. M. (2004). The role of cohabitation in family formation: The United States in comparative perspective. *Journal of Marriage and Family, 66*(5), 1214–1230.

Hill, H. D. (2007). Stepping out: Infidelity and sexual jealousy among unmarried parents. In P. England & K. Edin (Eds.), *Unmarried couples with children* (pp. 84–103). New York: Russell Sage.

Johnson, M. P., Caughlin, J. P., & Huston, T. L. (1999). The tripartite nature of marital commitment: Personal, moral, and structural reasons to stay married. *Journal of Marriage and Family, 61*(1), 160–177.

Johnson, C. A., Stanley, S. M., Glenn, N. D., Amato, P. R., Nock, S. L., Markman, H. J., et al. (2002). *Marriage in Oklahoma: 2001 baseline statewide survey on marriage and divorce (S02096 OKDHS)*. Oklahoma City, OK: Oklahoma Department of Human Services.

Kamp Dush, C. M., Cohan, C. L., & Amato, P. R. (2003). The relationship between cohabitation and marital quality and stability: Change across cohorts? *Journal of Marriage and Family, 65*(3), 539–549.

Kiernan, K. (2002). Cohabitation in Western Europe: Trends, issues, and implications. In A. Booth & A. C. Crouter (Eds.), *Just living together: Implications of cohabitation on families, children, and social policy* (pp. 3–31). Mahwah, NJ: Lawrence Erlbaum.

Kline, G. H., Stanley, S. M., Markman, H. J., Antonio Olmos-Gallo, P., St. Peters, M., Whitton, S. W., et al. (2004). Timing is everything: Pre-engagement cohabitation and increased risk for poor marital outcomes. *Journal of Family Psychology, 18*(2), 311–318.

Lindsay, J. M. (2000). An ambiguous commitment: Moving into a cohabiting relationship. *Journal of Family Studies, 6*(1), 120–134.

Manning, W. D., & Smock, P. J. (2005). Measuring and modeling cohabitation: New perspectives from qualitative data. *Journal of Marriage and Family, 67*, 989–1002.

Monte, L. M. (2007). Blended but not the Bradys: Navigating unmarried multiple partner fertility. In P. England & K. Edin (Eds.), *Unmarried couples with children* (pp. 183–203). New York: Russell Sage.

Pearson, M., Stanley, S. M., & Kline, G. H. (2005). *Within my reach leader manual*. Denver, CO: PREP.

Rhoades, G. K., Stanley, S. M., & Markman, H. J. (2006). Pre-engagement cohabitation and gender asymmetry in marital commitment. *Journal of Family Psychology, 20*, 553–560.

Rhoades, G. K., Stanley, S. M., & Markman, H. J. (2009). Couples' reasons for cohabitation: Associations with individual well-being and relationship quality. *Journal of Family Issues, 30*, 233–258.

Smock, P. J. (2000). Cohabitation in the United States: An appraisal of research themes, findings, and implications. *Annual Review of Sociology, 26*, 1–20.

Stanley, S. M. (2005). *The power of commitment: A guide to active, lifelong love*. San Francisco: Jossey-Bass.

Stanley, S. M., Amato, P. R., Johnson, C. A., & Markman, H. J. (2006). Premarital education, marital quality, and marital stability: Findings from a large, random, household survey. *Journal of Family Psychology, 20*, 117–126.

Stanley, S. M., & Markman, H. J. (1992). Assessing commitment in personal relationships. *Journal of Marriage and Family, 54*, 595–608.

Stanley, S. M., Rhoades, G. K., & Markman, H. J. (2006). Sliding vs. deciding: Inertia and the premarital cohabitation effect. *Family Relations, 55*, 499–509.

Stanley, S. M., Whitton, S. W., Low, S. M., Markman, H. J., & Clements, M. L. (2006). Sacrifice as a predictor of marital outcomes. *Family Process, 45*, 289–303.

Stanley, S. M., Whitton, S. W., & Markman, H. J. (2004). Maybe I do: Interpersonal commitment and premarital or nonmarital cohabitation. *Journal of Family Issues, 25*(4), 496–519.

Teachman, J. (2003). Premarital sex, premarital cohabitation and the risk of subsequent marital dissolution among women. *Journal of Marriage and Family, 65*(2), 444–455.

Thomson, E., & Colella, U. (1992). Cohabitation and marital stability: Quality or commitment? *Journal of Marriage and Family, 54*(2), 259–267.

Waller, W. (1937). The rating and dating complex. *American Sociological Review, 2*, 727–734.

Whitton, S. W., Stanley, S. M., & Markman, H. J. (2002). Sacrifice in romantic relationships: An exploration of relevant research and theory. In H. T. Reiss, M. A. Fitzpatrick & A. L. Vangelisti (Eds.), *Stability and change in relationship behavior across the lifespan* (pp. 156–181). Cambridge, MA: Cambridge University Press.

Woods, L. N., & Emery, R. E. (2002). The cohabitation effects on divorce: Causation or selection? *Journal of Divorce and Remarriage, 37*(3–4), 101–119.

Galena K. Rhoades
Department of Psychology
2155 S. Race Street
Denver, CO 80208
USA
E-mail: grhoades@du.edu

New Approaches to Assessment

Power and Arousal

New Methods for Assessing Couples

Brian Baucom

University of California, Los Angeles, CA, USA

Abstract

Power and emotional arousal are well-documented correlates of relationship quality. Existing work on power has used one of two assessment techniques, either self-report questionnaires or time-consuming behavioral coding; likewise, existing work on emotional arousal has generally been based on either invasive physiological measures or self-report questionnaires. Though these methods of capturing power and arousal have led to a rich line of discovery, each is subject to limitations that restrict when and how each can be used. This chapter describes new methods for assessing power processes and encoded arousal during interaction that circumvent the restrictions of traditional methods. Example applications of these methodologies in studies of the demand/withdraw interaction pattern and response to couple therapy are presented. Results of the example applications are briefly discussed, and future directions for the study of romantic relationships using these approaches to measure power and emotional arousal are offered.

> "The fundamental concept in social science is Power, in the same sense in which Energy is the fundamental concept in physics." – Bertram Russell

As epitomized by Russell's observation, couple researchers and therapists have long considered power to be a central aspect of romantic relationships. Results of empirical studies have supported this assumption, documenting many significant correlations between aspects of power and relationship functioning. The interactional use of power, or power processes (Cromwell & Olson, 1975), has been found to have particularly important consequences for relationship quality. Though much significant progress has been made in the study of power processes in romantic relationships, standard methods for assessing power have imposed limitations on many studies. Recent advances in the field of computational linguistics provide alternative methods for studying power processes that overcome many of the limitations of standard assessment tools.

The importance of conflict-related physiological arousal for relationship functioning has been introduced more recently in relationship science and practice. A host of physiological measures (such as heart rate, skin conductance, blood pressure, and cortisol (see Kiecolt-Glaser & Newton, 2001 for review)) have been found to be associated with overall relationship quality. While these measures are well-validated indices of arousal, the equipment and methodology required to capture the data for these measures makes them impractical for many researchers and in some research designs. Vocal parameters of speech are well-validated, alternative measures of arousal that have recently been applied to the study of romantic relationships and are practical options for many researchers for use in a wide array of experimental designs.

This chapter will first briefly review the importance of power and arousal in romantic relationships. Alternative methodologies for assessing power and arousal will then be described in detail. The goals of these sections are to provide the reader with: (1) an understanding of the requirements for collection of the necessary data for these methods, (2) basic knowledge of the way each of these methods generates a summary score along with the substantive meaning of the summary score, (3) description of recent applications of these methods in treatment-seeking and community couples, and (4) suggestions for future studies of power and arousal in romantic relationships using these methodologies.

Power

Russell neatly captures the essence of interactional power in romantic relationships by likening power to energy. Interactional power is the means by which influence is achieved and things are made to happen in a relationship. Romantic relationships are often one of, if not the, most important relationships in adulthood. Much of this importance is born of the fundamental property of exclusivity in monogamous relationships; they are the only relationship that has the potential to meet many important needs. When a romantic relationship is not meeting the needs of one or both partners, power processes are the ways that partners attempt to change their relationships to better meet their needs. Power processes are also used to resolve conflict. Most theoretical perspectives on relationships assume that all relationships will have to negotiate conflict, and there is consensus among couple researchers and therapists that the process of resolving conflict, i.e., the way that partners use power, is a significant aspect of relationship quality.

A substantial body of empirical evidence has documented significant associations between interactional power and relationship quality. A number of specific power processes have been tied to overall relationship satisfaction. For example, using fewer indirect, fewer unilateral strategies, more direct, and more bilateral strategies have been found to be associated with greater relationship satisfaction (e.g., Rosenbluth & Steil, 1995).

Measures

Existing work on power processes has generally used either self-report measures or observational coding schemes. Though these methods have been used in a large number of studies of power processes, they are problematic in several important and meaningful ways. As is the case with many self-report measures, agreement across spouses on power processes is typically low to minimal (e.g., Butterfield & Lewis, 2002). The frequently used self-report measures of power processes appear to be much better indicators of individual perspectives on power processes and less effective measures of actual use of power. Observational coding methods are highly time intensive. Many observational measures of power processes generate data for each action sequence, such as a talk turn, during an interaction. Given that a typical 10-minute conversation contains anywhere between 100 and 300 talk turns, the amount of time needed to code interactions using such time intensive measures makes coding a large number of interactions in this fashion impractical and very expensive.

Linguistic Analysis

An alternative method for assessing power processes is to use objective, observational measures of actual interactions that are not dependent on coders, such as linguistic analysis. Linguistic analysis treats the verbal content of an interaction as a behavior in and of itself that carries with it important psychological meaning beyond just the semantic meaning of each word (Atkins, 2006).

One highly reliable and efficient method of conducting linguistic analysis is to use computational linguistic programs. Computational linguistic programs measure a set of parameters, such as the number of negatively valenced words, within a sample of text, such as the transcript of an interaction. They are ideal methods for the analysis of power processes because they can quickly and objectively quantify power-related verbal behaviors over the course of an entire interaction.

Another important aspect of studying power processes by means of linguistic analysis is that linguistic analysis is flexible and adaptable to studying power processes from both a microanalytic and a macroanalytic perspective. Microanalytic measures of power processes are based on discrete behaviors, such as using specific words, or enacting specific behaviors, such as interrupting. One frequently occurring microanalytic measure of power are hedges, which are words or phrases that indicate uncertainty or weaken the strength of a statement. Examples of hedges are the modal verbs (would, could, and should) and short phrases such as "a little bit," "sort of," and "kind of." Research has shown that the more often an interlocutor uses hedges, the lower that person's power and the less powerful his or her message. For example, less frequent hedging has been judged as more persuasive in a number of different types of language samples, including written as well as spoken messages advertising new products (Areni & Sparks, 2005), and tape recordings of crisis intervention phone calls (Bradac & Mulac, 1984).

Word Counting Programs

Word counting programs, such as Linguistic Inquiry and Word Count (LIWC; Pennebaker, Francis, & Booth, 2001), are a good option for measuring microanalytic power processes like hedges in a transcript because existing research has generated large lists of specific hedges that can be used to define exactly which words and short phrases LIWC should count. When LIWC is used to analyze a transcript, the summary score it generates represents the percentage of the total words that the parameter of interest accounts for in the sample of analyzed text. For example, a hedge score of 0.1 would mean that one in every ten words was a hedge.

In contrast to the specific behaviors that are of interest in a microanalytic approach, macroanalytic power processes, or influence tactics, are broad and general tactics for creating influence during an interaction. Kipnis and colleagues (e.g., Kipnis & Schmidt, 1988) proposed a parsimonious, one-dimensional model of influence tactics which suggests that influence tactics can be thought of in terms of one primary dimension, the amount of freedom that tactics leave influences targets to respond to influence attempts. The two poles of this dimension are referred to as hard and soft. Hard tactics are controlling and coercive, leaving the target of influence very little freedom of choice when responding while soft influence tactics are collaborative and less restrictive, leaving the target of influence greater freedom in responding. More frequent use of soft influence tactics and less frequent use of hard influence tactics are typically associated with having greater power. For example, individuals who use hard influence tactics more often have significantly lower salaries, and therefore lower power, compared to others who have the same position and use fewer hard influence tactics (Kipnis & Schmidt, 1988).

Latent Semantic Analysis

Word counting programs are not a viable alternative for measuring influence tactics as the complexity of the phrases and statements used to create influence is beyond their programming capacity. What is needed is an objective method for determining the contextual meaning of words and phrases. Latent semantic analysis (LSA; Landauer, Foltz, & Laham, 1998) is one option for conducting context sensitive analyses of text.

The underlying idea in LSA is not all that different from LIWC. The goal of both approaches is to give meaning to the words that interlocutors use in a conversation. In LIWC, words are grouped *a priori* into categories by a researcher based on his or her theoretical notions about language use. In LSA, words are described by a number of empirically derived factors rather than being grouped into categories.

LSA accomplishes this by using a "semantic space" to derive the meanings of words. A semantic space is a large compilation of text that was generated and analyzed by the creators and developers of the LSA program. For example, the literature semantic space is composed of 5.7 million words and 104,852 terms from 942,425 works of English and American literature. LSA derives the meanings of words by analyzing the contexts that words appear in and are absent from in a semantic space. For example, suppose that a speaker said "I love you" and "I care about you" repeatedly. LSA would be able to determine that the words love and care meant similar things, or, in other words, score highly on the same semantic factor.

LSA uses the factors defined by the semantic space to compare samples of text for similarity. The central role of the semantic space in the comparison of text samples makes it very important to select an appropriate semantic space. One way to make sure that a semantic space is appropriate is to find out the words LSA associates with a given text sample. For example, suppose you are interested in hard influence tactics. It is possible to generate a text sample that describes methods that a person might try to use hard influence tactics (e.g., commanding and claiming authority) and have LSA tell you the words that it associates with that text sample in a given semantic space using a near neighbor analysis. If the words that LSA generates are consistent with an experimenter's conceptual understanding of hard influence tactics, such as superiority and disregard, then one can be confident that LSA is understanding a text passage in the intended way in that semantic space.

Mathematically, LSA relies upon singular value decomposition to represent a semantic space in terms of a greatly reduced number of factors and to compare samples of text for similarity. Singular value decomposition is a statistical technique that is similar to the data reduction techniques used in factor analysis. The end result of this process is a matrix that approximates the original raw data using a reduced number of dimensions. This property is important because it allows LSA to estimate the similarity of words that do not actually appear together in any of the contexts used in the analysis (Landauer et al., 1998).

Once the semantic space has been analyzed and reduced to a smaller number of factors, LSA uses these factors to compare two samples of text by calculating the dot product of the text samples' factor scores as defined by the semantic space. One way to conceptualize this phase is to think about the factors in a semantic space as subscales of a measure. It is possible to get a score on each factor, or subscale, for the passages of interest with greater length indicating greater presence of that factor in the text passage. Then these measurements for each passage can be combined into a single score by calculating a dot product. A dot product represents the magnitude and direction of the resultant matrix that is created when two matrices are combined. Therefore, the dot product for similar samples of text is higher than the dot product for dissimilar samples of text.

LSA has been used for a number of purposes and a thorough review of these efforts is beyond the scope of this chapter (see Landauer et al., 1998 for a review). The most pertinent set of findings involving LSA to its use as a measure of influence tactics is related to demonstrations that LSA is able to approximate the similarity of the contextual meanings of passages to a degree that is highly similar with human judgments. Landauer, Laham, and Foltz (1998) used LSA to assign holistic quality scores to essays written by students. A number of essays were graded by experts and used as standards for comparison in LSA for a number of additional essays on a wide variety of topics, such as physiology, psychology, and American history. Grades were assigned by clustering groups of essays that had very similar dot products. The grades assigned in this manner were more highly correlated with individual experts than the experts' ratings were correlated with one another.

Linguistic Analysis and the Demand/Withdraw Interaction Pattern

Baucom (2008) used these linguistic approaches to explore associations between the demand/withdraw interaction pattern and power processes in treatment-seeking and community couples. The demand/withdraw interaction pattern occurs when one partner, the demander, nags, criticizes, or complains to the other in an attempt to create change, whereas the other partner, the withdrawer, withdraws from or terminates the interaction in response (Christensen, 1988). Frequent occurrence of the demand/withdraw interaction pattern has been shown characteristic of distressed relationships. Power has been hypothesized to be an important component of the occurrence of demand/withdraw behavior as well as of the tendency for partners to assume behavioral roles, i.e., the likelihood of being a demander versus a withdrawer, when engaging in the interaction pattern (see Eldridge & Christensen, 2002 for a review). The treatment-seeking couples were severely and stably distressed married, heterosexual couples who took part in a treatment outcome study of two couple therapies (Christensen et al., 2004). The community couples were moderately satisfied to moderately dissatisfied married and dating heterosexual couples, lesbian couples, and gay male couples. Demand/withdraw behavior was observationally measured in two identically structured conflict interactions using similar coding systems in both samples of couples. Finally, power processes were assessed in the same manner in both samples of couples. Microanalytic power processes were assessed using observationally coded interruptions and hedges (measured using LIWC); macroanalytic power processes were assessed using hard and soft influence tactics (measured using LSA).

The total amount of demand/withdraw behavior exhibited by couples in both samples was significantly associated with hedge use and soft influence tactic use in both samples. Specifically, greater frequency of hedge use and higher levels of soft influence tactic use were associated with lower levels of total demand/withdraw behavior in both samples. More frequent interrupting behavior and higher levels of hard influence tactic use were significantly associated with higher levels of demand/withdraw in the treatment-seeking sample, but these results did not replicate in the community sample. There were no significant differences in the associations between total demand/withdraw behavior and power processes across couple types in the community sample.

Baucom (2008) also examined associations between the distribution of power processes across partners and the tendency of partners to take on either demanding or withdrawing roles during interactions. Demanders were found to use significantly more hard influence tactics than withdrawers in both samples. Demanders were also significantly more likely to use hedges and soft influence tactics than withdrawers but only in the community sample. Relative interrupting behavior was not associated with demand/withdraw roles in either sample. There were no significant differences in the associations between demand/withdraw roles across couple type in the community sample.

Taken together, these results indicate that demand/withdraw behavior is associated with both microanalytic and macroanalytic power processes. Sharing power, demonstrated through more frequent use of hedges and greater use of soft influence tactics, was associated with lower levels of demand/withdraw behavior while asserting power, demonstrated through more frequent use of interruptions and greater use of hard influence, was associated with higher levels of demand/withdraw behavior.

Sharing and asserting power by these linguistic means is likely to be involved in the demand/withdraw interaction pattern by being associated with reactance, or doing the opposite of what was requested. A problematic aspect of demand/withdraw is that when partners feel pressured to make a change, they often attempt to resist making that change by becoming more extreme in their own perspective, which is frequently the opposite of what was requested. Sharing power is likely to be associated with lower levels of demand/withdraw behavior by reducing the tendency of partners to do the opposite of what was requested. Consistent with this notion, using lower levels of hard influence tactics and higher levels of soft influence tactics has been found to be associated with lower levels of reactance (Blickle, 2003).

Power processes were also associated with the behavioral roles that partners assume when engaging in demand/withdraw behavior. Demanders used more hard influence tactic language than withdrawers. This finding suggests that when demanders ask for a change from their partners, they do so by frequently using strong emotional terms and by leaving very little room for negotiation in their request. It is also consistent with the finding discussed above that demonstrates that using hard influence tactics is an ineffective strategy for creating influence and is likely to result in the target of influence doing the opposite of what was requested (Blickle, 2003).

Arousal

The physiological arousal level of partners during conflictual interactions has been linked to concurrent and long-term relationship functioning in a large number of studies (see Kiecolt-Glaser & Newton, 2001 for review). Higher levels of arousal are associated with lower levels of concurrent relationship satisfaction and with poorer long-term relationship satisfaction and stability (e.g., Levenson & Gottman, 1985). Arousal level has also been hypothesized to be related to specific conflict behaviors, such as the demand/withdraw interaction pattern. Gottman and Levenson's (1988) escape conditioning model suggests that when a partner's arousal level gets too intense, he or she may use withdrawal as a method for lowering his or her arousal level by separating from the arousing stimulus, the conflict.

Measures

The measures of physiological arousal typically used in studies of romantic relationships include indices such as blood pressure, heart rate, skin conductance, and cortisol. These measures are complicated, time consuming, and expensive to collect and additionally they are removed from the process of communication. The invasive nature of the equipment and setup necessary for collecting these measures does not make them good candidates for collection during conflict interactions or therapy sessions. An alternative measure of arousal, fundamental frequency (F_0) is easily collected, noninvasive, and more directly involved in the process of communication and has been shown to be associated with traditional measures of physiological arousal, such as heart rate, skin conductance, and blood pressure, under conditions of psychological distress (Johannes, Petrovitsh Salnitski, Gunga, & Kirsch, 2000). Fundamental frequency refers to the pattern of vibration created by the vocal folds during phonation when the larynx regulates the outward flow of air from the lungs and is highly correlated with perceived pitch (e.g., Juslin & Scherer, 2005).

Fundamental frequency can be calculated for speakers in an interaction by analyzing a digital recording of the interaction using Praat (Boersma & Weenink, 2005), a free Windows based program available on Internet (http://www.praat.org/). No additional equipment is required beyond a good quality audio recording device and a computer. Many, if not all, experimental protocols that involve interaction include a method for recording interactions that minimizes couples' awareness of the recording equipment. In contrast, standard physiological measures of arousal typically use highly distracting and invasive apparatus, such as electrodes. The minimal, noninvasive data collection requirements of F_0 make it ideal for measuring arousal in interactions while minimizing the impact of data collection on interactions.

Another advantage of F_0 is that it is directly involved in the process of communication itself. While there is solid evidence that standard measures of physiological arousal are related to communication behaviors, none of the standard measures of physiological arousal actually communicate information from one person to another. Given the assumption that partners are not only behaving based on their own level of arousal but also reacting to their partners' levels of arousal, it is worth noting that F_0 allows researchers to measure arousal using information that is known to both parties in an interaction.

The use of F_0 as a measure of encoded arousal grew out of the basic emotion literature. Scherer and colleagues (see Juslin & Scherer, 2005 for a review) conducted a number of studies in an attempt to establish "vocal fingerprints" for different emotions. Though specific patterns of vocal parameters do not appear to reliably differentiate emotions, increased F_0 has been shown to be a reliable indicator of increased arousal across a wide variety of emotions (both positive and negative) using several different methodological paradigms.

Some of the earliest studies of F_0 and arousal utilized recordings made during naturally occurring events. For example, Williams and Stevens (1969) analyzed recordings of conversations between pilots and air traffic controllers prior to fatal crashes of the aircraft involved. Mean F_0 was found to increase over time relative to a baseline measure, calculated before the onset of the event that led to the crash, for both pilots and aircraft controllers (Williams & Stevens, 1969).

Similar results to those found in studies of naturally occurring stressors have been found in studies that asked participants to portray emotions while reading an emotionally neutral script. For example, Banse and Scherer (1996) asked 12 German actors to convey hot anger, cold anger, panic, anxiety, despair, sadness, elation, happiness, interest, boredom, shame, pride, disgust, and contempt while reading a paragraph of nonsense words. Normalized mean F_0 values were found to be positive for hot anger, cold anger, panic, despair, and elation; normalized mean F_0 values were found to be negative for anxiety, sadness, happiness, boredom, shame, pride, disgust, and contempt. With the exception of contempt, more intense versions of similar positive and negative emotions, e.g., panic and anxiety, elation and happiness, were found to have higher mean F_0 values.

Induction studies of F_0 have used several methodologies for experimentally manipulating arousal level. The most frequently used strategy has been to have participants complete some sort of stressful task or to view affect laden images in a laboratory setting. Bachorowski and Owren (1995) asked participants to judge whether two words were real or nonsense words. Stress was created by presenting the two words for a short enough period of time that participants were unable to be certain of the accuracy of their responses. Participants received feedback after each trial on the accuracy of their answer. Congruency between correct responses and positive feedback induced positive emotions while incongruence between response and feedback and difficulty with the task induced negative emotions. Mean F_0 was significantly elevated for both men and women during the stressful task relative to their baseline values.

It is important to note that there are several different indices of F_0, including mean, maximum, floor, range, and variability, which have been found to be related to arousal level. Mean F_0 has the largest amount of evidence linking it to arousal. In a recent authoritative chapter on the use of F_0 as a measure of arousal, Juslin and Scherer (2005) recommended the use of F_0 range. Future research would likely benefit for the inclusion of both mean F_0 and F_0 range to allow comparison of findings with existing studies that used mean F_0 and to allow transition to a "cleaner" index of F_0.

Fundamental Frequency and the Demand/Withdraw Interaction Pattern

Baucom (2008) examined the associations between arousal, measured using mean F_0, and demand/withdraw in the same sample of treatment-seeking and community couples described above in the section on power. Mean F_0 was found to be associated with overall demand/withdraw behavior in both samples of couples. Specifically, higher levels of mean F_0 were associated with higher levels of total demand/withdraw behavior. Differences in mean F_0 were also found to be associated with the tendency to take on a demanding or a withdrawing role during conflict. Directly opposite of what would be predicted by the escape conditioning model, demanders were found to have significantly higher F_0 than withdrawers in the treatment-seeking sample. There was a nonsignificant trend of approximately the same magnitude in the same direction in the community sample. No significant differences were found across couple types in the community sample in the associations between F_0 and either total demand/withdraw or tendency to take on a demanding or a withdrawing role during conflict.

These results are consistent with a large body of empirical evidence that has linked conflictual interaction to arousal (see Kiekcolt-Glaser & Newton, 2001 for a review) and with the hypothesis that demand/withdraw behavior is associated with arousal level. However, the finding that higher levels of F_0 are associated with an increased tendency to assume a demanding role is directly opposite of what would be predicted for the escape conditioning model.

One possible explanation for this counter-intuitive finding is that arousal contributes to demand/withdraw roles in a more complicated manner than was hypothesized. The hypothesis that withdrawers would be more aroused than demanders was based on a model which suggests that when individuals experience high levels of physiological arousal during interaction, they may withdraw from the interaction in an attempt to remove themselves from the arousing stimulus. Because withdrawers withdrew, they were, *ipso facto*, more aroused. No attention was paid to the emotion corresponding to arousal for either demanders or withdrawers in this model.

Demanders and withdrawers are engaging in different behaviors stemming from fundamentally different experiences. Demanders feel that their expectations are not being met to a degree that is so distressing that they engage in pursuing behaviors to force a change to happen. This sort of experience is likely to be accompanied by hot emotions such as anger and frustration. In contrast, withdrawers are likely to feel annoyed by and anxious about the frequent requests they are denying. A multilevel model of emotions associated with demanding and withdrawing behaviors using self-report emotion data collected after each interaction with the Post-Discussion Questionnaire (PDQ; Heavey, 1991) in the community sample provided support for this hypothesis. The results demonstrated that anger is only associated with demanding behavior while controlling for anxiety and that anxiety is only associated with withdrawing behavior while controlling for anger. While these results must be considered as tentative given their exploratory nature, they suggest that arousal may be associated with different emotional states for demanders and withdrawers.

Fundamental Frequency and Response to Couple Therapy

Results of a randomized clinical trial of two behaviorally based couple therapies, integrative behavioral couple therapy (IBCT; Christensen & Jacobson, 2000) and traditional behavioral couple therapy (TBCT; Jacobson & Margolin, 1979), have shown that both therapies create improvement in relationship functioning that is maintained over a period of 2 years after treatment termination (Christensen, Atkins, Yi, Baucom, & George, 2006). Atkins and colleagues (2005) examined demographic, intrapersonal, and interpersonal variables taken from a pretreatment assessment as predictors of treatment response at termination. Treatment condition, gender, years married, distress level, and a sexual satisfaction by treatment condition interaction emerged as significant predictors of the rate of improvement in relationship satisfaction (Atkins et al., 2005).

Recent work by Baucom, Atkins, Simpson, and Christensen (2009) examined prediction of treatment response 2 years after termination in the same randomized clinical trial of IBCT and TBCT using the same set of pretreatment variables as Atkins et al. (2005) with the addition of F_0 range and several other empirically based predictors from the same pretreatment assessment. Study findings showed a strong predictive relationship between wife's pretreatment F_0 and 2-year outcome for moderately distressed couples in both therapies. Higher levels of arousal during pretreatment conflict interactions were associated with less positive response to both therapies. For every standard deviation above the mean on F_0, couples were over two and a half times more likely to be in the deteriorated category (the worst treatment response category) relative to all other treatment response categories.

The results of this study demonstrate a strong negative association between high levels of pretreatment arousal in response to relationship conflict and less positive long-term response to couple therapy. This finding is consistent with studies that have documented long-term associations between higher levels of conflict-related arousal and an increased likelihood of divorce (e.g., Levenson & Gottman, 1985). While the pathways that link arousal to treatment outcome are currently unknown, it may be that when spouses are highly aroused by their own sources of distress, they are unable to effectively join emotionally with their partners or to problem solve during therapy sessions. The emotional and cognitive demands of therapy may be too great when spouses are already using all of their available coping skills to handle being in a highly aroused emotional state.

Future Directions

Power Processes

Christensen, Jacobson, and Babcock (1995) have suggested that the polarization process is an integral part of what develops into relationship distress in mature relationships. The polarization occurs when individual differences that were initial sources of attraction develop into sources of distress over time. When partners make requests to change those individual differences, they are often met with resistance and frequently result in reactance. When reactance occurs, each partner intensifies both the strength and frequency of his or her requests for or resistance to change. This cycle results in both partners becoming more extreme in their positions, or polarized, over time with each believing more strongly in his or her own point of view and becoming less open to considering his or her partner's perspective.

Viewed through the lens of power, polarization may occur when partners ineffectively use power processes to create changes in their relationships. As noted above, power processes are known to be related to the occurrence of reactance within romantic relationships. It may be that couples who frequently use low levels of hard influence tactics and high levels of soft influence tactics are better able to adapt their relationships to changing demands or circumstances. However, it is not currently known if using particular types of power processes are related to polarization, and, if so, whether certain power processes are protective factors in the long-term stability and quality of romantic relationships or not.

Arousal

Fundamental frequency has interesting potential for further study of arousal in couple therapy. An important component of successful couple therapy is likely to be a reduction of arousal in response to the same conflict area over time. A number of therapies are based on the notion of reducing arousal over time. This is particularly true of behavioral interventions for specific anxiety disorders such as post-traumatic stress disorder. Exposures are interventions designed to gradually decrease the amount of arousal experienced by a client in response to interacting with a feared stimulus. Other forms of therapy also place a great deal of importance on the reduction of arousal over the course of treatment for less well-defined conditions. The notion of a "corrective emotional experience" in time-limited psychodynamic therapy (TLDP; Levenson, 1995) is one such example. It is likely that successful couple therapy also involves reduction of arousal during discussions of long-standing conflict but this possibility is yet to be explored. Fundamental frequency is a good candidate for use as a measure of arousal for this purpose as it has been shown to decrease over time in successful individual therapy (Tolkmitt, Helfrich, Standke, & Scherer, 1982).

References

Areni, C. S., & Sparks, J. R. (2005). Language power and persuasion. *Psychology & Marketing, 22*(6), 507–525.

Atkins, D. (2006). Extension of the topics model to couple interactions. In S. Steenwick (Chair), *The language of relationships: Using computational linguistics to study couples and couple therapy.* Symposium conducted at the annual meeting of the Association of Behavioral and Cognitive Therapies, Chicago, IL.

Atkins, D. C., Berns, S. B., George, W., Doss, B., Gattis, K., & Christensen, A. (2005). Prediction of response to treatment in a randomized clinical trial of marital therapy. *Journal of Consulting and Clinical Psychology, 73*, 893–903.

Bachorowski, J., & Owren, M. J. (1995). Vocal expression of emotion: Acoustic properties of speech are associated with emotional intensity and context. *Psychological Science, 6*(4), 219–224.

Banse, R., & Scherer, K. (1996). Acoustic profiles in vocal emotion expression. *Journal of Personality and Social Psychology, 70*(3), 614–636.

Baucom, B. (2008). *The language of demand/withdraw: Verbal and vocal channels of expression in dyadic interactions*. Unpublished doctoral dissertation, University of California, Los Angeles.

Baucom, B., Atkins, D., Simpson, L., & Christensen, A. (2009). Prediction of response to treatment in a randomized clinical trial of couple therapy: A 2-year follow-up. *Journal of Consulting and Clinical Psychology, 77*, 160–173.

Blickle, G. (2003). Some outcomes of pressure, ingratiation, and rational persuasion used with peers in the workplace. *Journal of Applied Social Psychology, 33*(3), 648–665.

Boersma, P., & Weenink, D. (2005). Praat: Doing phonetics by computer (Version 4.3.27) [Computer program]. Retrieved October 7, 2005, from http://www.praat.org/.

Bradac, J. J., & Mulac, A. (1984). Attributional consequences of powerful and powerless speech styles in a crisis-intervention context. *Journal of Language and Social Psychology, 3*(1), 1–19.

Butterfield, R., & Lewis, M. (2002). Health-related social influence: A social ecological perspective on tactic use. *Journal of Social and Personal Relationships, 19*(4), 505–526.

Christensen, A. (1988). Dysfunctional interaction patterns in couples. In P. Noller & M. A. Fitzpatrick (Eds.), *Perspectives on marital interactions* (pp. 31–52). Clevedon, England: Multilingual Matters.

Christensen, A., Atkins, D. S., Berns, S., Wheeler, J., Baucom, D. H., & Simpson, L. E. (2004). Traditional versus integrative behavioral couple therapy for significantly and chronically distressed married couples. *Journal of Consulting and Clinical Psychology, 72*, 176–191.

Christensen, A., Atkins, D. C., Yi, J., Baucom, D. H., & George, W. H. (2006). Couple and individual adjustment for 2 years following a randomized clinical trial comparing traditional versus integrative behavioral couple therapy. *Journal of Consulting and Clinical Psychology, 74*(6), 1180–1191.

Christensen, A., & Jacobson, N. S. (2000). *Reconcilable differences*. New York: Guilford Press.

Christensen, A., Jacobson, N. S., & Babcock, J. C. (1995). *Integrative behavioral couple therapy*. New York: Guilford Press.

Cromwell, R., & Olson, D. (1975). *Power in families*. Beverly Hills, CA: Sage.

Eldridge, K. A., & Christensen, A. (2002). Demand-withdraw communication during couple conflict: A review and analysis. In P. Noller & J. A. Feeney (Eds.), *Understanding marriage: Developments in the study of couple interaction* (pp. 289–322). New York, NY: Cambridge University Press.

Gottman, J. M., & Levenson, R. W. (1988). *The social psychophysiology of marriage*. Clevedon, England: Multilingual Matters.

Heavey, C. L. (1991). *Causes and consequences of destructive conflicts in romantic relationships: Cognitive, affective, and behavioral predictors of course and outcome*. Unpublished doctoral dissertation, University of California, Los Angeles.

Jacobson, N. S., & Margolin, G. (1979). *Marital therapy: Strategies based on social learning and behavior exchange principles*. New York, NY: Brunner/Mazel.

Johannes, B., Petrovitsh Salnitski, V., Gunga, H., & Kirsch, K. (2000). Voice stress monitoring in space-possibilities and limits. *Aviation, Space, & Environmental Medicine, 71*(9), A58–A65.

Juslin, P., & Scherer, K. (2005). Vocal expression of affect. In J. Harrigan, R. Rosenthal, & K. Scherer (Eds.), *The new handbook of methods in nonverbal behavioral research* (pp. 65–136). New York: Oxford University Press.

Kiecolt-Glaser, J. K., & Newton, T. L. (2001). Marriage and health: His and hers. *Psychological Bulletin, 127*(4), 472–503.

Kipnis, D., & Schmidt, S. M. (1988). Upward-influence styles: Relationship with performance evaluations, salary, and stress. *Administrative Science Quarterly, 33*(4), 528–542.

Landauer, T., Foltz, P., & Laham, D. (1998). Introduction to latent semantic analysis. *Discourse Processes, 25*, 259–284.

Landauer, T. K., Laham, D., & Foltz, P. W. (1998). Learning human-like knowledge by singular value decomposition: A progress report. In M. Jordan, M. Kearns, & S. Solla (Eds.), *Advances in Neural Information Processing Systems 10* (pp. 45–51). Cambridge: MIT Press.

Levenson, H. (1995). *Time-limited psychodynamic therapy: A guide to clinical practice*. New York: Basic Books.

Levenson, R. W., & Gottman, J. M. (1985). Physiological and affective predictors of change in relationship satisfaction. *Journal of Personality and Social Psychology, 49*(1), 85–94.

Pennebaker, J. W., Francis, M. E., & Booth, R. J. (2001). *Linguistic inquiry and word count (LIWC): LIWC 2001*. Mahwah, NJ: Erlbaum.

Rosenbluth, S., & Steil, J. (1995). Predictors of intimacy for women in heterosexual and homosexual couples. *Journal of Social and Personal Relationships, 12*(2), 163–175.

Tolkmitt, F., Helfrich, H., Standke, R., & Scherer, K. (1982). Vocal indicators of psychiatric treatment effects in depressives and schizophrenics. *Journal of Personality and Social Psychology, 35*, 345–350.

Williams, C., & Stevens, K. (1969). On determining the emotional state of pilots during flight: An exploratory study. *Aerospace Medicine, 40*, 1369–1372.

Brian Baucom
Department of Psychology
University of California
Los Angeles
1285 Franz Hall
Box 951563
Los Angeles, CA 90095-1563
USA
E-mail: bbaucom@ucla.edu

Couple/Family-Based Assessment Strategies for Individuals with Psychological Problems

Steffany J. Fredman

National Center for Posttraumatic Stress Disorder, Women's Health Sciences Division, and Boston University School of Medicine, MA, USA

Abstract

A taxonomy for categorizing couple/family-based interventions for individual psychopathology has been in existence for more than a decade, but to date, no framework has been developed to classify assessment strategies within the field of couple/family psychopathology. To address this gap, this chapter offers a heuristic for conceptualizing differences among assessment strategies by distinguishing between those that are broadly applicable across psychological problems (non-disorder-specific strategies) and those that are focal to a particular form of psychopathology (disorder-specific strategies). As reviewed in this chapter, the bulk of family psychopathology research has been conducted using non-disorder-specific instruments that characterize the overall emotional climate of patients' family environments. Less work has been done using disorder-specific measures that assess family processes focal to a particular form of psychopathology. Nonetheless, as suggested subsequently, it is important to include such approaches in the array of available assessment strategies to facilitate the implementation of couple/family-based treatments for individual psychopathology that are as targeted and, therefore, as potent as possible.

It is well known among clinicians that one's interpersonal environment can have a profound impact on that person's functioning and well-being. This is especially true for individuals suffering from psychopathology, where relationships can serve as a resource by helping them address and manage the difficulties associated with their condition, or the relationship can serve as an impediment to recovery by creating high levels of stress or by interfering with behavioral changes that the individual needs to make. Numerous research studies support the idea that the family environments of individuals with psychological disorders do indeed matter and have important implications for treatment outcome, substantiating many of the clinical impressions of therapists working with patients and their families. Accordingly, a variety of couple/family-based interventions have been developed to assist families in which one member is coping with a psychological disorder (Snyder & Whisman, 2003).

As reviewed by Baucom, Kirby, and Kelly (this volume), when one member of a couple or family has an individual psychological problem, the goals from a couple/family perspective are to decrease existing relationship conflicts that serve as a broad stressor and then to use the relationship to help the individual with the disorder make and sustain behavior changes or other needed ways of adapting to their condition. Depending on the extent of coexisting relationship discord and/or disorder-relevant issues that affect the relationship, different types of couple/family-based interventions may be needed. These interventions can take the form of (a) *partner-assisted interventions*, in which the partner or family member functions as a "coach" or surrogate therapist to assist the identified patient with individual behavior change (e.g., helping a depressed person get up at a regular time every day and stay active rather than engage in passive withdrawal); (b) *disorder-specific interventions*, in which treatment attempts to decrease problematic relationship issues focal to the individual's psychopathology (e.g., in the case of obsessive-compulsive disorder (OCD), decreasing partner or family participation in rituals) or increase relationship behaviors that can assist the patient in improving; and (c) *couple therapy*, in which the intervention is used to decrease relationship distress and to promote more harmonious and supportive interactions among family members (Baucom, Shoham, Mueser, Daiuto, & Stickle, 1998).

Corresponding with this investment in creating and disseminating couple/family-based interventions for individual psychopathology, clinical researchers have developed a variety of assessment strategies to help clarify and operationalize therapists' clinical impressions, or even the observations of untrained lay individuals who might say to one another, "This family seems really healthy" or "Something is not right in the way this family relates." This is important because, as a field, we are committed to observing and understanding how people interact with one another so that we can help individuals with psychological problems and their families to experience a better quality of life. The more precise we become at pinpointing the specific domains in which individuals with psychological problems need to make changes and understanding how family members can help with those changes, the better we will be at refining existing couple/family-based interventions so that they are as effective as possible.

In this chapter, I will first offer a framework for conceptualizing differences among assessment strategies in the context of couple/family-based psychopathology research, as informed by existing couple/family-based treatments for individual psychopathology. In particular, I will make a distinction between assessment strategies that are broadly applicable regardless of the specific form of psychopathology and those that are focal to a particular form of psychopathology. To clarify this heuristic, I will first review some well-developed and widely applied measures that may aid clinicians and researchers in characterizing the emotional climate of patients' family environments and how these relate to treatment outcome. I will then discuss assessment strategies that are specific to particular forms of psychopathology, highlighting the fact that this area is not as well developed as the more global measures that can be used across patient populations. An assessment strategy that my colleagues and I developed will be discussed in more detail to provide an example of how to create a measure that assesses family interactional patterns related to a specific form of psychopathology. Finally, I discuss the ways that this approach can help us, as a field, to broaden our array of available assessment strategies so that information from assessment tools can help couple/family-based interventions for individuals with psychopathology be as directed as possible.

Using Couple/Family-Based Interventions for Individual Psychopathology as a Model for Understanding Couple/Family-Based Assessments for Individual Psychopathology

Couple/family-based treatments for individual psychopathology tend to consider simultaneously both the broad emotional climate in which the identified patient resides and particular relationship processes focal to specific conditions. The case of OCD, an anxiety disorder characterized by the presence of intrusive distressing thoughts and/or repetitive, ritualistic behaviors (compulsions), provides an illustration of how relationship processes focal to the disorder can affect the individual's recovery from the condition. In OCD, individuals commonly use rituals or compulsions to help themselves feel less anxious in the moment, and as a result, they are more likely to continue engaging in the rituals over time. Unfortunately, because the individuals either avoid situations that make them feel anxious in the first place or use compulsions to make themselves feel better once they become anxious, they never learn to evaluate the actual degree of risk associated with certain situations and to learn that they are safe. To help address this problem, individually based treatment for OCD usually takes the form of exposure plus response prevention, in which patients are encouraged to confront situations that they are afraid of (the exposure component) without using their usual anxiety-management strategy of compulsions or other ritualistic behaviors (the response prevention component). For treatment to be maximally effective, it is critically important that individuals participating in exposure-based therapies not engage in avoidance or rely on inappropriate safety behaviors like compulsions so that they can fully test out their beliefs about the relative danger or safety of feared situations. Otherwise, they may conclude that they are safe only as a result of their compulsions or other safety behaviors (e.g., someone with OCD believes that the only reason her child is alive and healthy is that she is careful to minimize contamination through avoidance and compulsions).

When patients live in negative environments, couple/family-based treatment targets and attempts to decrease those behaviors in the environment that may serve as a broad, diffuse stressor to the individual with the disorder. However, even in the absence of a negative environment or relationship distress, family members may inadvertently interfere with treatment if they help the patient avoid the very thing that he/she is afraid of. For example, a patient with OCD might be asked to touch various objects in the house that the patient has avoided for years (e.g., dirty dishes and counters) and then not wash his or her hands for some specified period of time afterward. However, if the partner washes the dishes and wipes down the counters so that the patient can be spared discomfort, the potency of the exposure plus response prevention has been decreased because the patient did not learn that he or she is safe despite not using compulsions or other ritualistic safety behaviors. To design an effective treatment for the couple, it is essential to assess these specific ways of interacting so that they can be targeted for change.

As noted above, couple/family-based interventions tend to consider both the broad positive/negative emotional climate the patient resides in and unintended but potentially problematic relationship patterns that may interfere with treatment (e.g., accommodation to symptoms). However, a single *assessment* strategy within the area of couple/family psychopathology has tended to focus on one or the other. There are a variety of possible reasons for this approach, not the least of which is that it is difficult to develop an instrument that is broadly applicable and relevant to a wide variety of psychopathologies and simultaneously assesses interpersonal processes focal to specific disorders. Indeed, this issue has been discussed within the context of classical test theory for many years and has been labeled the *bandwidth-fidelity dilemma*, a reference to the fact that as more songs were recorded onto 33-speed vinyl records, the lower the fidelity or quality of each song on the record (Cronbach & Gleser, 1965). Applied to the field of couple/family functioning and psychopathology, one is confronted with this same challenge in that the more one tries to assess at one time, the lower the quality or fidelity. As a result, within the context of any psychological assessment, one is forced to make an analogous tradeoff: either (a) gather as much broad-based data as possible using tools that are applicable to a wide variety of people and domains but have fewer details about individually specific processes or (b) gather information that is more detailed and individually specific but is less broadly applicable to other disorders or conditions.

Within couple/family psychopathology research, considerations regarding breadth versus depth can arise when trying to select instruments to assess clinically important couple and family processes. One heuristic for thinking about how to choose among available assessment tools in the area of couple/family psychopathology is to consider whether the assessment instrument is applicable across a wide variety of conditions (i.e., a non-disorder-specific assessment tool) or focal to a particular form of psychopathology (i.e., a disorder-specific assessment tool). This parallels the distinction within the couple intervention field between general couple therapies designed to address relationship distress broadly (e.g., cognitive-behavioral couple therapy; Epstein & Baucom, 2002) and partner-assisted or disorder-specific couple/family-based interventions that are designed to address specific processes and issues focal to the particular condition under investigation (e.g., family-focused therapy for bipolar disorder; Miklowitz & Goldstein, 1997).

Both types of assessment instruments are needed, as each offers potentially important clinical information. Regardless of whether one hopes to gather information about the overall emotional climate of the home or information related to family processes focal to a particular form of psychopathology, a variety of approaches can be taken, and some representative strategies are reviewed below.

Non-Disorder-Specific Methods of Assessment

To assess broad-based, global characteristics of the family environment, researchers have used different methods, including interview, self-report, and observational coding of patient-relative interactions. Among non-disorder-specific assessment strategies, it has been common to focus in one way or another on the presence or absence of relationship distress or overall negativity/positivity of the environment in which the patient lives, typically with an emphasis on negative attitudes and behaviors exhibited by family members. A prominent paradigm for examining this is the construct of expressed emotion (EE; Leff & Vaughn, 1985), the extent to which relatives display criticism, hostility, or emotional overinvolvement (EOI) toward patients. Following are several assessment strategies for assessing the overall emotional tone of the family environment, using the framework of EE, beginning with an interview-based instrument.

The gold standard measure of EE is the Camberwell Family Interview (CFI; Vaughn & Leff, 1976), a semi-structured interview conducted with the relative in the patient's absence. Relatives who make a high number of critical comments, exhibit hostility, or display marked EOI are considered to be high in EE. Consistent with the general finding that high levels of criticism and contempt among partners is a potent predictor of poor outcome for couples, a large body of research conducted over more than three decades has found that, across multiple psychiatric populations, patients from High EE families tend to have poorer outcomes than do patients from families low in EE (Butzlaff & Hooley, 1998). This broad-based, non-disorder-specific interview has yielded much understanding and led to efficacious family-based treatments for a number of psychiatric disorders (Baucom et al., 1998).

Self-report measures provide another way to broadly assess the extent of negativity in the home; for example, patients can be asked to share their perceptions of how they interact with relatives. A commonly used self-report measure that quickly and efficiently assesses the global emotional tone of the home is the perceived criticism measure (PCM; Hooley & Teasdale, 1989). The PCM is a one-item measure that asks patients to rate on a 10-point Likert-type scale how critical a relative is of them. On this scale 1 represents "not at all critical" and 10 represents "very critical indeed." Studies with a variety of patient populations support the utility of using a brief self-report measure like the PCM to assess the degree of negativity in the home and make predictions about which patients are at risk for poor outcomes (see Renshaw, 2008 for a review).

Couple/family psychopathology researchers also have relied on direct assessment of patient-relative interactions to investigate the extent to which negative environments and problematic communication patterns characterize the interpersonal relationships of individuals with psychopathology. The general assumption in conducting this type of research is that individuals with psychological problems are going to find it harder to recover from their conditions if they are being chronically stressed by relationship and family conflict. Examples of negative, problematic communication behaviors include family members criticizing one another, having trouble making constructive decisions together, or being unable to de-escalate or redirect negative conversations in a more neutral or positive way.

One of the most commonly used observational measures to assess communication patterns among the families of individuals with psychopathology is the KPI (Kategoriensystem für Partnerschaftliche Interaktion – "Interactional Coding System" – Hahlweg, 2004), which provides a frequency count of positive, negative, and neutral verbal and nonverbal communication behaviors (e.g., criticisms, agreements, problem description, and positive and negative solutions), typically during a 10-minute problem-solving interaction between two family members. Although originally developed in the context of studying marital distress more broadly, the KPI has been widely used in the family psychopathology area as a way of measuring the emotional climate of the patient's family environment through direct assessment of how patients and relatives engage with one another. This is in contrast to relying solely on attitudes and behaviors expressed by the relative in the patient's absence, such as in the CFI, or on patients' questionnaire-based reports of how relatives behave toward them, such as in the PCM.

A large body of research supports the usefulness of observational measures to address questions about basic communication processes in families in which at least one member suffers from a psychiatric condition (see Hahlweg, 2004 for a review). However, simple frequency counts of negative and positive communication between the patient and family member based on the KPI have rarely predicted whether a psychiatric sample will respond to treatment (D. L. Chambless, personal communication, April 6, 2006; K. Hahlweg, personal communication, April 12, 2006). Based on these findings, it appears that a non-disorder-specific observational coding system such as the KPI can readily assess particular communication behaviors that occur between individuals with psychological disorders and their families; however, to predict response to treatment, it might be more useful to observe how patients and family members interact in domains specific to the disorder.

The CFI, PCM, and KPI are representative examples of different methods that can be used to assess the extent of negativity in the family environment across a wide variety of psychiatric conditions. Findings from studies using these instruments clearly underscore the notion that high levels of negativity in the living environment are a general stressor for individuals with psychological difficulties and must be addressed. At the same time, these instruments were not developed to tell us about family processes that are specific to a given disorder that can influence treatment outcome. For instance, the KPI provides researchers with the ability to make detailed ratings about patterns of positive and negative communication that couples and families exhibit, but it was not developed to provide us with ratings of how adaptively or maladaptively family members respond to issues focal to a specific form of psychopathology, such as the tendency to avoid and use inappropriate safety behaviors in anxiety disorders or the inclination to withdraw in depression. To achieve such goals, other more disorder-specific instruments must be developed, as described below.

Disorder-Specific Methods of Assessment

In addition to understanding the basic psychopathology of the condition under investigation and what affected individuals need to do to improve, it is critically important to understand the ways that the condition pulls for certain types of family responses and the effect that relatives' behaviors have on the condition. That is, we need to have a clear idea of the ways that family members are impacted by the disorder and the extent to which family interaction patterns are conducive to facilitating and maintaining changes that the individual needs to make to recover from their disorder. Likewise, we must understand the extent to which family interactions interfere with or undermine the changes the identified patient needs to make. This is important because we will then be in a better position to determine if an individually based psychological intervention will be sufficient to help address the identified patient's problems or if couple/family-based treatment is needed and, if so, how best to implement that treatment.

To understand the impact of particular forms of psychopathology on families and the ways that family members' responses are adaptive or maladaptive for individuals with psychological disorders, it is helpful to have a way of operationalizing these processes. Within couple/family psychopathology research, investigators are beginning to develop tools to help us assess these clinical phenomena as precisely as possible within the context of specific psychiatric conditions so that couple/family-based interventions can be as targeted as possible. The same broad methods used in non-disorder-specific assessment strategies (e.g., interviews, self-report questionnaires, and observed interactions) are appropriate for disorder-specific assessment measures as well. However, there are few currently existing disorder-specific measures. Below I review examples of several disorder-specific measures. I will then discuss why we, as a field, should think about creating more disorder-specific assessment strategies to complement the array of available non-disorder-specific measures.

As noted earlier, clinicians have found that there is a strong pull for family members to participate in compulsions or otherwise alter their own routines to temporarily minimize OCD patients' distress or to decrease conflict with patients. The Family Accommodation Scale (FAS; Calvocoressi et al., 1999) is a clinician-administered interview that is often used as a relative self-report measure to assess the amount of accommodative behaviors that relatives of individuals with OCD engage in. Findings to date indicate that understanding this specific form of family interaction is valuable. For instance, research using the FAS has demonstrated that family accommodation in OCD is related to greater symptom severity and poorer functioning at baseline (Calvocoressi et al., 1999) and greater symptom severity following treatment (Amir, Freshman, & Foa, 2000), substantiating the clinical impressions of many therapists working with the families of individuals with this disorder but also providing a nuanced and detailed understanding of the relation between family behaviors and patient functioning as related to OCD. In turn, these research findings offer clinicians a formalized framework for thinking about family processes to identify and address in treatment.

Within the disorder-specific realm, we can also perform observational coding to examine how family members interact around issues focal to particular forms of psychopathology by using knowledge of the disorder and how it operates within the family. Although this approach has not been commonly used in the field of couple/family psychopathology research, it can be quite fruitful. Following is an example of how we developed a disorder-specific observational coding system, using bipolar disorder as our area of focus.

Bipolar disorder is a severe and recurrent psychiatric disorder characterized by episodes of extreme highs (manias or less severe hypomanias) and lows (depressions). The goal of treatment is to facilitate mood stability, typically by taking mood-stabilizing medication and maintaining a regular routine. Individuals with bipolar disorder are quite susceptible to psychosocial stress, especially stress related to living in a highly negative environment (e.g., Kim & Miklowitz, 2004). Nonetheless, even in the absence of extreme negativity, family members' responses can affect how a person with bipolar disorder recovers from a manic or depressive episode. To determine which behaviors by relatives can facilitate or, conversely, interfere with mood stability, it is important to consider the ways that family members are impacted by the disease and the behaviors that this can pull for in relatives. We can then generate likely behaviors that one might expect to observe in the course of watching patients and relatives interact with one another and make predictions about how these behaviors might, in turn, affect the patient.

There are a number of ways that the severe and episodic nature of bipolar disorder can affect family members. For instance, patients with bipolar disorder may show extremely poor judgment when manic by engaging in spending sprees, reckless driving, extramarital affairs, and they can be at increased risk of suicide when depressed. Further, because of the episodic nature of the illness, family members' roles and responsibilities shift when patients are sick versus well, and relatives often worry that even small changes in patients' emotional states are signs of an impending recurrence. Given the potentially negative consequences to both patients and relatives, in certain instances, relatives who develop a strong investment in patients' remaining well and make efforts to prevent manic or depressive recurrences may be behaving quite reasonably (e.g., reminding patients to take medications, taking over some of patients' responsibilities to reduce patients' stress). However, these same behaviors, if performed to excess or not commensurate with the patient's needs and current level of functioning, may be counterproductive. However, there has been little research conducted regarding the specific circumstances under which these types of behaviors are helpful or, alternatively, unhelpful to patients with bipolar disorder, perhaps because existing family psychopathology measures have focused primarily on criticism and other negative behaviors and were not developed to provide a way of examining behaviors reflecting different types of involvement or their appropriateness or inappropriateness within a disorder-specific manner.

To examine different types of involvement by relatives of individuals with bipolar disorder and the ways that these relate to how patients recover after a manic or depressive episode, we (Fredman, Baucom, Miklowitz, & Stanton, 2008) developed an observational coding system to assess both appropriate and inappropriate emotional involvement. Prior to this study, the only existing observational measure of emotional involvement was a scale that helped to assess the ways that family members could be highly involved in inappropriate ways. This measure was originally developed in a sample of anxious individuals and their relatives (Fredman, Chambless, & Steketee, 2004) and provided separate ratings for relatives' inappropriate intrusiveness (giving unsolicited advice, checking on patients), excessive self-sacrifice (inappropriately putting the patients' needs above their own), and exaggerated displays of emotionality regarding the patients' well-being. However, because we felt that it was sometimes reasonable for relatives of individuals with bipolar disorder to show high levels of unsolicited advice, sacrifice their own well-being to promote the patients' well-being, or demonstrate significant distress when patients are not doing well, we modified the measure so that coders could make ratings for both appropriate *and* inappropriate displays of (a) unsolicited advice giving or checking on the patient (*intrusiveness*); (b) willingness to endure negative consequences as a result of the patient's illness or to sacrifice his or her own well-being to promote the patient's well-being (*self-sacrifice*); and (c) concern for the patient's well-being or identification with the patient (*emotional response*), within the context of bipolar disorder.

This coding system was applied to a sample of recently episodic patients with bipolar disorder and their key caregiving relatives who had participated in one of two family-based treatment outcome studies for the treatment of bipolar disorder (Miklowitz, George, Richards, Simoneau, & Suddath, 2003; Miklowitz, Richards, et al., 2003). To distinguish between appropriate and inappropriate behaviors, coders made judgments based on a general understanding of bipolar disorder and the patient's current level of functioning. This understanding was applied to 10-minute patient-relative problem-solving interactions to assess the extent to which family members' responses were reasonable given the particular circumstances of the patient and family at that moment in time. To be able to train coders unfamiliar with the emotional involvement construct and the ways that it might operate in the context of bipolar disorder, training involved not only readings on emotional involvement and its behavioral manifestations (e.g., Fredman et al., 2004; Leff & Vaughn, 1985) but also extensive education about the psychopathology of bipolar disorder and the relationship issues that it can engender (e.g., Miklowitz & Goldstein, 1997). These considerations were then used to determine if certain behaviors by relatives were appropriate or inappropriate within the context of a particular patient-relative interaction.

For example, because emotional and behavioral stability are key in bipolar disorder, relatives whose behaviors facilitated this by giving something up or doing something the relative did not want to do if it helped the patient in a reasonable way were rated as showing appropriate self-sacrifice. In some families, this took the form of relatives' liquidating investments to help patients pay for mood-stabilizing medications. In others, relatives who did not like to exercise agreed to go for walks with patients to help them combat depression through behavioral activation. Similar judgments were used to decide whether certain behaviors by relatives interfered with emotional stability and were unreasonable in the context of bipolar disorder. For instance, a relative who allowed a patient to live at home rent-free, not work, smoke marijuana, and sleep late into the afternoon even though the patient was capable of working was rated as showing a high level of inappropriate self-sacrifice.

Applying this coding system to interactions between patients with bipolar disorder and family members indicated that it is possible to reliably code different behaviors reflecting emotional involvement and that doing so helps to provide important information about family processes in bipolar disorder. For instance, several of the ratings were related to both the CFI EOI score, the current gold standard measure of emotional involvement/over-involvement, and relatives' self-reports of how they behave toward patients (Fredman et al., 2008). Regarding the latter, relatives who were observed by coders to be appropriately intrusive during the problem-solving task were likely to rate themselves as being "active" toward patients, whereas relatives who were judged by coders to be inappropriately intrusive were likely to rate themselves as "contrarian" and "irritable" and unlikely to rate themselves as "getting along," being "friendly," and being "good-natured" toward patients. In contrast, the CFI EOI score was not related to any of relatives' self-reported behaviors toward patients. This set of findings suggests that making separate, nuanced ratings of relevant relatives' behaviors within the context of a particular form of psychopathology can provide distinctive information about the family environment of that disorder, such as how relatives might perceive their own behaviors.

Results related to treatment outcome further support the idea that disorder-specific assessment strategies are potentially valuable methods for understanding family processes within the context of a particular disorder, and, more importantly, for generating ideas for how to intervene with families directly and how to make decisions about allocation of limited resources. For instance, Miklowitz and colleagues (Miklowitz, George, et al., 2003; Miklowitz, Richards, et al., 2003) showed that patients who received family-based psychotherapy as an adjunct to mood-stabilizing medication fared better with respect to their manic and depressive symptoms over a 2-year period than did those who received crisis management (i.e., mood-stabilizing medication plus contact with a therapist in the event of a mood crisis, designed to emulate standard community care for bipolar disorder). To determine whether there were families that were in particular need of family-focused therapy, we examined the role of the emotional involvement observational variables in predicting the circumstances under which differences between patients in family-based treatment and those in crisis management would be most pronounced. We found that relatives' displays of emotional involvement before treatment differentiated between those patients who needed to be in family-based treatment to get better and those who did not (Fredman, Baucom, & Miklowitz, 2007). Broadly, findings revealed that patients with relatives high in inappropriate emotional involvement and/or low in appropriate emotional involvement did not improve or, in some cases, actually became more ill over time, unless they received family-based psychosocial treatment. In contrast, patients with relatives low in inappropriate emotional involvement and high in appropriate emotional involvement improved whether or not they received family-based psychosocial treatment as an adjunct to medication. However, the standard measure of emotional involvement, the CFI, did not predict changes in manic or depressive symptoms over time, perhaps because it does not differentiate among the different ways that relatives can be involved (intrusiveness, self-sacrifice, or distress related to the patient's well-being) or the appropriateness/inappropriateness of these behaviors within the context of bipolar disorder. This highlights again that, when one wants to investigate processes focal to a specific form of psychopathology, a disorder-specific measure that assesses relevant family processes within the context of that disorder can be more useful than a general, non-disorder-specific measure like CFI EOI that fails to make these distinctions.

These findings suggest that honing in on behavioral domains that are focal to a particular form of psychopathology in a disorder-specific manner can have potentially important clinical implications. First, in addition to clinicians' attending to broad-based negativity in patients' interpersonal milieus that may serve as a general stressor, it may also be possible to sensitize them to relatives' appropriate and inappropriate behaviors within the context of a particular form of psychopathology. By providing a framework for further operationalizing what many therapists see on a day-to-day basis in their clinical practices (e.g., family accommodation in the case of OCD or emotional involvement, in the case of bipolar disorder), clinicians might well be able to pick up and assess the intensity of relatives' behaviors in the context of psychosocial treatment planning for an individual with a psychological disorder. This is possible even if they do not formally use observational coding, as conducted in this study.

Second, these clinical impressions could be used to identify high-risk families (i.e., those high in global negativity, inappropriate emotional involvement, and/or those low in appropriate emotional involvement) and steer them toward family-based treatment. Given the difficulty of providing couple/family-based therapies on a large-scale basis and the fact that some patients do experience significant improvement even in the absence of family-based treatment, the use of indicated family-based interventions for high-risk family systems might be an efficient use of limited clinical resources in a way that benefits families most in need.

Where Do We Go from Here?

There are a number of assessment strategies available within the area of couple/family psychopathology, and these can be grouped broadly into whether they are widely applicable across a range of disorders (i.e., non-disorder-specific) or are focal to a particular form of psychopathology (i.e., disorder-specific). Non-disorder-specific methods tend to assess the global negativity/positivity of the patient's interpersonal milieu and help to identify characteristics in the living environment that may serve as broad, diffuse stressors to patients. There are a number of measures that investigators can choose from to assess the overall emotional climate in the home, but these do not necessarily address relationship processes focal to particular forms of psychopathology. To examine variables other than negativity/positivity requires the use of disorder-specific assessment strategies, but there are few available. Therefore, we, as a field, need to devote increasing attention and resources to developing measures that help us to understand constructs relevant to a given form of psychopathology and the ways that these family processes relate to treatment outcome. That way, in addition to having different methods for assessing the emotional climate in the home, we will be able to identify ways that family members can be involved to optimize outcomes for patients.

To do this, though, requires resisting the temptation to use a "one size fits all" approach. For instance, the methodology used to study appropriate and inappropriate emotional involvement in the context of bipolar disorder (i.e., observational coding) is portable across different psychiatric conditions, and the conceptual distinctions between appropriate and inappropriate involvement may be applicable when considering the family environment of multiple forms of psychopathology. However, the issues that are relevant in the context of bipolar disorder may not be applicable to another disorder; as a result, what is considered appropriate in bipolar disorder may be considered inappropriate in an anxiety disorder, for example. Taking over chores and responsibilities to help an individual with bipolar disorder feel less stressed may be considered appropriate if it helps patients to recover from a manic or depressive episode by promoting rest and behavioral and emotional stability. In contrast, doing things to help patients feel less distressed in the context of an anxiety disorder is generally considered inappropriate because patients who have historically avoided anxiety-provoking situations need to engage, rather than avoid, triggers for their feeling anxious. Accordingly, how measures are developed and the ways that raters are trained to use them will vary across different patient populations. Although this may require an investment of time upfront, information generated by the use of disorder-specific assessment strategies, coupled with findings from measures that globally assess the emotional climate in the home and help to identify broad-based stressors to patients, can help us ensure that our treatments and assessment strategies go hand in hand and benefit the greatest number of patients and their families as possible.

References

Amir, N., Freshman, M., & Foa, E. B. (2000). Family distress and involvement in relatives of obsessive-compulsive disorder patients. *Journal of Anxiety Disorders, 14*, 209–217.

Baucom, D. H., Shoham, V., Mueser, K. T., Daiuto, A. D., & Stickle, T. R. (1998). Empirically supported couple and family interventions for marital distress and adult mental health problems. *Journal of Consulting and Clinical Psychology, 66*, 53–88.

Butzlaff, R. L., & Hooley, J. M. (1998). Expressed emotion and psychiatric relapse: A meta-analysis. *Archives of General Psychiatry, 55*, 547–552.

Calvocoressi, L., Mazure, C. M., Kasl, S. V., Skolnick, J., Fisk, D., Vegso, S. J., et al. (1999). Family accommodation of obsessive-compulsive symptoms: Instrument development and assessment of family behavior. *Journal of Nervous and Mental Disease, 187*, 636–642.

Cronbach, L. J., & Gleser, G. C. (1965). *Psychological tests and personal decisions* (2nd ed.). Urbana, IL: University of Illinois Press.

Epstein, N. B., & Baucom, D. H. (2002). *Enhanced cognitive-behavioral therapy for couples: A contextual approach*. Washington, DC: American Psychological Association.

Fredman, S. J., Baucom, D. H., & Miklowitz, D. J. (2007, November). *Emotional involvement in relatives of patients with bipolar disorder: Implications for treatment outcome*. Paper presented at the annual meeting of the Association for Behavioral and Cognitive Therapies, Philadelphia, PA.

Fredman, S. J., Baucom, D. H., Miklowitz, D. J., & Stanton, S. E. (2008). Observed emotional involvement and overinvolvement in families of patients with bipolar disorder. *Journal of Family Psychology, 22*, 71–79.

Fredman, S. J., Chambless, D. L., & Steketee, G. (2004). Development and validation of an observational coding system for emotional overinvolvement (EOI). *Journal of Family Psychology, 18*, 339–347.

Hahlweg, K. (2004). Kategoriensystem für Partnerschaftliche Interaktion (KPI): Interactional Coding System (ICS). In P. K. Kering & D. H. Baucom (Eds.), *Couple observational coding systems* (pp. 127–142). Mahwah, New Jersey: Lawrence Erlbaum Associates.

Hooley, J. M., & Teasdale, J. D. (1989). Predictors of relapse in unipolar depressives: Expressed emotion, marital distress, and perceived criticism. *Journal of Abnormal Psychology, 98*, 229–235.

Kim, E. Y., & Miklowitz, D. J. (2004). Expressed emotion as a predictor of outcome among bipolar patients undergoing family therapy. *Journal of Affective Disorders, 82*, 343–352.

Leff, J., & Vaughn, C. (1985). *Expressed emotion in families: Its significance for mental illness*. New York: Guilford.

Miklowitz, D. J., George, E. L., Richards, J. A., Simoneau, T. L., & Suddath, R. L. (2003). A randomized study of family-focused psychoeducation and pharmacotherapy in the outpatient management of bipolar disorder. *Archives of General Psychiatry, 60*, 904–912.

Miklowitz, D. J., & Goldstein, M. J. (1997). *Bipolar disorder: A family-focused treatment approach*. New York: Guilford.

Miklowitz, D. J., Richards, J. A., George, E. L., Frank, E., Suddath, R. L., Powell, K. B., et al. (2003). Integrated family and individual therapy for bipolar disorder: Results of a treatment development study. *Journal of Clinical Psychiatry, 64*, 182–191.

Renshaw, K. D. (2008). The predictive, convergent, and discriminant validity of perceived criticism: A review. *Clinical Psychology Review, 28*, 521–534.

Snyder, D. K., & Whisman, M. A. (2003). *Treating difficult couples: Helping clients with coexisting mental and relationship disorders*. New York: Guilford Press.

Vaughn, C. E., & Leff, J. P. (1976). The measurement of expressed emotion in the families of psychiatric patients. *British Journal of Social and Clinical Psychology, 15*, 157–165.

Steffany J. Fredman
National Center for PTSD
Women's Health Sciences Division
VA Boston Healthcare System
150 South Huntington Avenue (116B-3)
Boston, MA 02130
USA
E-mail: Steffany.Fredman@va.gov

Transmitting Programs

Serving Rather Than Recruiting Couples

Thoughts on the Delivery of Current and Future Couple Interventions

Brian D. Doss,[1] Kathryn Carhart,[2] Annie C. Hsueh,[2] and Kristen P. Rahbar[2]

[1]University of Miami, Coral Gables, FL, USA
[2]Texas A&M University, College Station, TX, USA

Abstract

Despite the proven efficacy of empirically based couple interventions, only approximately 31% of couples seek premarital education and only 37% of couples seek marital therapy before filing for divorce. We suggest that a primary reason for this low rate of help seeking is that couple interventions are not designed or delivered in a way that makes them attractive to couples. In this chapter we review the existing literature on the reasons couples seek relationship-focused interventions, the steps and manner in which they seek these interventions, and which types of couples are especially likely and unlikely to seek couple interventions. From this literature, we conclude that these interventions would reach more couples if: (a) they were advertised in different ways, (b) resources were provided during the help-seeking process, (c) barriers to these interventions were reduced, and (d) special efforts were made to encourage high-risk couples to participate. Based on these conclusions, we present three approaches to further the reach of these interventions. Specifically, we review examples and advantages and disadvantages of three potential approaches: (a) dissemination of empirically based interventions to "real-world" settings, (b) modify empirically based interventions so they can be delivered by nonprofessionals in novel settings, and (c) adapt empirically based interventions into self-help formats.

Because of the impact of close romantic relationships on physical, mental, and child functioning, reviewed in the first section of this book, the potential effect of marital and family interventions delivered on a broad scale is enormous. However, couple interventions have an important limitation – most couples do not use them.

Number of Couples Who Seek Relationship Interventions

Couple Therapy

Previous research suggests that only approximately 37% of couples in the US (e.g., Johnson et al., 2002) seek relationship counseling or therapy before getting divorced. When those couples that did not seek therapy were asked why, the most common response was that it was too late to do anything to save the marriage; their reasons reported for not seeking therapy before getting divorce included that the other spouse was unwilling to go to therapy and that they did not think anything was wrong in their relationship when their spouse filed for divorce (Wolcott, 1986).

Couple therapy is also underutilized by intact couples. Although approximately 40% of new marriages in the US will end in divorce, only 19% of married couples report having ever sought couple therapy, with approximately half of those couples going to a therapist and half going to a clergy member (Johnson et al., 2002). Furthermore, preliminary research suggests that the average couple waits 6 years to seek help after serious relationship problems first develop (Notarius & Buongiorno, 1992, as cited in Gottman & Gottman, 1999). This delay is important given that, the more distressed couples are entering therapy, the less likely they are to be satisfied with their relationship at the end of therapy.

Primary and Secondary Couple Interventions

In the US, random-digit dialing methods yield estimates of 31% of couples receiving premarital education (Stanley, Amato, Johnson, & Markman, 2006); couples who married more recently appear to have higher rates of seeking premarital education than couples who have been married for longer periods of time (Johnson et al., 2002). Sampling from marriage records, Halford, O'Donnell, Lizzio, and Wilson (2006) found a participation rate of 29% in Australia.

Implications of Help-Seeking Rates

Given the above data, it appears that no matter the importance of marital distress or how effective our interventions are, relationship researchers' impact on the general public will be minimal unless we can dramatically improve our ability to help couples access our interventions. Consistent with previous calls, we believe the central task of the couples' intervention field in the next 10 years will be to apply our current knowledge and intervention techniques to more, and higher-risk, couples. Here, we would like to focus on what we see as one of the most important barriers to this goal: *Our current interventions are not designed or delivered in a way that is consistent with couples' relationship help-seeking behaviors*. In the past decade, the field has become concerned with external validity, as well as internal validity, so that we can be assured that our interventions would be effective if they were delivered outside of the research study. However, with a few notable exceptions, we do not take that next step – actually delivering those interventions to the general public outside of a research setting (or training others to do so). As a result, there is a lack of scientific attention paid to the best ways to *serve*, rather than *recruit*, couples with our interventions. Below, we review what we know about couples' relationship help-seeking behaviors and then present three approaches that we believe would be fruitful in aligning our interventions with these behaviors.

Couples' Relationship Help-Seeking Behaviors

There is a growing literature on couples' help-seeking motivations and behaviors when they decide they need external assistance for their relationship. To better design and deliver effective couple interventions, it is necessary to know why couples seek assistance, the process they take in seeking that assistance, and the types of couples who typically do and do not seek assistance.

Why Do Couples Seek Couple Interventions?

Deciding to seek outside assistance for one's romantic relationship can be an emotionally difficult thing to do. For distressed couples seeking therapy, it requires admitting to oneself that there is a problem, that this problem is unlikely to be solved by itself, and that there are sufficient reasons to try and solve that problem rather than to terminate the relationship. For nondistressed couples, deciding to seek outside assistance requires one to recognize that there is a possibility that relationship problems may develop in the future.

Couple Therapy

To determine why couples seek couple therapy, Doss, Simpson, and Christensen (2004) surveyed 147 therapy-seeking couples about their reasons for seeking help. In open-ended, qualitative reports, the majority of couples reported lack of emotional affection and poor communication as reasons for seeking therapy. Other reasons reported by > 30% of couples included divorce/separation concerns, desires to improve the relationship, arguments/anger in the relationship, desire for external help, specific relationship concerns, and concerns about children. The reasons for seeking therapy differed somewhat by a couple's level of marital distress. There was little agreement about the reasons for seeking therapy within individual couples, suggesting that motivations for therapy are largely individual. Finally, there was little overlap found between reported reasons for seeking therapy and elevated scores on self-report standardized measures of relationship functioning tapping similar constructs (e.g., communication). Therefore, it may be that perceptions of relationship difficulties, rather than higher levels of problems compared to other couples, may be more important in understanding the help-seeking process. However, this study was limited because it did not include a sample of couples who did not seek therapy. Additionally, although reports were collected during the help-seeking process, they required couples to report on reasons for seeking therapy after the couples had taken several steps in that direction.

To build upon this earlier study, Doss, Rhoades, Stanley, and Markman (2009) examined relationship help-seeking behaviors in a longitudinal sample of couples followed for 5 years after marriage. Couples who reported higher levels of relationship distress and depression were more likely to seek couple therapy in the subsequent year. Additionally, after controlling for global relationship distress, couples with higher levels of self-reported negative communication were more likely to subsequently seek couple therapy. Interestingly, neither negative nor positive observed communication predicted seeking therapy in the subsequent year. Therefore, it may be that the perception of communication problems is sufficient to encourage couples to seek therapy regardless of whether they reach objective levels of poor communication.

Primary or Secondary Couple Interventions

Although couples' reasons for seeking other types of couple interventions have not been investigated, the importance of various characteristics of premarital education in attracting couples has been examined. When engaged couples were asked about the importance of various characteristics of premarital counseling, qualities of the leader emerged as the top three items (Sullivan & Anderson, 2002). Specifically, a leader that was deemed "trustworthy," "professional," and "experienced" was rated by approximately 90% or more of participants as important or very important; however, whether the leader was an individual or a couple was only infrequently rated as important. The educational content of the interventions was also deemed important by almost 90% of individuals; communication, finances, and problem solving were all rated highly. Finally, usefulness ratings and success rates of previous participants were deemed as important or very important by the majority of individuals. Results were generally consistent across cohabiting status and gender (with only "insight-oriented content" rated as more important by women than by men). Furthermore, age, income, and education were not generally related to the importance of various program characteristics (Sullivan & Anderson, 2002).

How Do Couples Seek Couple Interventions?

A second factor to consider in designing future couple interventions and attracting more couples to them is the process that couples take to seek the interventions that are presently available.

Couple Therapy

Doss, Atkins, and Christensen (2003) found there to be three steps in seeking therapy: (a) recognizing there was a problem in the relationship; (b) realizing that therapy might help and communicating this to the spouse; and (c) actively seeking marital therapy. Across couples, there was a consistent pattern of wives being more active in seeking therapy;

67–73% were classified as wife-led couples at each of the three steps. However, within individual couples, a different pattern emerged – there was little to no relation between which spouse first recognized there was a problem and which spouse actually first considered and sought marital therapy ($r = -.17$ to .34).

To understand how to facilitate the treatment-seeking process, it is useful to examine predictors of which spouse are more active during each of the three steps. In addition to demographic factors (younger husbands and more educated wives) and higher levels of relationship distress, husbands' dissatisfaction with sexual activity significantly predicted being more active in the problem-recognition phase. For the second step, global relationship distress and specific problems with sexual dissatisfaction and communication were related to a higher likelihood of considering seeking therapy. Finally, in the third step – seeking treatment – husbands' less traditional gender roles and more dissatisfaction with sex were related to an increased likelihood of them actively seeking therapy; interestingly, global relationship distress was not directly related to treatment seeking for either spouse.

Another way to map the help-seeking process is to explore the sequencing of couples' help-seeking behaviors. In one study, the majority of couples seeking marital therapy reported previously seeking other forms of relationship help (Doss et al., 2009). Specifically, 37% had read a relationship-oriented book, 27% had attended a relationship-oriented workshop or retreat, and 20% had done both. Therefore, it appears that these alternative forms of help seeking serve as a gateway to couple therapy for many couples.

Primary or Secondary Couple Interventions

Unfortunately, little is known about the process of seeking premarital counseling or other types of couple education. Studies suggest that more than three-fourths of couples who received premarital counseling do so through a religious organization (e.g., Stanley et al., 2006). Therefore, in the US at least, religious organizations play a central role in the delivery of premarital education. Furthermore, in order to marry through that religious organization, many couples are required to attend premarital counseling; indeed, some studies estimate that 75% of couples who marry through such organizations are required to participate in premarital counseling (Sullivan, Pasch, Cornelius, & Cirigliano, 2004).

What Types of Couples Seek Relationship Interventions?

A third factor to consider in making our current interventions more accessible (or designing future interventions) is the types of couples that are currently attracted to couple interventions. It may be that certain demographic factors may facilitate or impede treatment seeking for one's relationship.

Couple Therapy

Couples who seek marital therapy offered as part of a research study tend to be upper-middle class, Caucasian, and college educated. However, there is currently only one study that examines which types of couples do and do not seek marital therapy in the community. When age, ethnicity, education, relationship length, religiosity, and presence of children were separately used to predict seeking marital therapy, only age marginally predicted help seeking, with older couples being somewhat more likely to seek marital therapy (Doss et al., 2009). In considering the results of this study, however, it is important to recognize that the sample was 85% Caucasian so ethnicity was dichotomized. Additionally, the average education was 16 years with limited range. Therefore, statistical power to detect differences by ethnicity and by education was low. Clinical experience and recruitment rates for research studies of marital therapy would suggest that ethnic minorities and individuals with less education (or lower income) are less likely to seek marital therapy. However, these clinical impressions have yet to be substantiated empirically.

Primary or Secondary Couple Interventions

Research suggests that couples seeking premarital counseling are generally at lower risk for developing subsequent relationship problems than couples who do not seek this counseling (e.g., Stanley et al., 2006). Other studies have found couples who are less religious (Halford et al., 2006; Stanley et al., 2006; Sullivan et al., 2004), cohabiting (Halford et al., 2006), and African-American (Stanley et al., 2006) tend to be less likely to participate in premarital interventions. Furthermore, perceived barriers (such as not being convenient or affordable) and not having the program recommended by someone they respected were also negatively related to seeking premarital counseling (Sullivan et al., 2004).

Less is known about seeking couple interventions after marriage. Johnson et al. (2002) reported that two-thirds of individuals currently in a committed romantic relationship said they would consider using relationship education to strengthen their relationship. More favorable attitudes toward relationship education were found in those who were younger or never married, more religious, with children, more educated, and had previously received government assistance. In a longitudinal study exploring numerous demographic and relational predictors of attending relationship-oriented workshops or retreats, only longer relationship duration and higher religiosity predicted attendance (Doss et al., 2009).

Conclusions from the Couples' Help-Seeking Literature

Although the existing literature on couples' help-seeking reasons and behavior is limited in important ways, it suggests several avenues that may aid in additional couples receiving services:

Modify How We Advertise Interventions

Armed with an understanding of why couples seek interventions, it may be possible to more effectively advertise couple interventions. First, by framing interventions to be consistent with couples' expectations or desired topics (e.g., communication and emotional distance), it may be possible to serve more couples similar to those that already seek services. Second, by advertising interventions as targeting other topics, it may be possible to attract different types of couples. For example, sexual dissatisfaction was a consistent predictor of husbands' involvement in seeking couple therapy but was listed by only 16% of men as a reason for seeking that therapy; if couple therapy was advertised as targeting the sexual relationship, would more male-led couples seek couple therapy?

Provide Resources During the Help-Seeking Process

Given that the therapy help-seeking process seems to be composed of distinct steps, it would be prudent to increase the resources for couples as they move through each of these steps. Additionally, because existing evidence suggests that one partner does not consistently lead the couple through the help-seeking steps, it will be especially important to increase the motivation and resources of both partners. For therapy, one promising method to accomplish these goals would be to incorporate resources and guidance into relationship-oriented books and workshops. To facilitate seeking workshops or premarital counseling, other methods to deliver these resources could be used (e.g., distributed with marriage licenses or at childbirth classes).

Reduce Barriers to Interventions

Given the psychological barriers couples experience in the help-seeking process, it may be effective to reduce the external barriers to couple interventions. Cost, an important barrier in seeking premarital counseling (Sullivan et al., 2004) and likely couple therapy, could be reduced as described in more detail below. Additionally, by making interventions more flexible with fewer initial commitments, couples would find it easier to initiate interventions on a trial basis. Finally, even if it is not as effective, interventions that work with only one partner may be better than no intervention in cases where the other partner is unwilling to participate.

Reach Out to High-Risk Couples in Appropriate Ways

Premarital education may also need to reach out to other types of couples, especially high-risk couples. It may be possible that some of the above suggestions may facilitate this outreach; however, as described below, new types of interventions may need to be developed. The limited existing research on couple therapy suggests that these concerns may not be as striking as they are for premarital counseling; however, clinical experience suggests that ethnic minority couples and couples with lower incomes tend to seek therapy at lower rates. Finally, in our efforts to serve new types of couples with our interventions, we should be mindful that our interventions have been found to be effective with couples who willingly participated; it is unclear what effect they would have with couples who felt they were being forced to participate.

What Do We Still Need to Know About Couples' Help-Seeking Behaviors?

As the field revises existing couple interventions and develops new ones, it will be important to have an understanding of several aspects of the help-seeking process that have not yet been adequately explored. One aspect of relationship help seeking that deserves additional attention is the role of informal help seeking from friends and family. One would imagine that friends and family are central to the problem-recognition, treatment-consideration, and treatment-seeking phases of seeking couple therapy. What aspects of social support, instrumental support, and social comparison facilitate or hinder seeking couple therapy? Within the premarital intervention literature, there is preliminary evidence to suggest that important others can have a significant impact on the help-seeking processes. Specifically, whether or not premarital counseling was recommended by a "respected" other was one of the strongest predictors of whether or not a couple actually participated in premarital counseling (Sullivan et al., 2004).

Other important sources of help seeking for couple relationships are relationship-oriented books and magazine articles. Doss et al. (2009) found that more couples read relationship-oriented books than attended couple therapy or relationship-oriented workshops or retreats during the first 5 years of marriage. Importantly, reading a relationship-oriented book in the following year was predicted by significantly higher levels of negative communication and physical aggression and marginally predicted by lower levels of global relationship satisfaction and confidence in the relationship. Therefore, reading a relationship-oriented book seems to be a form of help seeking for relationship difficulties rather than relationship enhancement. Unfortunately, nothing is currently known about how couples select a certain book from the myriad of choices available to them. It is also unclear how helpful reading a relationship-oriented book is in preventing or improving relationship problems.

Third, little is known about couples' relationship help-seeking behaviors over the Internet. However, it seems that couples are increasingly turning to the Internet for assistance in many areas of their personal life (e.g., WebMD and Match.com); therefore, it would be reasonable to expect that the Internet is increasingly serving as an important source of relationship information. Indeed, the attraction of the Internet for relationship information and feedback was demonstrated by Doss and Christensen (2006), who had more than 13,000 individuals participate in an online study in return for feedback about their relationship. This same study demonstrated that the Internet can reach diverse or high-risk couples that typically do not seek in-person couple interventions. In the same web site sample described above, there were almost 2,000 minority participants, more than 3,000 unmarried cohabiting participants (300 with children), over 1,500 participants with a high-school education or less, and over 1,500 participants who reported an annual household income of less than $40,000. Although this evidence should be considered preliminary, it suggests that the Internet may be an important tool in future couple interventions.

Three Potential Approaches to Reach More, and Higher-Risk, Couples

Based on couples' help-seeking behaviors and the nature of existing interventions, we present three approaches that we expect could improve the ability of current and future couple interventions to reach more, and higher-risk, couples. Where possible, we review ongoing efforts within these three veins.

Disseminate Empirically Based Interventions to Sources Where Couples Already Seek Help

Dissemination of empirically based treatments for individual psychological disorders has been discussed extensively in the literature and advantages and barriers to this approach have been well documented. However, there have been notably fewer dissemination efforts involving empirically supported couple interventions. There have likely been several reasons for this omission. *First*, delivery of couple therapy in the community is generally not centralized within large organizations as it is for other treatments. For example, most treatment for severe psychological disorders is likely delivered in hospitals or community mental health centers; couple therapy for relationship distress is often not available in these settings. Instead, in the US, couple therapy tends to be administered by individual private practitioners in the community. Given this dispersion, systematic training and evaluation of dissemination efforts become more difficult. *Second*, many primary and secondary couple interventions (e.g., premarital counseling and relationship workshops) are delivered by clergy or other individuals without extensive mental health training. Coordination with these professionals will likely require a different approach than that used in previous dissemination efforts. Finally, a *third* barrier to dissemination efforts has been the fact that, while interest in dissemination has increased in the larger field of clinical psychology, US federal funding for trials of couple therapy targeting relationship distress has been virtually eliminated. Fortunately, funding for trials of primary and secondary couple interventions has increased in recent years with the federal Healthy Marriage Initiative. Under this program, hundreds of millions of dollars were provided to community agencies to promote and strengthen marriage and responsible fatherhood.

Example of a Dissemination Approach

Perhaps the most notable published dissemination project to date in the couples' field is the effort to train clergy members to deliver the Prevention and Relationship Enhancement Program (PREP) as part of their standard program for couples getting married in their religious organization. Clergy were receptive to the training and a year after the intervention, couples who received PREP administered by both clergy and university staffs were doing significantly better on a number of self-report and observed measures than couples who had received the care-as-usual premarital counseling. Furthermore, there were no significant differences between the clergy-administered and university-administered PREP conditions (Laurenceau, Stanley, Olmos-Gallo, Baucom, & Markman, 2004).

Advantages of a Dissemination Approach

There are two advantages to disseminating empirically based couple interventions to existing service providers. *First*, the availability and infrastructure of those providers are already established, making delivery of these new interventions more rapid than some of the other approaches. *Second*, for the most part, the couple interventions do not need to be significantly modified before they can be disseminated. Of course, interventions may be strengthened by tailoring the general concepts and skills of a particular intervention to a specific population. For example, particular religious or cultural concepts, ways to handle common stressors in that population, and reframing certain skills or lessons could all be productive. Although most existing interventions may not need significant modification, there is one important exception – most empirically based couple therapies will need to be significantly shortened to correspond to the treatment lengths in most community settings.

Disadvantages of a Dissemination Approach

Despite these advantages, there are several disadvantages of a dissemination approach to future interventions. Perhaps most importantly, the studies cited above suggest that many couples who would potentially benefit from couple interventions do not seek them. Therefore, even if we improve the effectiveness of couple interventions by disseminating empirically supported programs, we will still not reach the thousands of couples who do not seek the interventions in the first place. A second important disadvantage is that many of the barriers to dissemination that have been encountered in dissemination efforts in the individual psychotherapy literature will likely also be experienced in dissemination of couple therapy. Specifically, research has suggested that the workshop training model of dissemination for individual psychotherapy, perhaps the most straightforward approach, is effective in increasing knowledge and skill but does not translate into client gains (e.g., Miller, Yahne, Moyers, Martinez, & Pirritano, 2004). However, these training concerns may not be as pressing for the more skills-based primary and secondary couple interventions; a 3-day training has been shown in previous studies to be an effective training method, at least for one premarital intervention (Stanley et al., 2001). Finally, in the individual treatment literature, practitioners have routinely expressed reservations about adopting manualized empirically based treatments; practitioners of couple interventions may have similar reservations. However, given that most psychotherapy training programs and seminaries do not generally emphasize couple interventions, it may be that practitioners will view couple intervention manuals more as a resource than as a restriction on their current theories or techniques.

Modify Existing Services So They Can Be Delivered by Professionals in Other Settings

In addition to disseminating our existing empirically based couple interventions to settings where couples currently receive services, additional couples can be served by modifying those treatments and delivering them in new settings or situations. Additionally, by tailoring these interventions to match couples' situations such as the birth of their first child, they can be delivered at times when the couple is receptive to relational change.

Examples of a Modification Approach

In recent years, several novel modifications to traditional couple interventions have been developed and tested; two promising types of interventions will be presented here. First, several researchers have targeted the transition to parenthood in an effort to intervene at a time of stress with couples who would not typically seek assistance for their relationship. The transition to parenthood has been repeatedly demonstrated to be a period of increased relationship stress and deterioration; additionally, it is one of the few times in the US where couples jointly complete education classes (i.e., childbirth education); therefore, it provides a unique opportunity to add relationship education onto existing services at a time when couples are already seeking outside assistance. Research on the effectiveness of couple interventions is still in its early stages, with some interventions showing significant effects while others do not. With several other programs of research currently ongoing, we expect the efficacy of intervening with couples during the transition to parenthood to become clear over the next few years.

Rather than targeting a particular event, two exciting new approaches deliver couple interventions to couples who would be otherwise unlikely to seek services. The first is the Marriage Checkup (Cordova et al., 2005). As part of the Marriage Checkup, couples respond to advertisements offering couples a free assessment of their relationship; this assessment consists of an extensive battery of both observed and self-report measures of relationship functioning. Cordova and his associates have found that 61–77% of couples who participate in the Marriage Checkup report at least moderate relationship distress; however, the level of relationship distress is less than what is typically seen in couples seeking couple therapy (Cordova et al., 2005). Results indicate that couples show small but significant decreases in relationship distress at the end of feedback; however, the long-term effects of the intervention have not yet been examined. A second novel approach to the delivery of couple interventions is Couple CARE. This program, a hybrid of self-help materials and therapist phone calls, has been found to significantly increase relationship satisfaction and decrease relationship instability at posttreatment, especially in couples presenting with lower initial satisfaction (Halford, Moore, Wilson, Farrugia, & Dyer, 2004). With greater accessibility than traditional couple interventions, Couple CARE represents an important advance in couple interventions.

Advantages of a Modification Approach

The primary advantage of this approach is that it addresses the central limitation of existing couple interventions – many couples who would benefit from couple interventions simply do not seek them. At the same time, delivering these interventions in other settings may reduce many of the barriers (e.g., transportation and cost) and stigma associated with participation – especially interventions for distressed relationships. A second advantage of modifying our existing interventions is that it becomes possible to tailor them to specific transitions (e.g., parenthood), events (e.g., serious illness), and even specific presenting problems (e.g., sexual difficulties). This tailoring, in turn, may create the potential for these interventions to have a larger impact on couple functioning. Additionally, certain topics (e.g., physical aggression and substance use) may not be relevant for certain couples but may be central for others. Finally, modifying our interventions may allow them to better fit into couples' help-seeking behavior. For example, the Marriage Checkup (e.g., Cordova et al., 2005) targets couples in the problem-recognition and treatment-consideration stages by including motivational interviewing techniques. By requiring those couples to only want more information about their relationship (they do not have to commit to any further intervention), it becomes possible to assist couples who are not yet in the action stage. Similarly, in our laboratory's transition to parenthood interventions, we stress the importance of couple functioning on infant development so that couples are willing to participate on behalf of their baby; they do not need to define their couple relationship as needing assistance.

Disadvantages of a Modification Approach

However, there are several important questions about this approach that remain unanswered. Perhaps the most pressing concern is one of sustainability. Most of these efforts have been supported by research funds to fund advertising, materials, and delivery of services – what happens when those research funds end? Would couples be willing to pay for these modified services if they do not recognize that there is a relational problem to prevent or fix? A second limitation of the modification approach is that, if the intervention becomes widely available, it is unclear how practitioners will be trained and supervised in the intervention. As noted above, the typical brief workshop training model has been demonstrated to be ineffective in improving client outcomes (e.g., Miller et al., 2004); however, more intensive trainings have been shown to be effective in the premarital intervention literature (e.g., Stanley et al., 2001). Finally, as the interventions are developed and delivered, it will be necessary to demonstrate that they attract couples who are at risk for, or currently experience, the relationship problems targeted by the intervention. Previous research has demonstrated that many couples who seek premarital interventions are not at high risk for subsequent relationship problems (e.g., Halford et al., 2006). Furthermore, preliminary data on the Marriage Checkup suggest that presenting couples are largely Caucasian and college educated (e.g., Cordova et al., 2005).

Modify Services So They Can Be Delivered in Self-Help Formats

In considering the future of couple interventions, one exciting possibility is to shift our focus away from couple interventions delivered by trained professionals and toward an emphasis on self-help formats. In the individual literature, self-administered interventions have generally been found to be significantly more effective than no treatment and not significantly different from therapist-administered treatments. Unfortunately, very little is known about how effective self-help couple interventions would be, the most effective method of delivery, or how many couples would seek these interventions.

Examples of a Self-Help Approach

The most established self-help couple intervention is relationship-oriented books; more couples read relationship-oriented books than attend marital therapy or relationship-oriented retreats or workshops (Doss et al., 2009). Fortunately, there are several excellent empirically supported books for couples dealing with a number of issues; however, the efficacy of these books has not yet been examined. Moreover, most couples likely read relationship-oriented self-help books that are not based on any empirical evidence (Doss et al., 2009).

Second, with the growing availability and technology of the Internet, couple interventions over the web are an exciting possibility. Like self-help books, web-based interventions are easy to access and inexpensive for the couple. However, in contrast to self-help books, web-based interventions have the possibility of being tailored to couples' specific presenting problems (e.g., Casey & Halford, this volume). Additionally, preliminary evidence suggests that couples find web-based couple interventions useful and these interventions improve couples' relationships (Markman, Rhoades, Delaney, White, & Pacifici, this volume).

Advantages of a Self-Help Approach

Perhaps the most attractive feature of self-help couple interventions is that they are much more sustainable over long periods of time than interventions that require the continued delivery of services by professionals. In other words, after an initial infusion of grant or publisher monies, these interventions would be available to couples for years via online bookstores or the Internet. Although a substantial investment may be necessary to develop the intervention, the longer timeframe of availability (and lower associated costs) could make such undertakings financial feasible.

Three additional advantages arise from the lower costs and sustainability of these interventions. *First*, a lower cost would remove one important barrier to couples seeking relationship-oriented interventions; Sullivan et al. (2004) found perceived barriers (especially expense) to be a significant predictor of reluctance to seek premarital therapy for men but not women. Furthermore, a lower cost would likely be especially important for couples of lower socioeconomic status – an important demographic that currently is not generally reached by couple interventions. *Second*, the low cost and sustainability of self-help interventions allow them to be more tailored to specific problems or populations than other types of couple interventions. As one example, PREP self-help books have been tailored for Christian couples and couples dealing with money problems, the birth of their first baby, and the children leaving home (i.e., empty nesters). The Internet provides even more possibilities for tailoring interventions. *Finally*, the accessibility of self-help interventions makes them an excellent gateway to more intensive couple interventions when necessary. For example, as noted above, 37% of couples who seek couple therapy report having previously read a book to improve their relationship (Doss et al., 2009).

Disadvantages of a Self-Help Approach

However, there are also several limitations to a self-help approach. Perhaps the most pressing concern is whether or not such interventions can be effective in improving relationship functioning. However, early results (cf., Markman et al., this volume) suggest that couples who complete an empirically supported couple intervention online report increases in relationship confidence and improved communication skills.

A second important disadvantage of self help interventions is that they are difficult to regulate. To sample the overwhelming experience of attempting to select an appropriate relationship-oriented book, one only needs to browse the "Relationship" and "Self-Improvement" sections in any national bookstore. Choosing an appropriate relationship-oriented web site is even more challenging. Typing "marriage therapy" into Google yields MarriageMax.com as the first link; this site, which claims to have helped over 75,000 couples, is not run by a psychologist but by a graduate of the Wharton School of Business. In short, helping couples to select appropriate and effective self-help interventions will be a central challenge to further development of relationship-oriented self-help interventions.

Conclusion

The possibilities for expanding our horizons into interventions that reach more and higher-risk couples dramatically increase our potential impact on real-world couples. Those possibilities also open up numerous lines of new and important research that will be needed to maximize the effectiveness of those interventions. The specifics of those interventions have yet to be finalized, but we are optimistic that the future is bright.

References

Casey, L. M., & Halford, W. K. (this volume). Couples and the silicon chip: Applying technology to couples relationship services. In K. Hahlweg, M. Grawe-Gerber, & D. H. Baucom (Eds.), *Enhancing couples. The shape of couple therapy to come*. Göttingen: Hogrefe.

Cordova, J. V., Scott, R. L., Dorian, M., Mirgain, S., Yaeger, D., & Groot, A. (2005). The marriage checkup: An indicated preventive intervention for treatment-avoidant couples at risk for marital deterioration. *Behavior Therapy, 36*, 301–309.

Doss, B. D., Atkins, D. C., & Christensen, A. (2003). Who's dragging their feet? Husbands and wives seeking marital therapy. *Journal of Marital and Family Therapy, 29*, 165–177.

Doss, B. D., & Christensen, A. (2006). Acceptance in romantic relationships: The frequency and acceptability of the partner behavior inventory. *Psychological Assessment, 18*, 289–302.

Doss, B. D., Rhoades, G., Stanley, S., & Markman, H. (2009). Marital therapy, retreats, and books: The who, what, when, and why of relationship help-seeking. *Journal of Marital and Family Therapy, 35*, 18–29.

Doss, B. D., Simpson, L. S., & Christensen, A. (2004). Why do couples seek marital therapy? *Professional Psychology: Research and Practice, 35*, 608–614.

Gottman, J. M., & Gottman, J. S. (1999). The marriage survival kit. In R. Berger & M. T. Hannah (Eds.), *Preventive approaches in couples therapy* (pp. 304–330). Philadelphia, PA: Brunner/Mazel.

Halford, W. K., Moore, E., Wilson, K. L., Farrugia, C., & Dyer, C. (2004). Benefits of flexible delivery relationship education: An evaluation of the Couple CARE program. *Family Relations, 53*, 469–476.

Halford, W. K., O'Donnell, C., Lizzio, A., & Wilson, K. L. (2006). Do couples at high risk of relationship problems attend premarriage education? *Journal of Family Psychology, 20*, 160–163.

Johnson, C. A., Stanley, S. M., Glenn, N. D., Amato, P. R., Nock, S. L., Author, H. J., et al. (2002). *Marriage in Oklahoma: 2001 baseline statewide survey on marriage and divorce (S02096 OKDHS)*. Oklahoma City, OK: Oklahoma Department of Human Services.

Laurenceau, J. P., Stanley, S. M., Olmos-Gallo, A., Baucom, B., & Markman, H. J. (2004). Community-based prevention of marital dysfunction: Multilevel modeling of a randomized effectiveness study. *Journal of Consulting and Clinical Psychology, 72*, 933–943.

Markman, H. J., Rhoades, G., Delaney, R., White, L., & Pacifici, C. (this volume). Extending the reach of research-based couples interventions: The role of marriage education. In K. Hahlweg, M. Grawe-Gerber, & D. H. Baucom (Eds.), *Enhancing couples. The shape of couple therapy to come.* Göttingen: Hogrefe.

Miller, W. R., Yahne, C. E., Moyers, T. B., Martinez, J., & Pirritano, M. (2004). A randomized trial of methods to help clinicians learn motivational interviewing. *Journal of Consulting and Clinical Psychology, 72*(6), 1050–1062.

Stanley, S. M., Amato, P. R., Johnson, C. A., & Markman, H. J. (2006). Premarital education, marital quality, and marital stability: Findings from a large, random, household survey. *Journal of Family Psychology, 20*, 117–126.

Stanley, S. M., Markman, H. J., Prado, L. M., Olmos-Gallo, P. A., Tonelli, L., St. Peters, M., et al. (2001). Community-based premarital prevention: Clergy and lay leaders on the front lines. *Family Relations, 50*(1), 67–76.

Sullivan, K. T., & Anderson, C. (2002). Recruitment of engaged couples for premarital counseling: An empirical examination of the importance of program characteristics and topics to potential participants. *The Family Journal, 10*, 388–397.

Sullivan, K. T., Pasch, L. A., Cornelius, T., & Cirigliano, E. (2004). Predicting participation in premarital prevention programs: The health belief model and social norms. *Family Process, 43*, 175–193.

Wolcott, I. H. (1986). Seeking help for marital problems before separation. *Australian Journal of Sex, Marriage, and Family, 7*, 154–164.

Brian D. Doss
Department of Psychology
University of Miami
P.O. Box 248185
Coral Gables, FL 33124-0751
USA
E-mail: bdoss@psy.miami.edu

Couples and the Silicon Chip

Applying Information Technology to Couple Relationship Services

Leanne M. Casey and W. Kim Halford

Griffith University, Mt. Gravatt, Australia

Abstract

Information technology (IT) is developing at a phenomenal rate and has the potential to play an important role in dissemination and enhancement of couple services. IT applications have the capacity to substantially increase availability of couple services and can be adapted to facilitate both two-way (professional and client) or multiple (group) communication. We review existing applications of IT in the couple relationship services literature and propose a number of ways in which IT could be used to enhance the quality and accessibility of couple services. Drawing our experience in developing IT applications, we discuss the challenges in designing such applications and suggest a number of issues that should be considered in order to maximize the potential of this new development in couple services.

A couple discuss the bitter divorces that they each witnessed between their parents when they were children, decide they want to manage their conflict more effectively, and search the Internet. They complete an online inventory that identifies that their current conflict management style is a risk for their relationship. The couple download audiovisual training materials and work through some exercises together, and have two telephone-based reviews with a psychologist on their progress. A woman, reeling from the discovery of her partner's infidelity, accesses the web in a desperate search for answers. She locates an online support group, finds the support she needs, and links to an e-book that provides her with useful information to help her understand and manage her distress. A couple struggle to cope with the husband's chronic illness. Unable to attend a clinic because of his restricted mobility, they locate an online therapist and use weekly webcam sessions to learn knowledge and skills that help them to cope.

These examples describe what is now available via information technologies (IT), and are representative of how increasing numbers of people seek psychological information and services. In this chapter we analyze the application of IT in the delivery of couple psychological services, describing the advantages of these applications and evaluating the available evidence for the effectiveness of such applications. We then consider possible future applications of IT to enhance the quality and accessibility of couple services, and review the challenges in developing such applications.

The IT Explosion and Couple Relationship Services

IT is developing and being adopted at a phenomenal rate. Figure 1 shows the rapid uptake of this new IT across the world for the period 1990–2003. It is clear that rapidly changing IT is making new means of accessing information available with unprecedented speed. The new IT is being used to provide information and services to couples, and already there is an extraordinary amount of information on couple relationship accessible via technology. We ran a Google search using the terms "couple therapy," "relationship education," and "relationship advice." Couple therapy returned 2.6 million hits (in 0.11 seconds); relationship education returned 14.4 million hits (in 0.16 seconds); and relationship advice returned 19 million hits (in 0.11 seconds). A brief inspection of a sample of these sites

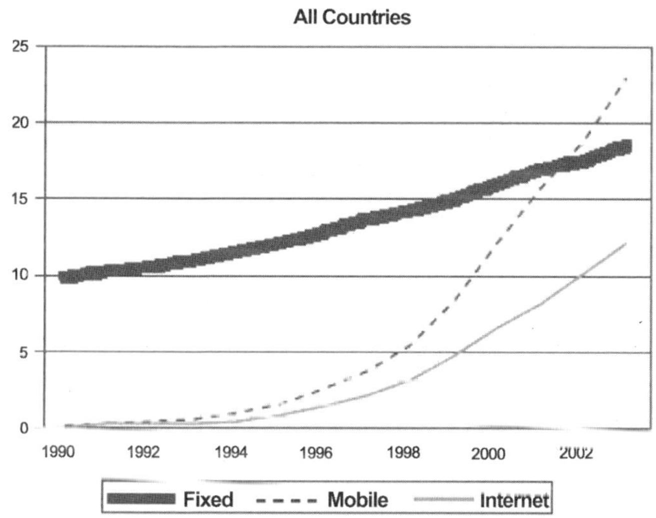

Figure 1. Fixed, mobile, and Internet subscribers per 100 people in the world. Source: Global Trends and Policies, World Health Bank (2006).

shows a bewildering array of advertisements, products and services, many promising enhanced or new relationships, or quick fixes for relationship problems. As we document below, systematic evaluation of the effects of these services is very limited, but the sheer amount of information is staggering.

Advantages of IT in Couple Relationship Services

IT is being used as a means to deliver a diverse range of psychological services including: Assessment and treatment for disorders including anxiety and depression (Spek et al., 2007), eating disorders (Taylor, Jobson, Winzelberg, & Abascal, 2002), problem gambling (Casey, Oei, Raylu, & Lim, 2007), and childhood anxiety (Spence, Holmes, March, & Lipp, 2006), and information, skill training, and support to cope with major stresses like cancer and heart disease (Lieberman & Goldstein, 2005); and educational and preventive interventions (Halford, Markman, & Stanley, 2008). The technologies being used for these new services are diverse and include mobile (cell) telephones (e.g., Leach & Christensen, 2006), Personal Digital Assistants (PDAs) (Newman, Consoli, & Taylor, 1999), video- and web-conferencing, Digital Video Discs (DVDs) (Halford, Moore, Wilson, Farrugia, & Dyer, 2004), and the Internet (e.g., Casey et al., 2007). This burgeoning diversity of technology applications reflects a growing awareness of the advantages of using IT in delivery of psychological services.

Availability

Technology can provide high availability in both a geographical and temporal sense. It removes the need for client and professional to be located in the same physical space and it enables clients to participate at any time they choose. A web site developed in Zurich can be accessed in Brisbane. A television program shown live last week can be accessed (podcast) at any time. An email written 3 days ago can be read in 2 weeks' time. A text message sent to a mobile telephone can be read at a convenient time.

Interactivity

Technology can allow interaction, for either two-way (between professional and client) or multiple (group) communication. A therapist can place assessment and homework tasks online for clients to complete. Internet chat rooms allow multiple users to discuss their difficulties together. Recent developments in Internet conferencing enable vision and dialog between therapist and clients to occur anywhere in the world with high-speed Internet access at low cost. A PDA can provide individually tailored suggestions of coping strategies as a client feels the need no matter where they are.

Multiplicity

The same content (whether this is assessment, information, or intervention) can be used multiple times by multiple clients, providing cost savings in both delivery and time. For the client, there are no waiting lists. For the service provider, there are no decisions to be made as to which clients get seen first, and which clients need to be referred elsewhere in an overstretched system.

Reliability

Barring technical difficulties that should occur less frequently as our mastery of technology increases, Internet content is delivered in exactly the way intended. It is not subject to fatigue, a bad mood, or the need for a holiday by a professional.

Content Updating Capability

Technology allows content to be updated on a regular basis, often at modest cost. Unlike a therapist who might require extensive retraining to deliver a new assessment, IT delivery of assessment can be easily standardized. It can provide structure to ensure new efficacious interventions are easy to deliver, and reduce the lag time between innovations in intervention and adoption in routine service delivery.

Flexibility

Technology can allow tailoring of content according to the client's needs and personal style. One couple might prefer to watch an audiovisual skills demonstration, while another couple might prefer to read a text-based description of the skill. Some clients may prefer face-to-face or telephone or email contact with a therapist whereas others may prefer anonymity and self-directed learning. Client preferences can be evaluated and accommodated in ways that are beyond the current capacity of most service providers of face-to-face services.

The above identified potential advantages in the use of IT to deliver psychological services in general, and couple relationship services in particular, probably explain the rapidly expanding use of IT for such services. However, systematic evaluation of the effect of use of IT on the effectiveness of couple relationship services has lagged substantially behind the applications.

Evaluation of the Use of Technology in Couple Relationship Services

In order to analyze the available evidence on the impact of the use of IT in couple relationship services, we conducted a literature search on the PsychINFO database using the terms "couples" and/or "marital" and "technology" or "software" or "cyber" or "Internet" or "web" or "computer" or "net" for articles published in refereed journals between 1980 and 2007. Before the current century there were only two examples of IT applications to couple relationship services, and only one of these was an evaluation of the effects of an IT-based relationship service. An early application of IT to couple services in the scientific literature was the use of computerized assessment and scoring of the Marital Satisfaction Inventory (e.g., Snyder, Lachar, & Wills, 1988). While this application has some of the advantages of IT in enhancing couple relationship services, the application does not use IT as means for delivering intervention. Ochs and Binik (1998) reported the first evaluation of an IT-based intervention study in which "Sexpert" (an expert computer system designed to counsel couples about their sexual relationship) was shown to assist couples to increase their knowledge about sexuality.

IT-based relationship education seems to be effective in producing short-term enhancement of couple relationships, as demonstrated in four randomized controlled trials. Halford et al. (2004) reported that Couple CARE, a self-directed couple relationship skill-training program using a DVD and telephone-based coaching, produced short-term increases in couple relationship satisfaction. RELATE, a web-based couple relationship assessment that provides a computer-generated downloadable report, which can be supplemented by a telephone call with an educator to assist interpretation of the assessment, also produces short-term enhancement of couple relationship commitment and satisfaction (e.g., Larson, Vatter, Galbraith, Holman, & Stahmann, 2007). Finally, a web-based adaptation of Markman, Stanley and colleagues' Prevention and Relationship Enhancement Program also produces short-term increases in individuals' relationship knowledge and satisfaction (Markman & Rhoades, this volume). While each of these applications of IT shows some immediate benefits from IT-based relationship education, long-term benefits have not been demonstrated.

We were unable to find published evaluations of IT-based couple therapy. This lack of scientific evaluation contrasts dramatically with the enormous amount of information available on the Internet that is presented as providing solutions to couple relationship problems. Given the modest amount of research on IT in couple therapy, it is useful to examine the research on IT-based psychological treatments more generally, to extract key principles that might have application to couple relationship services.

The nature of the presenting problem and the extent of therapist contact seem likely to moderate the effectiveness of IT-based psychological treatments. Much of the research on IT-based psychological treatment has reported effects within open trials using small sample sizes, and in many areas of application the evidence base is inadequate to draw meaningful conclusions (Spek et al., 2007). However, there have been 12 randomized controlled trials of Internet-based CBT of anxiety and depression that Spek et al. (2007) evaluated in a meta-analysis. They found interventions for depression had a small and heterogeneous mean effect size, $d = 0.32$, whereas interventions for anxiety had a large mean effect size, $d = 0.96$, with low (non-significant) heterogeneity. Secondary analyses showed the IT-based program's effects on depression with therapist support ($n = 5$) had a large mean effect size, while interventions without therapist support ($n = 6$) had a small mean effect size. The lower effect size for depression than for anxiety might reflect that different problems might be differentially responsive to IT-based intervention. The moderating effect of level of therapist contact on effect sizes in IT-based treatment of depression might reflect that people with depression need personal contact to benefit from treatment to a greater extent than people with anxiety.

In IT intervention for couple problems there might be heterogeneity in responsiveness moderated by level of therapist contact, analogous to that observed between depression and anxiety. For example, high conflict couples might need the presence of a therapist to provide structure and intensive coaching to prevent negative escalation, whereas couple lacking a sense of intimacy might be able to gather ideas for enhancing their relationship effectively from a web page without therapist contact. Therapist contact does seem to enhance web-based couple relationship education. Busby, Ivey, Harris, and Ates (2007) and Larson et al. (2007) both reported higher consumer satisfaction, and more gains in relationship satisfaction, when a telephone-based discussion with a therapist was added to provision of a computer-generated couple relationship assessment report.

In summary, preliminary reports of the effects of using IT to deliver psychological services are encouraging, and there have been some reports of successful applications to couple relationship services. Moreover, we suggest that couple therapists and educators are just beginning to explore the potential applications of IT to couple relationship services. This is not to suggest that IT-based services will replace face-to-face services, as inevitably there will be continuing demand from couples for traditional couple relationship education and therapy. However, IT can provide a new and different range of services, and it can assist, augment, and extend available face-to-face couple education and therapy services.

Possible Future Applications of IT in the Couple Area Improving Couple Health Literacy

In order for clients to attend relationship education or couple therapy, they must know that it is available and believe that it may be of help to them. Jorm and colleagues coined the term "mental health literacy" to refer to knowledge and beliefs about mental disorders which aid their recognition, management, or prevention (Jorm et al., 1997, p. 182) and subsequent research has supported the proposition that low mental health literacy has a negative impact on help-seeking behavior (Jorm et al., 2006). For example, in a study examining the barriers to initial help seeking in anxious and depressed individuals, Thompson, Hunt, and Issakidis (2004) found that the most frequent reason for delay in help seeking was lack of knowledge about mental illness or available treatment.

In a similar vein, we suggest that *couple health literacy* (i.e., knowledge and beliefs about couple difficulties and available treatment) is likely to impact on couple help-seeking behavior, and IT is likely to form an important strategy in addressing couple health literacy. Couple web sites are being used to attempt to improve couple health literacy by use of interactive checklists to identify couple difficulties, and provision of fact sheets, referral options, and general treatment resources. For example, Relationship Australia's web site http://www.relationships.com.au/advice/ and the US based Smart Marriages organization at http://www.smartmarriages.com/ both provide this sort of information. Unfortunately, there has not been any systematic scientific evaluation of the effects of such web sites.

The use of sponsored links to a couple web site could assist its influence to spread further. Halford et al. (2004) suggested that a promising means of extending reach is to target couples at transition points in their life, such as new parenthood, establishment of a blended family, retirement, or health crises. Web sites targeted at such change points could increase couples' knowledge regarding the availability of services. The addition of Really Simple Syndication which scans a site for updates to the content, and then delivers them to subscribers in the form of a list of headlines straight to their desktop could further enable couples in need to be advised of services and resources in a timely fashion.

Boosting "Treatment as Usual"

Clients who would benefit from relationship education or couple therapy are likely to present in a wide variety of settings. Yet unless the client initially presents to a specialized couple service, relatively few of these other settings are likely to provide specific couple-focused work as part of *treatment as usual* and referral to appropriate services may be restricted. Use of technology may provide adjunctive services in these situations where clients would otherwise receive only limited forms of treatment. For example, couple therapy is a highly efficacious treatment for depression (Gilliam & Cottone, 2005). Yet it is almost never offered to depressed clients. More generally, it is well recognized that clients with mental health problems who present in primary care often receive suboptimal treatment (Stein et al., 2004). Demonstrating the way in which technology can assist in this situation, Proudfoot et al. (2004) conducted a trial of computerized cognitive-behavioral therapy (C-CBT) in the treatment of anxiety and depression in primary care. Patients ($N = 274$) with anxiety and/or depression were randomly allocated to receive (with or without medication) C-CBT or treatment as usual. C-CBT improved depression, negative attribution style, work and social adjustment, without interaction with drug treatment, duration of preexisting illness or severity of existing illness, and outperformed treatment as usual in more severe anxiety cases. Use of IT-delivered couple interventions could similarly provide clients with services who would otherwise be unlikely to receive any couple-focused assistance. For example, a preliminary relationship assessment via the web (e.g., RELATE) could identify if there are couple difficulties contributing to the presenting problem. Halford (in press) reports the use of a DVD-based educational material from the Couple CARE program to structure couple therapy. It is easy to imagine web- or DVD-based interventions being used to assist delivery of therapy for specialized areas (e.g., alcohol use, depression, and anxiety) where a couple-focused approach may be useful.

Maximizing Use of Limited Resources

Provision of evidence-based couple therapy typically involves the use of highly trained therapists who can be in short supply. IT might reduce the duration of therapist contact needed without loss of efficacy by enabling clients to undertake at least some aspects of their treatment outside of sessions. For example, Spence et al. (2006) showed CBT partially delivered via the Internet halved the duration of therapist contact required to treat childhood anxiety from 10 to 5 clinic-based treatment sessions.

Effective use of the time between consultation sessions through therapeutic activities is an important issue across a range of psychotherapeutic approaches (Kazantzis & Ronan,

2006). IT is a useful way in which couples can be assisted to engage in tasks between sessions. IT can provide descriptions of core concepts via CDs, models of key skills by DVD, reminders and guidance for completion of homework tasks through mobile phones (Boschen & Casey, 2008), and support and feedback through emails or web-based programs (Casey et al., 2007). Face-to-face booster sessions enhance the long-term effectiveness of couple relationship education (Braukhaus, Hahlweg, Kroeger, Groth, & Fehm-Wolfsdorf, 2003). Couples might access booster sessions more easily and cheaply after therapy using web-based programs.

Providing Assistance to Clients Who Are Otherwise Unlikely to Present for Treatment

Technology can provide assistance to clients who are either unable or unwilling to attend face-to-face therapy. Some clients may live too far away from major centers to be able to access services easily. Some clients may be reluctant to seek professional support because this will involve acknowledging to others the nature of the difficulties that they are experiencing. For example, problem gambling is being increasingly recognized for its negative impact upon both individuals and their partners and yet only a small proportion of gamblers seek help (Productivity Commission, 1999). Shame and secretiveness about the extent of gambling problems have been identified as major barriers to people seeking treatment (Tavares, Martins, Zilberman, & el Guebaly, 2002). Internet-based treatment that can be undertaken in the privacy of their home offers individuals the chance to receive treatment who might not present at usual treatment facilities. Casey et al. (2007) are currently trialing an Internet-based CBT approach in this population called *Improving the Odds* and preliminary results are promising. Similarly, many couples that are unlikely to present for face-to-face treatment might access couple relationship education or therapy via such web-based programs.

Training

A fundamental issue in enhancing therapy outcomes concerns quality control in therapy delivery. Use of audiovisual demonstrations of therapy has been commonplace in therapist training, although there is little formal evaluation of the effects of such modeling. A more systematic approach to training therapists is possible through use of web based applications. For example, in the area of Dialectical Behavior Therapy, Linehan and colleagues have developed a site (http://www.behavioraltech.com) that provides details of DVDs demonstrating the approach, a schedule of training events, as well as an online training program. Development of similar programs in the couple area may be of considerable assistance in assisting the dissemination of evidence-based approaches in the couple area, particularly given the number of programs currently being used that lack validation (Halford & Casey, this volume). For example, a web site could be established to provide an easily accessible repository for research and resource updates on specific applications of couple education and therapy as well as an opportunity to undertake online training in these approaches.

Monitoring and Improving Outcomes

Despite overwhelming evidence that objective assessment of therapy progress and outcomes provides a more reliable gauge of therapy outcomes than relying on clinical impressions, many therapists fail to routinely measure outcome. In part, this failure may be associated with the time demands associated with administration, scoring, and interpretation of outcome measures. Use of technology can enable these tasks to be completed without adding to therapist burden and provide substantial improvement in client outcomes.

Lambert and colleagues (e.g., Lambert, Harmon, Slade, Whipple, & Hawkins, 2005) have conducted a series of studies that demonstrate monitoring and feedback of client outcomes to therapists in improving individual therapy outcomes. More recently, they have added web-based clinical support tools for therapists that suggest strategies to apply with clients who are not benefiting from therapy. The IT aspect of this process enables efficient collection and interpretation of therapy progress and timely delivery of assessment results to therapists.

One study applied Lambert and colleagues' approach to the couple area (Isakson et al., 2006). The data collected only focused on individual adjustment, rather than measurement of couple-based data. Female clients who reported clinical levels of disturbance at intake who had partners scoring in the normal range achieved better outcomes in individual rather than couple therapy. Regular monitoring and feedback of couple outcomes to therapists via use of technology could enhance therapists' responsiveness to couple needs and improve therapy outcomes. This feedback could be supplemented with clinical support tools, suggesting focus on specific areas (e.g., such as working alliance) or additional strategies (e.g., training in negotiating disagreements) that might enhance couple outcomes.

Alternative Forms of Intervention

Technology can provide us with radically new ways to offer couple services. For example, relationship education that could be particularly suitable for Net generation clients might use interactive gaming software embedding basic negotiation and relationship skills training in graphics rich environments. To illustrate, consider the highly popular "Sims" computer games, which allow users to construct their own characters and make choices that lead to certain outcomes. Imagine constructing such a game to enable the principles and skills of relationship education to be delivered on a similar platform. For example, such an application could allow users to construct characters based on their own interpersonal styles, and then engage in hypothetical situations with a partner where outcomes such as relationship benefits or breakdown could be made highly salient. Similarly, there are now literally millions of users online who are involved in "virtual communities" such as Second Life. These online environments may provide unique couple research and clinical opportunities (Yee, Bailenson, Urbanek, Chang, & Merget, 2007).

Expanding our conceptualization of couple services may also entail reconsidering the role of clients. The development of what has been termed "Web 2.0" has substantially expanded interactivity online, raising the possibility that clients now have far greater opportunities to become more self-directed participants in addressing couple issues. For example, there are now many online support groups, although there has been remarkably little research on effects of these groups. Clinically distressed populations do make use of these groups (Darcy & Dooley, 2007) and these groups can have a therapeutic value for their participants. For example, Lieberman and Goldstein (2005) examined the effects of online self-help groups in a sample of breast cancer patients and found significant improvements at 6 months in depression and psychosocial well-being. Online support groups could offer support and information to couples, which could incorporate professional input (Johnsen, Steinsvik, & Gammon, 2003).

Challenges in Applying IT in the Couple Area

Despite immense promise, implementing IT effectively is not without challenges. To illustrate, we examine the design issues that arose in developing two IT psychological applications, one an asynchronous web-based program for problem gamblers called *Improving the Odds*, and the other a DVD-based self-directed relationship education program called *Couple CARE*. The common element to *Improving the Odds* and *Couple CARE* was the use of interactive IT-based learning experiences to teach key knowledge and skills.

Content

One obvious place to draw guidance regarding content of IT-based programs is from evidence-based face-to-face intervention programs. In many areas of therapy and prevention, CBT has been identified as an intervention approach with considerable evidence for its efficacy (Nathan & Gorman, 2002). There are a number of characteristics of face-to-face CBT that make it well suited to IT applications. A fundamental premise of CBT is that the provision of information and skills can assist people to manage psychological difficulties, and often this is done in structured programs of defined duration.

CBT content information can be presented, and structured tasks can be used to develop skills, using a variety of IT such as online delivery. For example, in *Improving the Odds* gamblers were provided information on a web site about common cognitive distortions about gambling that often underpin problem gambling (e.g., gamblers often think they can "feel" a win coming on). Clients then self-assessed over the web their own gambling related thoughts and were taught to challenge unhelpful gambling related thoughts.

Format

There are considerable differences between delivering therapy face-to-face versus via IT. Content for IT applications needs to be engaging and interactive. However, much existing content on the Internet has been described as "shovelware," which is essentially content developed for other modes of delivery that is dumped wholesale onto the web (http://www.wordspy.com/words/shovelware.asp, retrieved 17/8/07). For example, large tracts of text often are lifted from books or handouts and simply uploaded to a web site. Such shovelware rarely sustains engagement or promotes learning. People are much more likely to learn when given new experiences that prompt reflection and analysis, when provided with opportunities to interact with others to consolidate learning, and when given opportunities to apply new knowledge and skills (Kolb, 1984). IT applications need to be structured to provide these processes.

Bearing in mind the goal of promoting new experiences, reflection and interaction to enhance new learning, IT provides myriad opportunities to provide these aspects in a psychological program. For example, use of questionnaires that give online feedback, and frequent opportunities for clients to enter text into the program at specific points, can be easily included to provide a more interactive experience that promotes reflection. Even didactic presentation of key ideas can be done in engaging and interactive formats. In *Improving the Odds*, suggestions for coping with gambling urges are illustrated graphically with depiction of how people might behave in particular situations, and clients identify (by clicking in particular boxes on the screen) strategies that they believe might work for them.

IT applications can also promote interactions with others to promote learning. Teaching effective couple communication in *Couple CARE* consists of the couple watching a DVD together that explains and demonstrates a range of communication skills, then the couple do a communication exercise, each self-evaluates their communication skills, and asks for feedback from their spouse. The couple's self-evaluation of communication is reviewed in a telephone call with an educator.

Pacing and Sequencing

An advantage of IT-based psychological programs is that they are often readily accessible at times chosen by the consumer. If the program is entirely IT based, clients potentially might access all or parts of the program as many times as they wish, take breaks and come back at any time that is convenient, and progress through in any sequence they chose. However, it is not clear that an entirely open access program provides optimal outcomes. Program designers can structure the timing or sequence of completion of particular units in a program (e.g., through making the next unit available only after previous unit has been completed). It is not entirely clear what level of structure of pacing and sequence of IT program delivery is helpful. In Couple CARE there are six units and initially couples were given the choice of timing of completing the program and its associated telephone calls. However, experience suggested that the lack of temporal structure often led to couples losing momentum and failing to complete the program. Now we recommend that a couple complete one unit per week, with a schedule of telephone call a professional educator. Couples report this structure keeps them on track, and the time-limited commitment to a 6-week program appeals to them (Wilson & Halford, 2008). Similarly, in *Improving the Odds,* content is delivered on a regular basis in the form of a weekly "session" in order to maintain momentum.

Technical Implementation

Developing IT-based applications is likely to involve collaboration with individuals who have expertise in areas like web design, audiovisual production, and the like. It has been the repeated experience of the current authors that accessing such expertise is essential to producing programs that utilize the capacity of IT to be engaging and interactive. Many psychologists and other mental health professionals simply do not know the possibilities of IT. Conversely, many IT experts have little understanding of the guiding principles of psychological service provision, such as the importance of providing evidence-based content. Learning to collaborate effectively with an IT design team is a challenging but crucial aspect of the development of IT-based psychological programs.

Extended discussion between IT experts and psychology program designers is often necessary to develop the desired design characteristics, and inspection of staged versions of the final product can help ensure it combines the right content with the right IT applications. In web design, psychologists need to become acquainted with key issues like appropriate site hosting, digital security of information, systematic collection and use of data provided by clients interacting with the program, and the range of media that can be used to present ideas. Such familiarity opens up creative possibilities. For example, well-designed web sites can automate many potentially time-consuming tasks, such as automatic registration for use of the web site, monitoring and reporting on use of aspects of the web site, automation of reminders to clients and professionals about key tasks, linking the program to important related content, and tailoring of content to address particular needs of clients based on their answers to web-based questions.

Contact with a Professional and Associated Ethical Issues

IT-based programs can provide anything from zero to considerable scope for contact with a professional. In the absence of any direct contact with a professional, there is the possibility that the program might not be appropriate for those accessing it, or that someone might have a need for assistance that the program cannot provide. Some IT programs are designed to be accessed without professional contact but provide a potentially important "manual override" so that clients can contact the professionals running the program, or *vice versa*. For example, in *Improving the Odds* gamblers received a contact telephone number and email addresses for reaching a therapist if they felt the need. Other programs include therapist contact as part of the program. For example, in *Couple CARE* couples have a regular (approximately weekly) telephone call with a professional educator.

Many traditional concepts that have guided the ethical and professional conduct of face-to-face psychological services seem equally applicable to IT-based service delivery. For example, the Australian Psychological Society (2004) guidelines for provision of psychological services on the Internet emphasize the need for psychologists to honor obligations to ensure the confidentiality of information provided by clients over the Internet, to present their professional qualifications and expertise in an accurate manner, and to present clear evidence on the effectiveness of treatment recommendations that allow clients to make informed consent. At the same time the guidelines make recommendations that are not supported by evidence and might need to be rethought. For example, the guidelines suggest that clients be informed that "online assessment is not a substitute for any psychological evaluation performed by a qualified professional," and that "psychologists should warn clients that certain problems are not suitable for online counselling." While these statements might prove to be true, it is far from established that this is the case.

Conclusions

Most web-based programs are attempts to transfer the traditional face-to-face experience of therapy online. As our experience grows in making use of IT, our conceptualization of what constitutes an intervention will likely develop to incorporate as yet unanticipated possibilities. Already IT programs are shifting in design with new conceptualizations of how technology can assist clients. For example, Halford et al. (2004) drew heavily on Kolb's (1984) experiential learning cycle of experience, reflection, and goal setting in the design of Couple CARE, and emphasize self-regulated learning. In a similar vein, Weingardt (2004) has advocated the use of instructional design principles in translating manualized therapy content to web-based technologies that allow much greater client self-direction of learning goals.

In summary, IT applications to couple relationship services are in their infancy but hold promise of many exciting possibilities. How we can best prepare couples for their journey together, and how we can best help couples when this journey becomes difficult, are fundamental questions that drive our work. Harnessing the power of technology for couples is likely to be an invaluable aid in our attempts to address these challenges.

References

Australian Psychological Society. (2004). *Guidelines for providing psychological services and products on the Internet*. Australia: Australian Psychological Society.

Boschen, M. J., & Casey, L. M. (2008). The use of mobile telephones as adjuncts to cognitive behavioural psychotherapy. *Professional Psychology: Research and Practice, 39*, 546–552.

Braukhaus, C., Hahlweg, K., Kroeger, C., Groth, T., & Fehm-Wolfsdorf, G. (2003). The effects of adding booster sessions to a prevention training program for committed couples. *Behavioural and Cognitive Psychotherapy, 31*(3), 325–336.

Busby, D. M., Ivey, D. C., Harris, S. M., & Ates, C. (2007). Self-directed, therapist-directed, and assessment-based interventions for premarital couples. *Family Relations, 56*, 279–290.

Casey, L. M., Oei, T. P. S., Raylu, N., & Lim, H. K. (2007). *Improving the odds: Internet-based treatment for problem gambling*. Paper presented at the 5th World Congress of Behavioural and Cognitive Therapies.

Darcy, A. M., & Dooley, B. (2007). A clinical profile of participants in an online support group. *European Eating Disorders Review, 15*(3), 185–195.

Gilliam, C. M., & Cottone, R. (2005). Couple or individual therapy for the treatment of depression?: An update of the empirical literature. *American Journal of Family Therapy, 33*(3), 265–272.

Halford, W. K. (in press). *Marriage and relationship education: What works and how to provide it.* New York: Guilford.

Halford, W. K., Markman, H. J., & Stanley, S. M. (2008). Strengthening couple relationships with education: Social policy and public health perspectives. *Journal of Family Psychology, 22*, 497–505.

Halford, W., Moore, E., Wilson, K. L., Farrugia, C., & Dyer, C. (2004). Benefits of flexible delivery relationship education: An evaluation of the Couple CARE program. *Family Relations, 53*(5), 469–476.

Isakson, R. L., Hawkins, E. J., Harmon, S., Slade, K., Martinez, J. S., & Lambert, M. J. (2006). Assessing couple therapy as a treatment for individual distress: When is referral to couple therapy contraindicated? *Contemporary Family Therapy: An International Journal, 28*(3), 313–322.

Johnsen, J.-A. K., Steinsvik, O. O., & Gammon, D. (2003). Health-care professionals' participation in an online discussion forum: The impact on structure, content and interaction. *Journal of Technology in Human Services, 22*(2), 31–44.

Jorm, A. F., Barney, L. J., Christensen, H., Highet, N. J., Kelly, C. M., & Kitchener, B. A. (2006). Research on mental health literacy: What we know and what we still need to know. *Australian and New Zealand Journal of Psychiatry, 40*(1), 3–5.

Jorm, A. F., Korten, A. E., Jacomb, P. A., Christensen, H., Rodgers, B., & Pollitt, P. (1997). "Mental health literacy": A survey of the public's ability to recognise mental disorders and their beliefs about the effectiveness of treatment. *Medical Journal of Australia, 166*, 182–186.

Kazantzis, N., & Ronan, K. R. (2006). Can between-session (homework) activities be considered a common factor in psychotherapy? *Journal of Psychotherapy Integration, 16*(2), 115–127.

Kolb, D. A. (1984). *Experiential learning: Experience as the source of learning and development.* Englewood Cliffs, NJ: Prentice Hall.

Lambert, M. J., Harmon, C., Slade, K., Whipple, J. L., & Hawkins, E. J. (2005). Providing feedback to psychotherapists on their patients' progress: Clinical results and practice suggestions. *Journal of Clinical Psychology, 61*(2), 165–174.

Larson, J. H., Vatter, R. S., Galbraith, R. C., Holman, T. B., & Stahmann, R. F. (2007). The relationship evaluation (RELATE) with therapist-assisted interpretation: Short-term effects on premarital relationships. *Journal of Marital & Family Therapy, 33*(3), 364–374.

Leach, L., & Christensen, H. (2006). A systematic review of telephone-based interventions for mental disorders. *Journal of Telemedicine and Telecare, 12*(3), 122–129.

Lieberman, M. A., & Goldstein, B. A. (2005). Self-help on-line: An outcome evaluation of breast cancer bulletin boards. *Journal of Health Psychology, 10*(6), 855–862.

Nathan, P. E., & Gorman, J. M. (2002). *A guide to treatments that work* (2nd ed.). New York, NY: Oxford University Press.

Newman, M. G., Consoli, A. J., & Taylor, C. B. (1999). A palmtop computer program for the treatment of generalized anxiety disorder. *Behavior Modification, 23*(4), 597–619.

Ochs, E. P. P., & Binik, Y. M. (1998). A sex-expert computer system helps couples learn more about their sexual relationship. *Journal of Sex Education and Therapy, 23*(2), 145–155.

Productivity Commission. (1999). *Australia's Gambling Industries, Report No. 10*. Canberra: AusInfo.

Proudfoot, J., Ryden, C., Everitt, B., Shapiro, D. A., Goldberg, D., Mann, A., et al. (2004). Clinical efficacy of computerised cognitive-behavioural therapy for anxiety and depression in primary care: Randomised controlled trial. *British Journal of Psychiatry, 185*(1), 46–54.

Snyder, D. K., Lachar, D., & Wills, R. M. (1988). Computer-based interpretation of the marital satisfaction inventory: Use in treatment planning. *Journal of Marital & Family Therapy, 14*(4), 397–409.

Spek, V., Cuijpers, P., Nyklicek, I., Riper, H., Keyzer, J., & Pop, V. (2007). Internet-based cognitive behaviour therapy for symptoms of depression and anxiety: A meta-analysis. *Psychological Medicine, 37*(3), 319–328.

Spence, S. H., Holmes, J. M., March, S., & Lipp, O. V. (2006). The feasibility and outcome of clinic plus Internet delivery of cognitive-behavior therapy for childhood anxiety. *Journal of Consulting and Clinical Psychology, 74*(3), 614–621.

Stein, M. B., Sherbourne, C. D., Craske, M. G., Means-Christensen, A., Bystritsky, A., Katon, W., et al. (2004). Quality of care for primary care patients with anxiety disorders. *American Journal of Psychiatry, 161*(12), 2230–2237.

Tavares, H., Martins, S. S., Zilberman, M. L., & el Guebaly, N. (2002). Gamblers seeking treatment: Why haven't they come earlier? *Addictive Disorders and Their Treatment, 1*(2), 65–69.

Taylor, C., Jobson, K. O., Winzelberg, A., & Abascal, L. (2002). The use of the Internet to provide evidence-based integrated treatment programs for mental health. *Psychiatric Annals, 32*(11), 671–677.

Thompson, A., Hunt, C., & Issakidis, C. (2004). Why wait? Reasons for delay and prompts to seek help for mental health problems in an Australian clinical sample. *Social Psychiatry and Psychiatric Epidemiology, 39*(10), 810–817.

Weingardt, K. R. (2004). The role of instructional design and technology in the dissemination of empirically supported, manual-based therapies. *Clinical Psychology: Science and Practice, 11*(3), 313–331.

Wilson, K. L., & Halford, W. K. (2008). Processes of change in the flexible delivery of couple relationship education. *Family Relations, 57*, 625–635.

Yee, N., Bailenson, J. N., Urbanek, M., Chang, F., & Merget, D. (2007). The unbearable likeness of being digital: The persistence of nonverbal social norms in online virtual environments. *Cyber-Psychology & Behavior, 10*(1), 115–121.

Leanne M. Casey
School of Psychology
Griffith University
M24 Mt. Gravatt Campus
Qld 4111
Australia
E-mail: l.casey@griffith.edu.au

Index

Christoph Flückiger · Günther Wüsten
Richard E. Zinbarg · Bruce E. Wampold
Resource
Activation
Using Clients' Own
Strengths in
Psychotherapy
and Counseling
HOGREFE